THE THREE K

DATE LABEL

slep

N

7. NOV. 196
-1 DEC. 196
DEC. 1969
1970

NORTH EAST I.

reat King

East Point

Hapuka Point

North West Bay

Farmer Rocks

South East Bay

Tasman Bay

The Cove

South Point

0   ¼   ½   ¾   1
MILE

85

THE *ELINGAMITE* AND ITS TREASURE

by
WADE DOAK

HODDER AND STOUGHTON
LONDON AND AUCKLAND

PRINTED IN GREAT BRITAIN FOR HODDER
AND STOUGHTON LIMITED, LONDON AND
AUCKLAND, BY C. TINLING AND CO. LIMITED,
LONDON AND PRESCOT

Author's Note

The writing of the *Elingamite* story would have been less satisfying were it not for the encouragement of fellow-diver and friend Kelly Tarlton, his enthusiasm in the pursuit of treasure, his technical ability and photographic skill.

Foreword

by Sir Douglas Robb

*An eminent New Zealand surgeon who was also for two terms chancellor
of the University of Auckland, Sir Douglas Robb has two close links
with the Elingamite. His mother and brother survived the wreck on the
remote Three Kings that foggy November Sunday in 1902. And he himself has twice visited the islands; the first time to see the area that his
mother had described in her writings and then, in 1968, to witness the
salvage of treasure from the wreck deep at the foot of the cliffs.*

To cruise slowly around the Western King on a windless summer
day and watch from a safe distance the diving operations was quite
an experience. First it was not all that calm and peaceful. Though
fog persisted in greater or less quantity most of the day—in shallow
layers at sea level or higher—there was ceaseless and terrifying
activity. The steady swell from the south-west kept up an unending
assault on the stern and rockbound face. Solid water, apart from the
creaming tops, seemed to climb up and down some thirty feet and
in clefts and at other points two or three times as high. This made the
surface, and I am told the bottom also, anything but peaceful, quite
apart from the tides that sweep past and around at four to five knots.

They had a couple of buoys, seemingly very close to the rocks,
to which a dinghy would cling, up and down whose anchoring ropes
the divers would ascend and descend. From a little distance out the
dinghy and the head of the diver who manned it went up and down
like a yo-yo, mostly lost to sight in the troughs of dark waters, but
occasionally silhouetted against the creaming top of the last breaker
high on the cliff wall.

The broad-bottomed scow, the mother ship of the divers, hovered
and circled between the dinghy and us and the cliffs, putting off and
taking on the divers in turn and collecting the proceeds of the hunt.
They kept a watch on times and pressures. Seagulls wheeled and
screamed, and the thin fog inescapably conjured up the Sunday
morning sixty-six years ago when the ship was wrecked.

I think these divers are gallant fellows. It is quite a feat to get
themselves to such a remote and inhospitable place in the first place.
Then to find and locate the flattened-out hull and propeller, and
finally to grope in detail for coins and other relics in such deep
water, using specially contrived tools, is wholly admirable.

Skill in photography, care and exactitude in managing the techniques of the diving itself, tenacity in what is most exhausting work physically—all these things contribute to an epic of which their fellow New Zealanders may be proud.

Acknowledgements

For sixty pages of foolscap in painstaking copperplate, countless letters and the loan of his grandfather's diary, personal visits and encouragement I owe deep gratitude to N. T. (Wally) Wetherilt of Trentham. Then a sea of names comes to mind: the numbers of people who have helped me research this book. Norman Cassrels, Sir Douglas Robb and Neil Robinson provided both information and inspiration when the task of fathoming more about the disaster seemed so hopeless. For the research facilities provided by Vernon Sale, editor of the *Weekly News*, and the use of the *Herald* reference room, the Auckland, Wellington and Dunedin reference libraries and the files of the *Northern Advocate* in Whangarei I am greatly indebted.

Then there are those scores of kindly people whose letters gave me new information and fresh leads to follow or who, like Mr Harper of Leigh, invited me into their homes and gave me their personal reminiscences and a cup of coffee.

The divers who joined our expeditions and the *Elingamite* syndicate members John Gallagher, John Pettit and Kelvin Tarlton, and our diver-cook Jeff Pearch provided many of the words in this book, both in written form or filched from them verbatim in the course of our activities.

Traditionally, treasure hunts have one added spark of excitement: the disputes and quarrels, double-crosses and treachery which big stakes are supposed to give rise to. Our *Elingamite* expeditions have been singularly lacking in such colour. As I write our group has come through it all with the warmest of friendships, bonded by shared risks, setbacks and success.

What do you do when you find a treasure such as that of the *Elingamite*? To untangle this novel situation took some eighteen months of gruelling endeavour on the part of Muir Douglas, Auckland manager of the Northern Assurance Co. Ltd. Just as this book is completed we learn that our syndicate now owns the *Elingamite* bullion. We owe an immense debt of gratitude to Mr Douglas for his efforts on our part. One condition of our ownership is that a few *Elingamite* relics and some treasure be displayed in a Northland museum. This we shall do with pleasure.

WADE DOAK

Contents

Illustrations

Credits for Illustrations
[1] Kelvin Tarlton
[2] Jaan Voot
[3] Wade Doak

Book 1

Chapter 1

IT'S NO SECRET really if I tell you where there is a ton and a half of pure silver lying off the New Zealand coast. At least there was a ton and a half, until we lifted three hundredweight out of the wreck. The rest can stay there for a while. Buried under a mountain of corroding iron plates and girders in the guts of the steamer *Elingamite* it is just too deep and too dangerous to get at. Already two divers have died in the attempt. And about 6,000 gold coins are down there too, still as mint and shiny as the day the ship sank. Kelly and Jag and John and I have taken twenty-one of them but that took us two years and 150 dives. We reckon the silver will do us—about £12,000 worth as metal, but some of these old Queen Victoria coins are a collector's delight, all encrusted with coral and sand, glass, coal and bits of seashell.

At 150 feet the sea can be a pretty hostile place to men. You don't see much there that's not eating or being eaten. There isn't much colour and it's always as cold as fish blood. You don't even feel like a human down there. No weight, nothing to plant your feet square on so you can size things up. Like a patient under an anaesthetic you have a mouthpiece between your teeth and the queer, thick stuff you breathe sets your lips tingling. You feel as if you're not inside yourself. Rather like after the first few drinks at a wedding party where you don't really feel wanted and you start analysing how alcohol is affecting your version of reality.

That's how it was when I came across the *Elingamite* treasure: finning quietly from rock to rock, feeling very wet and groggy, some part of the half-boozed brain still ticking over, sensible to the 150 feet of liquid cutting it off from the sky.

"Soon have to make it back up there again, but below it's so quiet and peaceful." I could easily have fallen asleep: no struggling in the fierce current up there and all the cold work of taking off my gear.

Life topside in the cramped quarters of the *Ahiki*, sleeping on the diesel fuel tank, was hell anyway. No really deep sleep such as seemed possible down below. Still that smart part of the brain kept the fins flicking and head swivelling among the wreckage.

"Feel like a blasted ballet dancer down here." Weightless and clad in tights, it was a lot easier to move with grace and poise in liquid space than to barge around like a he-man. I kept thinking I was a fish

15

as schools of red perch swam close in front of my mask, pirouetted around me or darted under a rock.

"Suppose it saves energy if you copy them." Besides, any sudden effort sent an icy squirt of water through the neck of my wet suit and sluicing around my armpits. Then I would get a bit dizzy and have to screw my mind into focus on what I was doing.

"Looking for the bullion. But there wouldn't be a chance of finding it amongst all this junk. The rest of the boys must be close by hunting for souvenirs. They don't reckon there's a tinker's chance in hell of finding the treasure here."

I'd passed Jag and John Pettit struggling in the current to attach a shotline to a couple of portholes. And Kelly was waltzing around with his huge camera rig and flash gun trying to get some smart pix of the wreck.

Trouble was this area of seabed didn't look much like a ship. Earlier in the dive I'd posed for Kelly with a few seagrowth-covered wine bottles gathered from under a rock. Nearby was a white, twisted length of lead plumbing. This would show we were actually over a wreck. Then we'd come across a huge, mossy mangle of wreckage which turned out to be the propeller, sitting boss uppermost, blades awry and jagged. While Kelly juggled with his light meter and aperture controls I'd balanced over the prop, holding on to the tip of one six-foot blade, like a gymnast doing a single-handed handstand. Then he had signalled me to snuggle up close to some more debris—some sort of winch bristling with sea eggs and finger sponges. Now as I swam by myself my fingers still burnt with those damned spines you pick up from touching sponges. "Like bits of fibre glass—spicules! Fancy my depth-fuddled brain throwing up that word! Not as water-logged as I thought."

Anxiety struggled to resist nitrogen narcosis: "Wonder how my air supply is lasting. Be good when it's cut and I can get out of here. I'm getting too cold to feel sleepy now." Trouble is the insulating bubbles in these wet suits get so squeezed up under pressure there's no warmth left in them.

I was starting to get clumsy. If I curved gracefully and swooped down under the rock ledges cold water would swill up and down my spine, so I moved as little as possible. Just my big flippers. They kept going without even thinking about it. Like the heart, a reflex action and a big drain on energy and body heat. The thick, compressed air which I gulped from my regulator was cold too, my lungs acting as a heat radiator with each breath.

I felt flayed and water-sodden. I tried to imagine sitting down to a good meal, all dry and warm in the cosy cabin. A bit of salty water in my mask made my eyes smart like onions as I wriggled under another rock.

"Body just keeps on working for me while the mind hikes off on little trips of its own. Like shelling peas. Why does a man like diving? What a hellish torment it can become near the end of a deep dive. Fortunately we forget this and remember only the pleasure.

"Hey! Can I really be here?" *Coins:* a mound of scattered discs in the white sand. This was like watching a film and telling yourself it was not real. But they were! A handful in my plastic bag. Gold? I plunged my hand back in feverishly. "Too light—just pennies. May as well keep digging. Could be something better below."

Varying sized coins began to tumble into view. These could not all be pennies but they were not heavy enough for gold. Everywhere in the rocky recess coins were scattered, coral encrusted or sulphated black.

"How the hell will I find this spot again when I go up?" I should have brought down a marker buoy to fix to the kelp growing on top of the rock.

"Hey—where are the other divers? Who can give me a hand before my air runs out? Need someone else to help me get a good fix on this spot."

This was the last dive of the expedition and I hardly dared leave off to call someone else in. Doubling sideways I saw John Pettit finning past. I gave him the "OK" sign, which means on a treasure wreck: *COINS.* Like a fish taking a bait he streaked beside me and we scrounged furiously in the sand together for more and more coin. We could not see much in the sandstorm of particles being stirred up, so we worked by touch, groping blindly until our fingers met. It did not feel deep any more. I was no longer cold. My brain was working perfectly and methodically—hyper-aware.

I knew my air was getting very low and I shepherded every breath. The decompression meter on my wrist indicated that ascent should be soon if I was to avoid a "bend".

John tapped my shoulder and signalled "up". His air was finished already as he had been toiling hard raising portholes. Off up into the blue tide race he went, to tell the boys we were on to it. Frantically I scooped up as much as possible, thinking: "This is our last dive here." That day the weather had begun to deteriorate and our supply of air tanks was finished.

A tap on my leg. I did not even react. Then it sunk in: I turned and there was Kelly wanting to know what I was doing. I flashed some coins at him. Gasping the remaining air from his tank he snapped some photos of me with his electronic flash, and ascended.

My own tank was giving me the last air we would be able to breathe on the *Elingamite* site.

"Pit-a-pit-a-pit", my sonic air pressure gauge triggered off its staccato warning, forcing me to accept that it was all over. Hiccuping bubbles it drew a cloud of fish around me as I made a last fossick through the sand, squeezed the water out of my coin bag and backed out from the underhang.

It was getting twilight and no one else remained below. A blue wall of current was sweeping down over the wreck. I kicked off into it but I could not rise far from the bottom with the weight of coins. Removing my mouthpiece, my chilled lips fluttered uselessly around the tube of my buoyancy compensator as I puffed in some air; like a yellow halter around my neck it swayed and tilted inflated by my exhaust. I lightened and lifted off. The current started to bear me away. Slanting up from the wreck I tried wildly to fix some landmarks in my mind. From forty feet above, the wreck looked so different: just jumbled rocks festooned with kelp plants streaming out in the current.

"The prop—can't miss that. One—two—three—four. Four rocks down the slope from the prop. A valley of girders, a square hatch cover to one side and"—but by then the wreck site was fading from view as I started to soar. My eyes lifted upwards towards the surface glitter: far above a buckling sheet of tinfoil, so good to see after a long dive. As the pressure of the water diminished, my compensator bulged tight around my neck. Reaching forty feet I purged the air from it so it would not rupture. Had I ascended too fast my own lungs would also have swollen and burst. I kept breathing steadily and the sonic air gauge kept up its staccato cluck, cluck warning. Attracted by this sound trevally and kingfish swarmed around me in the warmer surface waters. I clutched the precious bag firmly in my hand.

"Hell, when will I ever get back to what I'm leaving below me? Wait till the boys see this bullion!"

My mask burst through the surface into another world and a fresh set of problems. It was a mad, white confusion in the tide race. A wind could just be heard howling amidst the roar of the waves slamming into the face of the island. The *Ahiki* was soaring or plummeting with the deep swells as she cruised as close in as she dared. "Weather is brewing something up."

Despite the evening sunlight my yellow buoyancy compensator was quickly noticed. Sea birds swooped low over me. Bucking violently the *Ahiki* swung her bow around and came surfing down. One moment her red bottom was indecorously exposed, the next I was looking down on her foredeck winches and gear. It always seemed an impossibility to transfer from this mad welter of water on to that runaway stallion of a ship, wearing such a burden of lead and scuba tank. But this time I had only one hand free to snatch the ladder with.

18

"Time it right." I finned hard to close the gap between the ship and myself. Strangely it was not a matter of moving horizontally but getting on the same level as the ship even long enough to grab the diving ladder before she crashed below me. Alternately I soared high on a crest or dropped under her hull. She could not use her propeller in case it hacked into me, and I had to back off smartly to avoid her crashing bilge. "How could Kelly make it with his great, unwieldy camera rig?" flashed through my mind.

The current did not matter much now: both the ship and myself were being swept north, away from the sea-lashed island. With a series of strong fin thrusts I snatched the ladder and friendly arms reached down to help me aboard.

"Hey! Wait a minute," I yelled, letting drop my mouthpiece. My bullion hand was empty. They had grabbed the bag from me to safety. Well I now had two hands to hoist myself aboard with, so why worry! By the time I had flung my gear off the boys were crouched in a circle on the counter of the ship: John Gallagher (Jag), John Pettit, John Young, Kelly Tarlton, Jeff Pearch and Mr Tarlton, Kelly's father. On a sack in their midst was a small heap of gritty, rust-covered coin. Jag wielded a hefty diving knife and started to hack, scratch and gouge at a coin, hopeful of a golden gleam. The stainless blade flashed on the dirty coin. "Might just be a penny from a passenger's cabin," said John Pettit, voicing a thought in all our minds: "Could this really be the bullion?"

"It's silver," was Jag's verdict.

"More likely this is just the purser's change from the ship's bar," ventured Kelly, who remembered all the wine bottles I'd been posing with.

My heart was sinking as the flush of discovery started to fade away. I started to shiver in my wet suit. The sun was setting.

We were a lot of pessimists. First we had thought we would never locate the wreck, back in 1965 when we had made our first expedition and chanced upon the wreck's perimeter on our very last dive.

Now we thought we were never to find the bullion. Down below, they all admitted, no one else had given the least consideration to looking for coins. Artifacts: bath-tiles, wine bottles, portholes, or photos, that was all the *Elingamite* wreck seemed likely to yield. The search area was just too vast and too deep. At least the proverbial needle in the haystack was on dry land with no limit on time or air. Despite these doubts we were bursting to go below again, but this was impossible. Our skipper Peter Sheehan was tapping the glass. Our air supply was exhausted and the fine spell was over. Just as the year before, we were heading for home on the verge of a fresh discovery, scurrying into the shelter of North Cape before the storm broke.

The setting sun glowed red in our faces and our knives scraped and clinked. "Say—this one is a *half-crown*," said Jag. "Nineteen-hundred." Queen Victoria's stately plump head was just visible through a mud pack of corroded iron rust and adhering coraline growth.

Kelly's father, our boatman, was methodically scraping at a smaller coin. "This is a shilling," he announced. "Eighteen seventy-nine."

As others scraped clean more shillings, all with varying dates, 1880, 1875, 1899, things really began to look grim.

"This can't be the bullion. They wouldn't send a lot of old, used coins across from one bank to another," said Kelly. At that time we did not know much about the *Elingamite* or her cargo, except that her £17,300 consignment of specie was a mixture of silver coin and gold half-sovereigns, despatched from a Sydney bank to its New Zealand branch in 1902.

"Must be some passenger's savings. Still it *is* silver coin—let's count it," I urged, excitement still on the simmer. So over the small heap our hands plied until it was all sorted into coin piles. There were a few threepences and sixpences, a dozen pennies and the balance was shillings, florins and half-crowns, totalling in all £15 11s. 8d.

Some coins soon cleaned up handsomely, especially those stuck in clumps. Six shillings, cemented together by iron rust, readily fell apart with the tap of a knife to reveal blue-faced Queen Victorias oxided from the small amount of copper in each coin. Three differently designed heads marked successive mintings of the old monarch's likeness, each increasing in severity. My hopes sagged. Clearly this was not bullion: each shilling a different date, even when stuck together in lumps.

As more and more florins and half-crowns were cleaned it was noticed that these were all dated 1900: two years old when the ship sank. A new theory arose: "Surely no passenger or bar-till would hold so much silver of the same year?" Jag said.

"Might have been a collector with a craze for that date," John Young put in. John was the spearfisherman on our expedition, and a quiet humorist. We could not find a single florin, half-crown, three-pence, sixpence or penny which was *not* dated 1900.

The Bullion Theory began to gain deckspace. After all, the shillings could just have been despatched from circulated coin stocks held in the bank vaults. New Zealand and Australia were both using English coinage in 1902, and it was highly unlikely that all the other denominations were not part of a consignment of specie, being without exception of the same minting.

Anyway, while our expedition members argued and scraped and theorized, with a following sea the *Ahiki* surged southwards from the Three Kings Island to New Zealand. Once it grew too dark I went below to my bed on the diesel fuel tank and wrote up my diary for this final day of the trip.

There has always been a rather humorous pattern to our Three Kings diving trips. We have invariably started off pessimistically. Each time, on our last dive, we have been both staggered by a sudden success and frustrated by the relentless verdict of reality. In this remote and exposed area it says: "Get back to the shelter of New Zealand; you have no more air supplies and you can't dive anyway."

So it was in 1966 with this initial coin discovery. And in 1965 without a thought of treasure we had gone up to the Three Kings on a spearfishing safari, only to make a fluke discovery of the *Elingamite* on our very last dive.

In 1963 Kelvin Tarlton and Chris Busck had been the first to spearfish in these virgin waters. Held by the giant kingfish and schools of groper they had no serious thoughts of the *Elingamite*. They knew it was there, somewhere around the West King, but at about 200 feet. Kelvin had actually written to Lloyds of London for information about it, but when they saw the area concerned, any search seemed futile. They had not even bothered to take a single scuba tank.

When I look back on it all I can see that if it was not for the fantastic spearfishing available at the Kings we would never have laid hands on the bullion. To get up there involves a great expense and effort. Only some very powerful fish stories and a mad urge to test the truth of them with a speargun made it attractive. Chris Busck gave me an account of that first trip which was to fire Kelly and me to return. His story also provides some good background to the Three Kings:

"The chance of a lifetime came the way of Kelvin Tarlton and myself that summer when we accompanied an expedition of natural scientists to the Three Kings Islands to study the animal and plant life there. Kelvin had been asked along as photographer and I was lucky to be invited to make up the number when one of the team had a car accident.

"The islands are in an area of strong currents caused by tidal flow along each side of the New Zealand coast meeting off the north of the North Cape. We had reasoned that fish life should be prolific

21

because of this convergence, and tales of commercial fishermen confirmed our ideas. One fisherman brought back four tons of kingfish, averaging sixty pounds weight!

"Kelvin and I were going purely for spearfishing and photography while the rest of the party wanted to study the regrowth of plants and animal life on the islands since the extermination of the goat population by cullers in 1946.

"We left on Sunday, 30 December 1962, at dusk in the fifty-foot shark fishing boat *Ahiki* from Awanui, near Kaitaia. We sailed all night, reaching North Cape at 3 a.m. and then started on the forty-mile trip across to the islands. It was a fabulous experience sleeping on deck under a canopy of brilliant stars and a clear sky. The weather was perfect in the morning and we approached the largest island, with hopes of an easy landing.

"The Three Kings are made up of three main islands of diminishing size, the Great King, Middle King and West King, and numerous rocks, islets and reefs. They are rugged and inhospitable. There are no beaches, and near vertical cliffs with enormous boulders heaped at the bases form the coast.

"It was Abel Tasman, the Dutch discoverer of New Zealand who named these islands the 'Drie Cöningen'. Commissioned by Van Diemen, the Governor-General of Batavia, to find the Great South Land, Commander Tasman had first discovered Tasmania, which he modestly named Van Diemen Land. On the 13 December 1642 his 60-ton war yacht *Heemskirck* and the *Zeehaen*, the 100-ton store-ship, had sighted New Zealand, and sailed for three weeks along the west coast of the two main islands. By 4 January they were sailing north along the extreme northern tip of New Zealand homeward bound. Abel entered in his logbook:

January Anno 1643
4th day: In the morning we found ourselves near a cape (Cape Maria Van Diemen) and had an island north-west by north of us (Great King) so we hoisted the white flag for the officers of the *Zeehaen* to come aboard and with them we decided to touch at the island to see if we could get fresh water and vegetables there.

Towards noon we drifted in a calm and found ourselves in the midst of a heavy current which drove us westward. There was also a heavy sea running from the north-east, which gave us great hopes of finding a passage through here.

By evening we were close to this island, and from what we could see of it we feared there would be nothing there for us. So we sent the pilot-major and the secretary to the *Zeehaen* and asked her officers whether they thought it better to run on if we should

get a favourable wind during the night. The officers agreed.
5th day: In the morning we still drifted on a calm but about
9 o'clock we got a slight breeze from the south-east, so we agreed
with our friends on the *Zeehaen* that it would be wise to steer for
the island. About noon we sent the pinnace with the pilot-major
together with the *Zeehaen's* cockboat, commanded by supercargo
Gilsemans, to find out whether there was any fresh water there.

They returned towards evening aboard and reported that,
coming near the island they had kept close watch and taken precautions against sudden surprise attacks by any natives. They had
entered a small, safe bay where they had found good fresh water
coming down in great plenty from a steep mountain, but owing
to the heavy surf on the shore it was highly dangerous and
virtually impossible to obtain water. Therefore they had pulled
farther round the island to seek a more convenient watering place.
In several places they saw on the highest hills from thirty to thirty-
five persons, men of tall stature, so far as they could see from a
distance, armed with sticks or clubs, who called out to them in a
very loud, rough voice, certain words which our men could not
understand. Our sailors said that when these people walked they
took enormous strides. As our men were rowing about, a few
natives showed themselves here and there from the hilltops. From
this our men concluded that these natives must generally keep
themselves in readiness, with their assagais, boats and small arms
and that few, if any more people inhabited the island other than
those who showed themselves. In rowing around the island our
men nowhere saw any dwellings or cultivated land except just by
the fresh water referred to, where, higher up on both sides of the
running water, they saw everywhere square beds looking green
and pleasant, but owing to the great distance they could not tell
what kind of vegetables they were. It is quite possible that all the
island's inhabitants dwelt beside the fresh water.

In that bay they saw two prows hauled on shore, one of them
seaworthy, the other broken, but they saw no other craft anywhere. As soon as our men returned with the pinnace we did our
best to get our ships near the shore and by evening we had
anchored on the north-west side in forty fathoms, good bottom, at
a small swivelgun's distance from the coast. We then made
preparations for taking in water the next day.
6th day Early in the morning we sent the same two boats to the
watering place, each equipped with two *pederaroes* (guns which
fired stones) and six musketeers. The rowers carried pikes and
side arms. Our pinnace went too with Francoys Jacobsz, the pilot-
major, and Gerrit Jansz, skipper of the *Zeehaen* and carried casks

for getting fresh water. While rowing shorewards they saw, at various places on the heights, a tall man standing with a stick like a pike, apparently watching our men. As they rowed past he called out to them in a very loud voice.

When they got halfway to the watering place between a certain point and another large high rock or small island, they found the current to run so strong against the wind that even with their empty boats they had to do their utmost to hold their own. Because of this the pilot-major and the skipper agreed not to expose the small craft and the men to such great peril, seeing there was a long voyage ahead of them, and the men and the small craft were greatly wanted by the ships. So they decided to pull back to us, the rather as the heavy surf was rolling on the shore near the watering place. The breeze freshening we on the ship could only surmise that they had not been able to land. With the furled flag we gave the signal that they were at liberty to return, but they were already on their way back before we signalled.

When the pilot-major came alongside he reported that owing to the wind the attempt to land was too dangerous, seeing that near the shore the sea was everywhere full of hard rocks, without any sandy ground. It was too risky for the men and there was a danger of the water casks being damaged or stove in.

Straight away we summoned the officers of the *Zeehaen* and the second mates on board of us and convened a council, at which it was decided to weigh anchor directly and run on an easterly course as far as 220 degrees longtitude, then shape our course north-ward . . .

To this island we gave the name of Drie Cöningen Island because we came to anchor there on Twelfth-night eve and sailed thence again on Twelfth-day.

"This tribe of lofty Maoris described by Tasman was later mas-sacred by a raiding party from the mainland. Then in the 1800s a young Maori chief, christened Tom Bowling by the whalers for whom he had worked, lived there with his wife and four daughters until, after nearly starving to death, they were evacuated by mis-sionaries. In 1902 the steamer *Elingamite* struck the West King in a fog and sank in twenty minutes, many of the survivors perishing at sea. Of £17,320 in gold [sic!] aboard, only £4,000 was salvaged. The rest remains there. Les Subritsky of Auckland dived there recently but found only a few battered steel plates.

"Arrived at the island we had to throw all our gear piece by piece from the dinghy to a helper on a rock and then lug it up a 300-foot cliff to the camp site. This just about killed Kelvin and me. Con-

24

sequently we left most of the gear at the bottom including the ZCI transceiver which stubbornly refused to transmit. Lucky for us we had had to leave our scuba at home.

"The camp site was in a shady nook near running water in a saddle about 400 feet above sea level. Bellbirds and parakeets flew around us all day and large brown lizards scuttled everywhere, eating from our hands and pinching any uncovered food. Hundreds of blowflies which normally live on corpses in the large seagull colonies decided to try us instead. They swarmed all over us and made mealtimes quite a trial. Most of the party of eight suffered from a twenty-four-hour dysentery which we blamed on the flies. The silence of the night was broken by large crashings in the undergrowth and the appropriate noises as bug collectors lost their dinner each night!

"Each day the nature study boys clambered about the island, pouncing on unsuspecting beetles and other insects and promptly bottling them. Skin diving commenced when Kelvin and I clambered down the cliff and changed into our wet suits ready to dive in waters as yet untouched by man. We dived into cold water with visibility of eighty feet and more. Hundreds of jellyfish with eight-foot stinging tentacles floated in the sea and we had to dodge these as we swam. A forty-pound kingfish swam up to a yard from Kelvin's face, when he was looking the other way. He was so startled he almost forgot to pull the trigger. We decided to swim back to our base rock in case of sharks and as we neared it I speared another forty-pound kingfish.

"Despite the northern latitude the water was much colder than at the mainland and our feet were getting numb but we went for a short swim again before dusk. Schools of large trevally were everywhere. There were no crays or snapper in snorkel depth. Cutting the steaks from the kingies we wearily climbed the cliff again and started to prepare a dinner of bullybeef and potatoes. We spent the next three days exploring the main bay below the camp. As we had no dinghy we did not venture out into the currents. From the cliff tops the current patterns could be seen for miles out to sea and we had no intentions of swimming to South America!

"On the last day, however, the boat returned to take us to the Middle King where two of the scientists wanted to look for snails. While they went ashore Kelvin and I asked Peter Sheehan, the skipper, if he would watch us while we swam in the rip swirling around the island. He agreed, so we donned our gear and plunged in. With no jellyfish the water was sky-blue and it was as clear as any we had seen. No sooner had we broken the surface, than several small kingies of thirty to forty pounds circled us. We ignored them, deciding to wait for a monster, or get nothing at all, so we swam furiously to beat the current to the shelter of the rocks.

"Mao mao by the hundred and trevally swarmed round us with kingies manoeuvring amongst them as we swam along the cliff base where the current was least. As we rounded a small point some bigger kingfish of fifty pounds or so came to meet us and Kelvin raised his gun to fire at the biggest. I tried to signal to wait a while, but he took no chances and let fly. The spear hit the gill plate at an angle and skidded off. I then returned my attention to the school and saw circling up from the deep two large hapuka (groper to Southerners). One swam right up to me and I fired at point-blank range, the spear going through his skull between the eyes and nearly out the other side.

"I looked over to Kelvin who was still trying to load his gun. The other groper swam round him while he frantically tried to free the ferrule which had jammed on the end of the spear. Smothered obscenities poured through the end of his snorkel as he swam to the rocks and climbed out. I hauled my fish out, hardly believing my eyes, and laid it on a crevice. Kelvin having freed the ferrule, we reloaded and jumped back in.

"A small groper swam over a shallow reef but shied off as Kelvin approached it. We followed it into a natural gut about a hundred feet deep, and quite dark due to the overhanging cliffs. Far below us I could see a white shape catching the light as it moved. I looked again and saw it was another groper. I yelled to Kelvin and pointed. He dived towards it but the line to his float pulled taut at fifty feet and he surfaced to frantically unwind more line. Looking down again we saw not one but twenty or more white underbellies glinting in the light, and a school of groper rose slowly towards us, circling and twisting like trout at Rotorua.

"This was too good to be true; Kelvin swam down to the biggest and slammed a spear through it, just behind the gills. Releasing his gun he surfaced and the fish headed for the bottom, fighting nearly as well as a kingie. Kelvin tried to stop it from getting into the seaweed, but it caught the 300 pound breaking strain line round a rock and snapped it. Kelvin was quite ropable by now—the fish appeared to be bigger than mine which weighed in at fifty-four pounds. We took off for the boat for a new spear. Much to our dismay the skipper decided it was time to pick up the 'snail men' and we regretfully shed our gear. A while later we headed back to New Zealand after a fabulous week."

Chris and Kelvin organized a return trip the following year, but bad weather cancelled it. Tasman had discovered the islands in midsummer and this is the only time of year we have dared to plan a trip. At no other time can a reasonably long calm spell be expected in the area, and the abortive 1964 expedition established firmly in our minds that even at the ideal time all our planning, outfitting and supplies could be for nothing when the destination is the Three Kings. Over the following year Kelly, Chris and I, still eager for a spearfishing safari, managed to raise enough enthusiasm to man another expedition. It was a gamble on the weather and a diver stood to waste his whole Christmas holiday sitting on a boat tied to the Awanui wharf. Many a diver who turned down our invitation was to lament it bitterly later on. And pity help his wife if she had any part in the decision! Fortunately for me, my wife Jan is a keen scuba diver and is always glad to see me enjoy a diving holiday.

Chris arranged the food supplies and chartered the *Ahiki*, which they had taken on their first trip. Few men have a knowledge of the northern tip of New Zealand and the Three Kings area to match that of skipper Peter Sheehan. Fishing boats seldom visit these treacherous waters. The tides racing around the rocky extremity are unpredictable. Vast sandbanks shift and alter with the storms. The combination of tide and storm has kept a trawler steaming for thirty-six hours trying to make headway across the forty-mile stretch. In 1966 the collier *Kaitawa* was lost with all hands when she tried to round the cape in the teeth of a north-easterly storm. We were to learn just how tricky these waters can be, and especially to fear the north-easterly, from which there is no shelter.

One Sunday in January 1965 we assembled our rather unleadable crew of six spearfishermen on the Awanui wharf in the far north of New Zealand: Dave Barnett, then New Zealand spearfishing champion and holder of New Zealand records for an eighty-eight pound kingfish and a ninety-five pound groper; Chris who loves wrestling and cooking octopus; Jaan Voot; Derek Pollard; Kelvin Tarlton, New Zealand's top underwater photographer, who had made a New Zealand record snorkel dive to 104 feet; and myself, editor of *Dive* underwater magazine, thirsting for some good diving stories.

We all had at least ten years' diving experience and regularly used scuba to depths of 150 feet.

Before sundown we loaded our two runabouts (twelve-footers), outboards, gear, supplies and a mountain of over thirty scuba tanks aboard the *Ahiki*. Early the next morning we sailed with the tide for a twelve-hour thumpety thump seven-knot journey along the long sandy leg of New Zealand. It was sunny and just an easy swell was running as we sunbathed northwards, our course crossed by several sunfish.

After six hours we were off North Cape, where the sandy coast gives way to knotty hills and steep cliffs, before finally plunging headlong into the blue Pacific. So that was New Zealand! The boat suddenly felt very small. It was some hours before we caught our first

27

glimpse of the Kings. At ten o'clock on Monday night we crept blindly into the rather exposed south-east anchorage, using echo sounder. No lights on the islands which were just dark mounds on the sea. It was an anticlimax to arrive at night, unable to dive. We shone torches down into the black water: it was seething and boiling with red and green fireflies darting and swooping as thick as white bait in a bowl. We scooped some up—horrible centipede-like worms which we consigned to formalin before turning in to our bunks.

While breakfast was cooking two sharks were pulled in by keen divers. Our first dive that Tuesday was in a deep, eighty-foot clear cove out of reach of the tide-race which swept by at five knots. In the sheltered water trevally swarmed. Its clarity soon had us all snorkeling to eighty feet. Kingfish were so common none was reckoned worth shooting unless over seventy pounds. While Kelvin took photos of five hapuka, the largest eighty pounds, Dave shot a forty-pound hapuka. Just as in New Caledonia, the hapuka lay goggling in a cave. The spear of Dave's pneumatic gun penetrated the gill plate. Then he swam into the cave and wrestled his catch out.

Meanwhile Chris speared a sixteen-pound bass, quite a rare fish in New Zealand waters.

To bring in the big kingies a speared trevally was dangled down. Many made passes at it and the boys couldn't resist shafting a sixty-pounder.

That afternoon after a scuba dive to get pictures we dived in a tide-race where birds were madly working. On each occasion one poor wretch had to stay topside and look after the runabout, while the *Ahiki* circled close by. First Jaan Voot shot a deep-gutted eighty-five-pound kingfish at forty feet. He was using 140 feet of heavy nylon, a float he can ride on, a puny single rubber gun with a beautiful new drop-off, penetrator head and flick-out barbs. It took twenty minutes for Jaan to control his catch and heave him aboard. Swimming in these currents it would be folly to spearfish without a float. The short, sharp waves and confused water make it impossible to find a diver without one. I have seen a seventy-pound kingie explode a heavy reel, and in these deep waters a big fish takes out the full 140 feet. Without a float the diver would be dragged under and perhaps lose his gun.

Meanwhile the rest of us were swimming with tuna! They swarmed in around us. I was off to one side and had the fortune to have five circle round me. The first one came from behind me and hurtled under my feet like an express train, dashing off into the acres of trevally, then rocketed straight back towards me. I could see right down its mouth. Four others joined it and swept around me, their jagged scutes like saw teeth along their plump, thwacking tails; huge

28

cylindrical bodies hurtling about like fast, two-man submarines. These were blue fin tuna. I had several opportunities to spear one had I been carrying a powerful gun. Oh for a powerhead! The biggest one, eight feet long, I would conservatively estimate at 300 pounds, although I wouldn't be surprised if it was 400. Could a diver hold one? We saw none smaller than 150 pounds. Dave bounced his spear off two. They moved so fast that only a very manoeuvrable gun could be brought to bear. In the clear water, Dave said, those huge fish were deceptive, being further off than it seemed.

Wednesday arrived and after that night's bull session we were determined to get a tuna. Everyone had a different motive: Kelvin wanted a photo, I wanted a cover story for *Dive*, Dave wanted a fight...

We chased about all day, growing accustomed to brushing aside seventy-pound kingfish, which zoomed in to three-feet range, spoiling visibility. Not a tuna was seen, though we dived in the wildest rips. At one place the boys got into a whirlpool which bunched them altogether and spun them around, elbows and guns bouncing off one another, floats tangling. The runabout hovered nearby and plucked them out smartly. We wore life jackets and were easily identifiable by our floats, even though they can be a damned nuisance at times. Later in the day Jaan shot his second huge kingie. Right in beside a steep cliff it swept in on him. This time the struggle lasted for half an hour and Jaan was very exhausted. This catch was eighty-three pounds.

Chris fed us marvellously—not the usual rough tucker, but real cuisine, even if our dry red wine was a bit off and garlic ran short. For lunch each day we had a special high calorie diet, working on the theory that a heavy meal takes energy to digest, which we needed for diving. Chris mixed up flagons of glucose and orange cordial, which we used to wash down a huge block of chocolate each, besides nibbling dry apricots. This diet was amazingly good: at the end of a day we didn't get that drained out feeling.

Each night we anxiously listened to weather reports from distant New Zealand feeling very exposed and vulnerable away out there. So far the weather had been ideal, but now a change to north-east winds was coming, the worst weather for this area. We could have one more full day diving before heading home. To get three fine calm days up there is very rare and such weather is only likely in December or January.

On the final day of our expedition Kelly, Chris and I were curious to make a random dive at the West King in the general area where we thought the *Elingamite* might lie. We had only the faintest hope we might locate her, but in the cabin at night we three had yarned about her and dreamt of the £13,000 bullion still lying among her wreckage. While the others were reluctant to waste valuable spear-fishing opportunities, our pleading had prevailed.

It was sunny and calm, apart from the huge rolling swell. The wind had turned north-east which meant we had to head for shelter very soon. Wearing seventy cubic feet tanks and buoyancy com-pensators we swam on the surface from the *Ahiki* to get as close as possible to the side of the island. The ocean swells striking against solid rock produced a strong confused backwash and white water.

As soon as the bottom was visible, 100 feet below through the clear, black water, we submerged. Chris carried a powerful spring gun, trailing a float on 200 feet of nylon. This served to mark our position for the divers above. Kelvin clutched his Nikonos camera rig with twin flash guns.

We followed the bottom contours from 100 feet finning down the slope over huge house-size rocks. A kingfish above in the transparent water looked like a sardine flashing in the sun just beneath the sur-face. Chris resisted an impulse to ascend.

At 150 feet the slope became more gentle. A series of enormous rocks formed confused ridges, tending to run out at right angles from the island, and sloping down into even deeper water. Yawning caves and deep clefts cut into their bases. We dropped down into these and began to explore. Our masks nodded around in search of any coral and sea fans while I posed, careful to shoot out a stream of bubbles as Kelly's trigger clicked. We ignored the large groper lurking under ledges lined with pink corals.

Hunting within sight of each other, but individually, it is hard to say who first found the wreckage. I think it just dawned upon us gradually. My first sign was a piece of timber. Might it be a hand rail? Or just sunken driftwood? Then a circular stump of wood, blackened and eaten away internally. A bollard! Chris found bath tiles—yellow and blue, "Wedgewood" embossed on the underside. A bolt. A port-hole complete with glass! Lead piping. Huge girders, steel plates, shafts, beams and rods. This must be the *Elingamite*!

As our excitement grew our air supply dwindled. Just as things were becoming exciting Kelvin signalled us together. The decom-pression meter told us we had to surface. Clutching chunks of wreckage, we inflated our buoyancy compensators. It is a strange sensation to stand at 150 feet, holding a fifteen-pound chunk of lead plumbing, and feel yourself slowly become weightless, eventually wafting surfacewards, clutching the entrails of a sixty-year-old wreck.

Topside, the other three, Dave, Jaan and Derek, were not im-pressed at our delirious ravings about wrecks. Lead is not gold. I suppose wrecks either appeal to you or leave you cold.

30

With the last of the remaining air cylinders and little time to spare they descended the float line which Chris had left tied to the wreckage.

Derek and Jaan came up laden with huge pieces of lolly-pink coral. After having a vigorous look around down to the 200-foot level Dave surfaced saying: "There wasn't really any wreck to see. Let's go and shaft some big kingies", and they did that.

"But look here," we said, "That was the *Elingamite*. The gold's still there—somewhere."

"You find it: you can have it!"

Chapter 2

WITH THE FINDING of a famous bullion wreck it would naturally be expected that everyone would be fanatically keen to return for the treasure, but the *Elingamite* story is not like that at all. Of the divers on our spearfishing safari only Kelly and I were available for a return trip when the calm spells set in again a year later. We hunted around for a team enthusiastic enough to come up there with us. Still there was very little expectation of bullion. Kelvin and I knew the wreck would provide a good photo story for our diving magazine and there were many interesting subjects for photography at the Kings. We wanted good spearfishermen to make spectacular catches for us to film. We needed experienced deep divers to come down with us on the wreck site. They had to be true fanatics as the boat charter and expenses on a Three Kings trip are very high.

Precious few skippers would risk their boats or skins up there. We were so fortunate to have won the heart of Peter Sheehan on our last trip. A more honest, straightforward man does not sail the New Zealand coast and there was never any question of his giving away our secrets or taking anyone else up.

On the evening of Boxing Day 1966, the *Ahiki* again set off down the winding Awanui River for the Three Kings. For the long, uneventful cruise we all bedded down on whatever flat surface we could find. I propped myself up on my plank "bed" balanced athwartships on the diesel fuel tank and began a diary for my second trip to the *Elingamite*. Around me the others dozed fitfully. Sleep had to be snatched whenever available with eight people living on the comfortless *Ahiki*.

Reading quietly in one of the two bunks was Kelvin's father. Ewart Tarlton was a very valuable acquisition. At sixty-five he had spent a lifetime in small boats; he had lived for some time on remote D'Urville Island in Cook Strait, and was as fit as any of us. He shared Kelvin's interest and ability in photography and rock climbing. A skilled boatman, capable of handling a cockleshell in the most atrocious conditions, he was to spend hours pitching and tossing in whirlpools, tide-races and big swells, together with loads of divers, diving gear and big fish.

A good boatman at the Kings is essential. Our ship could not venture close in enough to the rocks, the risk being too great so far

On a calm day a great swell still flexes across the tide-race as the *Lady Gwen* approaches the wreck site on the West King in 1968, taking the same course as the *Elingamite*

A shroud of mist and spray overhanging West King

Before the *Elingamite* wreck was found, the amazingly varied sea life itself was the main source of interest

Jaan Voot and his second eighty-five-pound kingfish of the day

Wade Doak offers champagne to a blue cod

He hovers above the *Elingamite*'s winch

At first the wreck was scarcely discernible, heavily covered with marine growth and in the dim light of 150 feet down

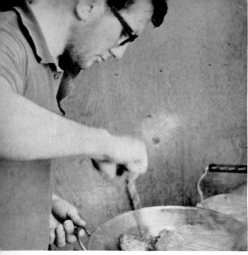

John Pettit

Jeff Pearch (cook-diver)

Wade Doak

Kelly Tarlton (cameraman master-blaster)

John Gallagher (Jag)

Ewart Tarlton (boatman)

Some members of the *Elingamite* diving team

from home. If a ship was holed at the Three Kings there would be no hope of beaching it. The cliff faces everywhere plunge straight down one hundred feet.

John Gallagher had not been hard to recruit. I had met him on a diving trip to White Island, the active volcano in New Zealand's Bay of Plenty. The Gallagher family of Hamilton own the 90-foot steel motor yacht *Hamutana* which frequently takes out a score of divers on long weekends. Each winter either John or his brother Bill go with her up to the New Hebrides for a family cruise, and deliver equipment to the mission stations as a charitable gesture.

I met John when invited to dive on the *Hamutana*, but didn't see much of him except underwater. Down below I soon learnt that he and his brother were superb divers, equally capable with a spear gun or camera. Topside I would see John only at mealtimes. He seemed as enthusiastic at eating as at diving. But then he would disappear. Only towards the end of the trip did I find that John had a bunk right up for'ard by the chain locker. When not eating or diving, I was to learn, John's favourite occupation is sleeping. While other poor divers endured the boredom of a six-hour voyage to White Island, John would escape to the "sack". At any available moment John would get his head on the pillow and we had to learn to copy him.

When Aucklander John Pettit joined us we decided to call our first John "Jag" and Jag he has remained for the rest of our diving trips.

John Pettit is a natural foil to Jag: when there's nothing to do Jag sleeps but John hops around as lively as a sparrow. He is always finding work and cleaning things up. When there's a job to do both he and Jag are dynamic.

John is an ex-policeman who decided there was a bigger opening in hothouses than jails. Over the last eight years he has built up a business as a nurseryman with a string of shops, glasshouses, vans and pots. A chance to come to the Kings was just what he needed to get a real break from his hothouse business and we acquired another first-class deep diver, with an unusual appetite, for a scuba man, for snorkeling a big kingfish or a groper—anything, so long as it would beat the club champion.

Kelvin and I were thinking of our stomachs when we invited Jeff. The year before our party of divers had camped for twelve days on a narrow ledge on the cliff face at the Poor Knights Islands, twelve miles out from Whangarei. And with us in that harsh place among the mutton birds, tuataras and giant wetas we had a treasure: our skindiving cook Jeff Pearch. After twelve days' deep diving to lay out a scientific grid survey of the undersea cliff face our eight divers all returned to the mainland having gained weight. Jeff is a trained chef and when it comes to roughing it he just has not got the message. None of this tinned meat, baked beans and indigestible lumps of spud cooked in salt water. No tired cabbage boiled until the blowflies came or anaemic tinned peas. Jeff is a Lancashire lad from Wigan and had never been camping in his life. When we shift out into the wilds he *does* take a kitchen sink. And a chopping board, special chef's knives, garlic, parsley, a black pepper grinder and enough dry red wine. We knew we could just leave Jeff to jack up the tucker and live like kings at the Three Kings.

On the verge of departure John Young had turned up. He had just stepped off a plane from New Guinea where he had spent a year working as a mission carpenter, and diving in his spare time. When he ran into us he had not really settled down to life in Hamilton so one very bronzed spearfisherman who didn't like garlic joined our expedition.

Kelvin Tarlton and I were both South Islanders who had shifted north five years earlier to be closer to our reigning passion: the clear blue Pacific Ocean.

I'd first met Kelly on a railway journey through the Southern Alps to Lake Moana. Our party of a dozen skindivers was going to explore the remains of ancient Maori war canoes. The story we had heard was that a tribe of Maoris lived on an island in the mountain lake. The route to the beautiful greenstone "jade", so highly esteemed as an ornament and cutting tool by Maoris throughout New Zealand, lay across this wide lake. From their fort on the island the Maori tribe would allow the toiling travellers past to hew and carry the greenstone out of the bush, but on the return journey they would ambush them, kill them and seize the stone.

So when Kelvin and I first met we were after treasure: big lumps of greenstone and carved Maori war canoes, which we would raise for the Canterbury Museum. But our rumoured canoes turned out to be sunken logs from the timber mill. Then the West Coast rains came down. We were flooded out and had to make a long gruelling walk waist deep through the flooded bush wearing our scuba gear on our chests, our packs on our backs and our lead weights on our aching hips.

But that triggered off our love for expeditions. Initially we dived all round the South Island seeking clear water. With Kelvin I dived at Stewart Island. With our friends we hewed a hole in frozen Lake Ida and made New Zealand's first sub-ice dive, and up in the Marlborough Sounds I stood on a launch and waited for Kelly to

34

surface after a snorkel dive to 104 feet. In those days this was only thirty feet off the world record so we were very proud of Kelly.

From the start he was the opposite to me: a telephone technician, he is a genius at wires, nuts, levers and resistances. He built the first underwater camera house I ever saw. A huge sphere with brass knobs on, it enclosed his father's precious Leica. Kelly was sure it would be safe though. A piece of blotting paper stretched between two springs would ensure this. Should a drop of water enter the housing the paper would snap, causing a current which would ring an electric bell mounted beside the camera. His father's camera never got wet but Kelly grew tired of rushing to the surface when that bell rang. Wryly he said one day: "It's all wrong. No use putting in warning systems in case of leaks. A housing should be designed to be one hundred per cent watertight!"

And he made one. In those days of underwater photography Kelly used to place all his accessories, light meter, view finder, flash batteries and capacitators, close-up lenses—the lot went inside his clumsy, huge housing. Then the amphibious Nikonos under-water camera arrived. Just a simple 35 mm camera, but watertight to 150 feet without any housing. Light, rugged and a joy to handle. Kelly mounted a light meter on it. Then he found he needed a special view finder to eliminate parallax errors; measuring rods for close-up work followed, plus close-up lenses to clip in the front. Finally he had to build a fifteen-pound electronic flash adjustably mounted on a nine-foot pole. So now his light, handy little camera fits inside a cluster of gadgets weighing nearly twenty pounds.

While I was at Canterbury University Kelly decided to organize a six-months diving expedition to the Hermit Islands, north of New Guinea. His diving friends and I assisted him in raising the money by running diving shows in a 10,000 gallon perspex-fronted tank.

It was during these shows that I learnt that Kelly can keep his head in an emergency.

Dennis Fowler, an Irish diver, stood at the ticket box at the front of our marquee: "Come on folks, step inside and see the skindivers underwater," he blared broguishly with the electric megaphone. But the public was too rapt in a free movie being projected by the Traffic Department. Again he urged them: "See the divers defy gravity under ten tons of water." This was better; a few turned and stared at Kelly and me out front in our dry suits, but no one moved. Incensed, our barking diver-showman muttered: "All right then you bastards, just stand there and bloody-well stare." But he still had his finger on the megaphone button. This torrent of abuse hit the public like a bucket of cold water, and quite a few automatically moved past a red-faced Kelly into our tent.

Once we had acquired an audience Kelly strode smartly into the tent to compere the show. A rope separated the audience from the ten tons of water. Kelly vaulted this barrier like a ballet dancer, caught his foot on it and fell flat on his face in the sawdust. The audience would have been hardened a little by the language outside the tent but Kelly's flood of imprecations must have been a little daunting. Gathering himself up with grace and aplomb Kelly cleared his throat. His beard matted with sawdust, apologetically he began his spiel. The first diver appeared up the ladder and paused at the rim of the huge floodlit cylinder of water.

"Good evening folks. Ah, the diver will now, ah, descend."

Our clumsy, great rubber-clad clot leapt from the ladder down into the diving tank, hooking the floodlights in his apparatus. There followed sparks, an explosion, hissing air and complete darkness. When Kelly succeeded in restoring order and light to the tent and managed to send out a mollified audience at the end, I knew my diving mate would rise to any emergency.

During his 1959 expedition to the remote Hermit Island Group with Dennis Fowler, Kelly had first tried his hand at filming with a 16 mm underwater camera. He brought back a dynamic footage of giant manta rays, countless sharks all mixed up with divers, multi-coloured fish, and corals. It had us enthralled but commercially it was a flop. Kelly learnt the hard way that a movie must have establishing shots, middle distance and close-up sequences; that the narrative must be carried by the film itself, not by an explanatory narrator. His manta-riding sequences needed to start with the divers donning diving gear in their dugout canoe, then gliding down from the surface of the lagoon. He had only the climatic scenes with no build up or linkage. But it was a grand experience.

From the islands Kelly wrote to me: "It was late in the afternoon, the ideal time to find mantas. Every few seconds a yell would go up and we would peer in the direction of the splash that had created the alarm. Generally it would just be a fish, though a few were no doubt mantas. However, they were always gone before we reached the spot.

"As our dugout rounded a point a simultaneous yell went up from the four of us. In front were dozens of fins breaking the surface in regular beats. It could be nothing but the wingtips of a shoal of mantas. Suddenly we saw the huge shapes passing under the canoe and we all hit the water at the same time. The sight was unbelievable: twenty or thirty mantas doing acrobatics, looping the loop, victory rolls, and peeling off in succession. From ten to twenty feet across they flew through the water effortlessly. Awe-stricken we did nothing but float there and gape. Then we all came to life at once. We dived down amongst them, swimming right up to their gaping mouths, peering inside and then dodging back at the last moment as they swished past. On occasions like this, depth does not seem to matter and only now and then do you come to the top for a breath. As I filmed I saw Dennis dive towards one: it changed course and headed straight for him. Only when it was almost touching him did it do a half roll and slide past him. As the big white belly trailing remoras glided by he reached out and touched. The manta suddenly accelerated with one mighty beat of its wings, then slowly swam back and joined in with the rest of the shoal. Dennis swam up for air and came down to grab another manta. This time he reached out and seized its tail. Giving several beats of its wings it spurted ahead, trailing Dennis. Bursting for air he soon had to release his grip and drop behind."

On the same expedition Kelvin wrote to me of his first attack of nitrogen narcosis. (This was to be one of the problems on our future *Elingamite* dives.) This diving hazard, aptly named by the French "rapture of the deeps", is caused by breathing compressed air at great depth.

Kelvin was making his first 200-foot descent: "Dennis and I swam on down. At 130 feet we began to feel the effects of nitrogen narcosis, a slight fuzziness in our heads as if we had had two or three drinks. At 180 feet we were feeling quite light-headed. The bottom was covered with small worm holes, but otherwise there was not much to see yet. It became hard to realize that we were swimming down a steep slope. My brain kept telling me we were swimming horizontally across a flat sea floor. Possibly my balance organisms were being affected by the narcosis. It was only by a concentrated effort that I forced myself to watch the hand of my depth gauge winding itself around.

"By now my tongue felt as if it was filling my whole mouth. Birds were singing in my head. A vision of a grove of trees with a small creek running through it kept drifting in front of my eyes. I knew I should be keeping a lookout for the large sharks we had often seen swimming in these deep waters but I could not be bothered to turn my head and look.

"The worms on the bottom almost invariably pulled themselves back into their holes as we approached but occasionally one did not, and I found myself trying to poke it back with my finger! Suddenly a wave of anxiety hit me and I forced myself to look at my depth gauge. The luminous paint on the dial was glowing like a neon sign with the needle swinging past the 200-foot mark. I tapped Dennis

37

on the shoulder—he jumped. I showed him the gauge and gave the
'going up' signal. According to my watch we had been descending
for fifteen minutes. I fastened my eyes on a small bubble and followed
it up.

"It was only when I had nearly finished decompressing at ten
feet on the anchor chain that the last of the narcosis left me."

In 1960 our annual series of four diving expeditions to New
Caledonia began, each time largely motivated by spearfishing.
Photography was struggling with our urge to catch big fish, and
greedily we tried to accomplish both. At this stage Kelvin was using
a still camera whenever we could afford the film. I had a Rolleiflex
and Rolleimarine housing but I still preferred to spear fish. After
one experience, while diving with Keith Gordon, our close diving
friend, I wrote home: "We Kiwis departed for Dumbea Passage
with Gus and M. Bequer. It was a long trip to the barrier reef but I
was absorbed watching the morning lights creep across the sea
towards us, while to the west Noumea still lay twinkling in the darkness. Over the sleeping town hung clouds shot with the glow of the
ever burning nickel furnaces which keep it prosperous.

"When we arrived at the pass, the sun was well up (6.30 a.m.)
and already intense. We piled into the gin clear water of the tide-
race teeming with fish as usual. I shot a fair-sized saumonee first.
It was beneath a mushroom coral, the underside packed with fish
like sheep under a tree. Then I glimpsed a twenty-pound loche
(spotted groper) which I chased around until it headed into a cave.
At the entrance I met Keith. We shook fists at one another—both
hunting the same fish. I motioned him to have first shot. He dived,
fired, but the spear pulled out. I fired into the head. It held when I
pulled on the spearline but the fish must have dilated his big gill-
plates there in the gloom. He would not budge. Keith meanwhile,
having searched around the coral clump, found another cave entrance,
and seeing a large groper tail, fired a shot up into the dark. Now
both of us were independently diving, yanking at our respective fish
and exchanging a gurgled commentary each time we surfaced
for air.

"Gradually the murk cleared enough for me to see my fish—no
twenty-pounder. This was a whopper! We continued tugging and
then something dawned on us: we both had the same fish!

"Now the tussle began in earnest. As a team we ripped off huge
chunks of coral to get closer and with a third gun, borrowed from
Kelly, put a spear into the eye. We had him properly now. Three
guns bobbed on the surface tethered to the vague shadowy mass
below. However, we had reached a stalemate—two guns were

38

attached from one side of the cave and one from the other. We decided to cut one loose and then we hauled together and gradually extracted an 80-pounder loche from the cave into which we had chased the 20-pounder. Whose was this one ?"

Now all this was a long way behind us and we were sailing northwards again to the Three Kings. I stowed my diary away and over the huddle of sleeping divers crawled from our tiny quarters and made my way along the deserted deck to the wheelhouse. Inside John Pettit and Peter Sheehan were yarning. Peter tirelessly spun the wheel spokes, waited for the bow to answer, then spun them again as she swung off course. The *Ahiki* is a very old vessel and really has to be steered every sea mile. As she chugged at seven knots into the darkness the four-knot tide rip running around the tip of New Zealand pushed her off course to the west; then, in the early hours of the morning to the east.

There were no lights on the Kings. Only Cape Reinga lighthouse, astern, pencilled the horizon in great arcs every few seconds. There was no moon. The ship's bows dipped and lifted into utter blackness, directed by the compass glowing quietly under Peter's eyes.

We passed close by the *Kaitawa*'s graveyard. On a pad beside the compass we had the exact bearings of the sunken collier which had disappeared one stormy May night in 1966 with all hands. Once we had photographed the *Elingamite* and speared plenty of big fish, we intended to try to locate the *Kaitawa* in quest of more photos. The Navy had reported that she was lying on her side in 120 feet of water, up against a huge rocky pinnacle. The current would be an obstacle, but no worse than at the *Elingamite* site. There would be little problem from the swell and no rocky shore to endanger our ship. We were as keen to dive on her as on the *Elingamite*.

Below we had jars and jars of alcohol from Auckland and Victoria universities. Another important objective was to collect corals, sponges, crustacea and other material from this seldom visited area. We knew that marine scientists would be overjoyed to receive a well-labelled collection of samples and we were very keen to help them. At the outset this expedition was certainly no treasure hunt.

When the *Ahiki* drew into the towering cliffs of the Great King at seven on Tuesday morning our first thought was to dive in the fabled Groper Gut, the rocky ravine in which Chris and Kelly had met a school of the big fish back in 1963. Poor Peter! For fourteen hours he had stood at the wheel, yet he was still keen to keep going. Trawler skippers get used to such punishment.

Three with guns and two with cameras, we leaped into the mouth of the Groper Gut and swept through in the current, itching to get among the big school Kelly had told us about. The sea was turquoise and wonderfully clear but it was colder than coastal waters in mid-winter. In the gut we clung to rocks, flapped in the current and waited. Not a sign of a groper. Packs of sleek trevally, pink mao mao, red sea perch, crayfish but nothing worth spearing. The huge basin-sized sea eggs took our interest. Once our hopes had cooled, we grabbed a couple of huge specimens to start our *marine* life collection and kicked hard up current back to the *Ahiki*.

Disappointed at spear fishing, we decided to make our way down to the West King, a nine-mile trip, to try a dive over the wreck. This, too, proved a waste of time.

Until the ship rounds the tip of West King Island and comes to the exposed western face, one does not know whether it will be possible to dive or not. The wind is no real indication. In a westerly wind we have hazarded a trip down there from our anchorage at Great King, only to be amazed by reasonable conditions. Another time, with hardly any wind, we have found it impossible to round the corner. The seas pounding the West King come from miles down the Tasman, perhaps even from Antarctica.

And so it was when we arrived at the wreck site for the first time on this 1966 expedition: the swells were cresting into breakers half a mile out from the cliffs and the area above the wreck was a maelstrom of incoming waves and backwash from the surge sweeping down over the switchback curved reef immediately above the wreck. The air was white with spray, and through the existing confusion the usual fierce tide rip was pouring. Diving was impossible.

Wednesday morning we returned to the wreck site. Conditions had improved considerably, but it was still a horrible looking place to dive. At this stage we had made only one dive in this area, right at the end of our last expedition. We were to learn later how to cope with conditions just as bad as this, and even worse, but it took knockbacks and experience to develop the techniques and special gear used on our later expeditions.

The *Ahiki* nosed cautiously in towards the wreck site. Jag, Kelly and I, all bristling with underwater cameras, flash units and bulbs, leapt into the tide-race and started finning furiously shorewards. Below us we could see nothing but a bottomless blue void. When we raised our head to get our direction there was no island in front of us. The whole ocean was sliding towards Australia. Our frantic efforts towards the West King were laughable. We relaxed in the current, buoyancy compensators inflated, and waited for the *Ahiki* to cruise in over the swells and rescue us. At times only her mast was visible as the ocean sagged and heaved around us. Trying

40

to make a dive in that place reminded me of the efforts of space scientists to pair up orbital satellites: the same huge areas, changing forces and shifting positions.

Aboard ship we decided to leave the wreck until later. Getting some good photos of groper was just as important as the *Elingamite*. So we sailed around to the lee of the West King. In the slick of calm water you can always find beside the worst current, Peter parked the *Ahiki*. It was too deep to anchor. His echo sounder showed 300 feet within fifty feet of the cliff face.

We were expecting to find some large schools of kingfish feeding in here. Seabirds were screaming over the backs of trevally packed fin to fin in a half-acre mass. Beneath them the kingies would be swooping about vying with the birds and trevally to devour bait fish sheltering from the current in a huge cloud.

While the other three went snorkeling among this frenzy of fish, Jag and I donned scuba. We swam into the cliff face, planning to glide down it for shelter from the current, in order to photograph the spearfishing action from below.

We sank down to a hundred feet, puffing a little air into our compensators *en route*. Then our breathing stopped short: a herd of over thirty huge hapuka was moving up the steep slope from the dim-clear depths. Jag and I perched dumbfounded on an outcrop while they swarmed over us, between us and round our legs. From forty to over one hundred pounds, their huge jagged dorsal fins filled our viewfinders in great inartistic masses. The best compositions formed up as we frantically changed flash bulbs. Some zoomed straight for us on collision courses and finned out at arm's distance. All around them cavorted trevally, dense packed and feeding. King-sized kingfish nosed in at us for their share of the camera. The light was almost blotted out by seething fishes' bodies. But for nearly ten minutes all Jag and I had eyes for was the hapuka. Individual 'puka are a rare enough sight in New Zealand, but to be schooled around by them was like some alcoholic dream. Jag's eyes were like saucers and I haven't the least memory of taking a photo of him holding a 'puka off with his outstretched flipper as he frantically fiddled a bulb into his flash socket he was worried that the fish would come too close to make a good picture. The 'puka looks quite tolerant as Jag's fin drapes across his back.

Gradually, as the tide slackened and the feeding frenzy diminished, the hapuka slipped back into the purple (300 feet plus) depths, leaving us to play with the tarakihi. In most locations we have great difficulty getting fish and diver into the same photo. We often marvelled at the luck or skill of overseas photographers who succeed. But in conditions like these such shots were obligatory.

41

It would be very difficult to photograph a lone diver. Every time Jag rubbed his fingers the tarakihi would move in to nibble them. Only a movie camera could have captured his reaction when one gave a determined nip.

One hundred feet above us Kelly was peering down. He had been trying to get among hapuka like these for years—ever since he saw them briefly on his first trip to the Kings with Chris Busck. He was furious at having jumped in to snorkel with the spearfishermen, John Pettit and John Young, hoping to get some action shots of them. Kelly had snorkeled to 104 feet but not wielding his huge electronic flash rig. John Pettit's description as he watched Kelly trying to reach us and our cloud of hapuka: "A bloody, great frame full of junk with a tiny Nikonos camera that does all the work buried in the middle."

Here is John's story:

"So Peter parked the *Ahiki* in the lee of the West King. The cliff face plunged sheer down through the transparent water to loss of view. Wade and Jag leapt over the side festooned with aqualungs, cameras, flashbulb holders, depth gauges, D.C.P. meters, the lot. John Young and I decided to snorkel with spearguns. Around us the water boiled with four to six pound trevally. Great schools of them making and breaking together. You could feel the activity of their frenzy, like electricity. In a few moments, in swept the kingies. I must say at this point that although kingies are most plentiful in this region I did not see any of the monsters speared by the previous expedition. It was just our luck to strike a period when the big 'uns had gone deep sea. None the less the adrenalin count rose as they swept around us. John Young planted one immediately; about a fifty-pounder. I watched from the surface as the kingie went through his death throes at about fifty feet.

"I always watch carefully at this stage as you can often get a good shot in at the curious big 'un that will always park alongside a freshly injured mate. Sure enough, through the trevally I could see a large shape having a gander at John's fish. I immediately stoked up, and down I went, easing off the safety catch, paying out some free line all ready for the kill shot. Suddenly I am there and as I sight up I realize that this is no kingie. A giant-size hapuka was hanging there gazing sorrowfully at John's kingie. I took aim as I swam closer but as I did a thought came to me. This hapuka would go at least 100 pounds. I was almost out of breath, about 200 feet of water lay beneath us and above, approximately fifty feet. My reel held 120 feet of braided nylon. This I realized, is how spearguns are lost. I broke the surface and tried to console myself; I had

42

lost an opportunity but retained a speargun. Was it good judgment or cowardice or plain meanness? Let's face it—spearguns are hard to buy at the Kings! I must say that this little episode left me somewhat depressed. This was my first sighting of a hapuka and to take one of that size on snorkel would most certainly raise a few eyebrows.

"John, meanwhile, had boated his kingie and was making his way back towards me when I half-heartedly speared a passing kingie. History now repeats itself as John dives down towards my wounded fish. A big 'puka moves back alongside and John lets him have it. I lost sight of the play at this stage as I suddenly realized that we were being swept by a steady current into a deep gut, which cuts through the southern end of the island. I could make little headway against it, particularly as my kingie wanted to go the other way and it was only after hailing the *Ahiki* that we were saved from a nasty experience. I must say at this stage that anyone venturing to dive at Kings should have a good boatman and never anchor or stop engines while divers are in the water as no swimmer, no matter how strong, could make headway for more than a few minutes against these rips. Sure enough, back on *Ahiki*, John Young dejectedly reported that he had lost his gun on the big 'puka.

"After picking up Wade and Jag, Wade by this time incoherent with excitement, John and I donned scuba gear and decided to do a quick dive to see if any 'pukas happened to be wearing spearguns at the moment. We worked down the same face that Wade and Jag had been working on. At ninety feet we stopped on a ledge. The slope continued steeply from here and looking down into that deep blue water it seemed bottomless. Great clouds of fish gathered about with kingies always in view. Beyond them I could see the 'puka, first one then another, looming up from nowhere, their great undershot jaws and gleaming gill plates adding a menacing look to their great dark metallic bodies.

"I turned towards John. Behind him a 'puka was gliding down the rock face. This fish looked bigger than John and with three kicks it was in range. Wham! In went the spear—deep into his broad fleshy back. Whrrr! Out went all the line in spite of the drag being wound on hard. I last saw my prize thrashing his way down the rock face into the deep blue abyss. I held ground by wedging the end of my speargun into a hollow in the rocks. After a while the tug of war ceased and I reeled in my bent and battered spear Was it sweat? Was my mask leaking? No, I think they were tears of anguish that ran down my cheeks as I set about trying to straighten my spear. I was unable to get out all the kinks but after a lot of trial and error I managed to get the spear jammed back in the gun.

"By this time John had gone, my air was getting low, and a bent

43

spear is no equipment to shoot fish with. I kicked off for the surface muttering diabolical underwater curses to myself. As I glided up the rock face I came across a baby 'puka swimming towards me so I nonchalantly planted my spear into him. Some baby—he almost wrenched my arms out as he took off. Where did all that power come from? I was being towed along at speed clutching my speargun in one hand and holding my mask with the other. I kept the line short and by planing my body upwards I was actually lifting both myself and the fish with the fish doing all the work. Gradually he stopped and as I worked nearer the surface, he was suddenly dead and floating upside down. My baby looked a little bigger on the surface and I was quite thrilled to see him tip the scales to sixty-three pounds. The boys on board the boat showed great enthusiasm and even helped me to weigh the fish.

"After the most profuse congratulations my shipmates invited me to take a look at the deck on the other side of the boat. I felt my little moment of glory collapse as I gazed on John Young's eighty-five-pound hapuka lying there in all its splendour."

That dive was the climax to our spearfishing at the Three Kings. It was also the last time we would take a speargun below.

Before the tide turned the *Ahiki* plucked us aboard and steamed back around the corner to the wreck site. Conditions were much better now. Only a slight current would run for the next few minutes of slack water. Five splashes and we strung out in line swimming north with the stream. Each diver was in visual contact with his neighbour so that we were like a human net angled downwards from 100 to 200 feet and moving along the flank of West King.

The water was very clear now. We could see 150 feet in every direction. After some five minutes of searching the first signs of the shipwreck appeared. A white porcelain lavatory, festooned with pink fan corals; scattered portholes, the brass gleaming from abrasive sea action even at 150 feet. As the wreckage thickened excitement rippled up the chain of divers and we broke up. With not the least thought of treasure, each diver sought a souvenir or a photo of this famous wreck. Swimming near Kelly I found a pile of sea-growth-covered bottles, swept under a rock ledge by the current. Two champagne bottles and a brandy bottle. For Kelly I removed my mouthpiece and took a pull on one bottle, while he extended the boom of his electronic flash six feet towards me and lit the sea up like lightning each time he triggered his camera.

Then we came across the propeller. A brilliant mosaic of sponges, anemones and sealife encrusted the huge blades. With my diver's knife I began scraping it away. Would it be cast iron or brass? A

44

brass propeller this size, about seven tons in weight would be very valuable as scrap metal. The metal gleamed golden. It *was* brass!

And this was the dive that culminated in my first coin finds, described at the start of this story; those dusky metal discs littered under the rock ledge which changed our lives so much.

From now on we were diving for *Treasure*.

Chapter 3

As the *Ahiki* wound its way up the slow skeins of the Awanui River we had an hourlong discussion on our plans. The *Elingamite's* gold was foremost in our minds now. No more spearfishing or "shutter bugging" at the Three Kings.

"How soon can you make it up there again?" Kelly asked Peter.

"Aw, should be right the week after next, Kel."

Peter was as keen as any of us to see that gold on his decks. We could not do better than take a skipper like him on our side. The way he had handled the boat in the confused seas alongside the West King and his tolerance of divers and their mountains of gear warmly endeared him to us. We appreciated what a worry it must have been to put men over the side of his boat in such a risky area and, ignorant of diving procedures, to cruise nearby waiting for us to surface again. We trusted his weather eye and deep knowledge of the sea coming from a lifetime afloat. While the *Ahiki* was old and slow, hardly designed for comfortable living, in Peter's hands she was the best treasure diving boat we could get. And Peter wanted to return.

We had a fortnight to prepare a full-scale attack on the wreck. "What if someone decides to beat us to it?" I worried. "Should we try to keep the whole thing a secret?"

"There wouldn't be a hope," said John Pettit. "Too many people know where we've been and would have a fair idea why we're returning."

Kelly reassured us: "No one would stand a show of finding that bullion, let alone the wreck. Our own luck has been terrific. Besides, most of the divers in New Zealand who can dive that deep are our friends."

That worry quelled, our old pessimism began to arise. Jag wondered if the treasure was still there. "Could have been raised by the Japs on the quiet. Sixty odd years seems a long time to leave a fortune on the bottom."

That was a possibility, but just another risk we would have to run. It seemed unlikely that, unnoticed, a ship could work the treasure site for the length of time necesary to recover the bullion. We knew that there had been initial salvage attempts in 1907.

Kelly and I were given the job of trying to trace the son of the diver, Harper, who had died at the wreck site. We had heard he was living at Leigh, fifty miles north of Auckland.

Jeff Pearch would arrange the provisions for our return trip. John Pettit and Jag would get all our air tanks refilled, and obtain as many extra ones as they could beg or borrow. Air we would need in great quantities. Jag would bring some large storage cylinders, each one equivalent to seven scuba tanks. Kelly said he would construct some airlifts.

I was appointed press spokesman for the expedition. Our first difficulty was to keep things quiet as the ship pulled into Awanui wharf. Someone on the wharf could be a newshound who would send our story all around New Zealand. A small crowd awaited our return. To sell our story and photos we had to control the release and find the best market.

So as we unloaded, slinging the frozen cadavers of the three huge groper and several large kingfish up on to the wharf, we raved about the fabulous spearfishing we had had at the Kings. Among the crowd I saw an eighteen stone Maori giant. He looked as if his ancestors had waved their spears at Abel Tasman's men from the cliff tops of the Great King. He grinned and I remembered we had given him one of Jaan Voot's eighty-five-pound kingfish on returning from our last spearfishing safari. I clapped the tail of another whopper into his hand. Delighted he told me; "Those Three Kings kingies are the fattest I ever knew. Big fellas like that are never hungry enough to take a hook. Have to spear them, ae." There was one guy on our side on the Awanui wharf.

During the next two weeks we all worked, slept, ate and dreamt treasure. The newpapers published our story. "Divers Enter Strongroom of Treasure Ship", said front-page headlines in New Zealand and Australia! The phone buzzed with interest, letters started to pile up from people with personal links with the ship, and our small pile of coins was handled and fondled by our diving friends.

Kelvin arrived at my Wellsford home with two airlifts. He had built them from fifteen-foot lengths of alkathene tube, three inches in diameter. There was an inlet pipe two feet from one end. A corrugated hose linked this with one exhaust port of the scuba regulator. When a diver exhaled, his exhaust air escaped through this hose and expanded up the alkathene tube, causing a powerful suction at the bottom end. He must keep his head tilted towards the tube so that the exhaust port linked to it was uppermost. Kelly had built two models, one having a complicated "baffle" system to prevent the suction effect (venturi principle) dragging

47

on the regulator. Otherwise he felt the suction might cause it to deliver a constant air flow similar to a diver inhaling continuously. This would swiftly empty a scuba tank at 150 feet.

The airlifts strapped from bumper to boot, we drove out to Leigh. We had two aims: To test our "goldsuckers" and to trace Mr Harper, son of the diver who had first worked on the *Elingamite* bullion.

It must have been a curious sight: two scuba divers walking into the sea trailing great lengths of black tube. Some new breathing system or perhaps the beginning of a new pipeline to Kawau Island? As we submerged we both had strong doubts that a system as beautifully simple as ours would work. Conventional airlifts function in much the same way, but instead of using fluctuating pulses of exhaust air, a separate tank of compressed air is discharged through the inlet pipe in a constant stream. This would be preferable, but quite impossible for us at the *Elingamite* site. The great depth would cause a tank to exhaust itself in five minutes. Besides, our supplies of air up there were too limited to be wasted in this way, and the strong current would make transporting an extra tank below a time-consuming struggle. Our exhaust-air sand dredges were truly Scottish in conception; we were hoping to get the very last bit of use out of our air.

I placed the tube on the sand, connected the bayonet fittings linking the exhaust port on my mouthpiece to it, and then erected the tube so that it curved slightly fifteen feet above me. I breathed out. With a rattling roar a two-foot diameter hole appeared in the sea bed, clean right down to the rocky substratum a foot below. The gentle curve of the pipe sent the debris well clear of me, sand and stones sifted and sank in a dense curtain ten feet away. This would be no worry if I worked up current. The vortex caused by my next breath exposed a strange snakelike eel which I had never seen before. The airlift was revealing an area of the seabed most inaccessible to scientists. The rock bottom beneath a foot of sand was bristling with life-forms.

Nearby Kelly had been testing his "baffle" model and to his surprise, it laid bare a length of very heavy galvanized anchor chain, presumably lost from a rather spacious yacht.

As we climbed out of our gear we chattered excitedly at the success of the dredge. Kelly said that for some models of regulator the baffle was essential to prevent it triggering off a constant delivery. My own Calypso regulator worked perfectly without it. The gold seemed closer to us now we had this new means to vacuum clean the sea floor.

At Leigh Post Office we asked the whereabouts of Mr Harper.

"There," said the postmaster, pointing towards the sea. "Just beside the cemetery on the hill."

We found the tall old man very willing to talk about his adventures at the Three Kings. On his kitchen wall was a framed photo of the schooner *Huia*, the salvage ship on which his father had died. We were keen to glean any details of those early diving operations which might help our own efforts.

"The gold was in the turret head, above the propeller shaft," said diver Harper's son. "Ted, my brother and I were in the longboat tendering Dad's hose. Two chaps were working the pump. A four cylinder job. Real old chaff-cutter. We could tell the depth by the amount of hose left in the boat. Twenty-four fathoms it was."

That tallied with the spot we were working in. We showed him a photo taken on the surface above our coin discovery, and he assured us we were in the right area.

"Dad said the bullion must have shot out when the turret head split open. There were fifty-two or fifty-four boxes, I can't remember. Our longboat was moored fore and aft. Four anchors. She was twenty-six feet long. Dad came up after the morning dive and we pulled up £804. He said there were half-sovereigns stacked on their edges sticking to the iron. He even found coins sticking in the prong of a fork."

When our questions neared the fatal dive Mr Harper began to tell us about the earlier salvage expedition when he went up on the *Young Bungaree*. We listened rapt to his disjointed account of earlier divers and their mishaps.

"That ex-man-o'war's man didn't even get to the bottom. He went down a little way, then he turned the air off on his helmet. Of course his suit ballooned out and he bobbed to the surface. Said he thought he was getting too much air. He was bleeding from the eyes and mouth so we had to sail down to Helensville to see a doctor, making sixteen knots in a north-west gale."

Kelly and I thought to ourselves how lucky this diver was to survive. A sudden ascent like that can often result in an air embolism. Expanding with the reduced water pressure, air in the lungs ruptures the capillaries and foams into the bloodstream leading to a rapid death.

"The Union Company man, an Aussie diver, was swept away when he was halfway to the bottom," Mr Harper continued. "Just a minute I'll get the half-sovereign my father gave me."

This old man made us very aware of the passage of time since the shipwreck as he talked about his father and we tried to imagine him as a boy at the wreck site.

He returned with a gold chain. On it dangled the first gold half-sovereign I had ever seen. Kelly and I lovingly fingered the embossed figure of St George and the Dragon. The date on the coin was 1902. It had sunk with the *Elingamite* the year it was minted, and had lain there for five years before diver Harper had plucked it off the rusting iron plate.

"Dad had been below for one and a half hours that day. He was a fine diver. He had worked in Ceylon laying twenty-five ton concrete blocks for a breakwater. Now he was using a marlin spike and hammer. Ted my brother signalled him to come up, but he wouldn't. He was too excited."

The old man's eyes misted as the death of his father aboard the *Huia* came back to his mind.

Kelly and I thanked him deeply and made him a gift of one of our own *Elingamite* coins, which he accepted with genuine pleasure.

As we drove home we seethed with renewed excitement. Our air-lifts worked well and now we felt sure we were really on to the bullion. The old man's story, his description of the actual wreck site, the depth—everything made us feel sure that we were taking up the work his father had been engaged in when he died. Our hopes were golden. We had fingered an *Elingamite* half-sovereign. We were sure we were going to be running our fingers through heaps of these golden discs in the next few days. To return to that rocky cleft, in which I had found the initial pile of silver was all that mattered.

Chapter 4

THE *Ahiki* PULLED OUT from the Awanui wharf, one hour up river from the sea and fourteen hours steaming to the *Elingamite*; and we stuck fast in the mud on a falling tide, twenty yards downstream opposite the dairy factory waste outlet. Two hours' vile stench and frustration followed before we got any closer to our goal.

So remote it had seemed during the days of preparation; to get to the Three Kings twice within a fortnight after being delayed for two years by bad weather and other contingencies, seemed to be asking too much. Yet everything rested on our return. It was a fluke to locate coins amongst an acre of wreckage strewn down the steep flank of West King Island but now we were prepared for a carefully planned series of dives to recover the bullion.

This time, as Kelly, Jeff and I dropped down from the madly tossing surface to the relative quiet of the wreck site, the gold seemed to be already in our grasp.

On the bottom at 150 feet we swam around looking for our bearings. Each diver in his silent blue world registered a private feeling of dismay. The powerful current billowing in our faces was changing visibility rapidly from forty to eighty feet in cloudy gusts. When we had fixed the position of the initial silver find visibility had been 150 feet. Now we had no way of determining that position. With rising fears we searched among the similar rocks, probed hopefully in the wreckage, and fossicked in crevices. Kelly found two threepenny bits in a crack.

I seized a golden looking cat's eye jubilantly. We surfaced in the rip tide. It was hard to break the news to John Pettit and John Gallagher waiting to descend with a golden glitter in their eyes; we'd failed to relocate the coin deposit.

Divers become accustomed to swift reverses of fortune but when ten minutes later those two divers broke the surface and came aboard, and John Pettit reached into his sack to flash a golden half-sovereign under our noses, we were bursting with excitement. Over 100 silver coins spilled on to the deck. He had refound the cleft. In prospecting nearby he had picked up the golden coin somewhere, but not recognising it immediately, could not say exactly where it had been. However a small buoy was now bobbing six feet above the coin deposit and that single coin made our hopes even more buoyant than

51

ever. It was the morale booster that galvanized us into five hard days' diving.

That night, in the crammed quarters of the *Ahiki* anchored in the lee of the Great King five sleepers tossed fitfully. "Millions of them," one muttered. Another had a nightmare in which he located a huge heap of half-sovereigns, but none of his mates would come off raking in silver to help him.

During the following days of gruelling diving activity, over fifty quarter-hour descents were made into the boiling rip that swirls around the West King. Our team accumulated over twelve hours at 150 feet.

By starting diving early in the morning and finishing at the last evening light we were able to dive three times a day, in two shifts. Slack water was essential for descent but the second shift of divers often had to ascend after the rip had set in.

Swirling on the surface like a maelstrom it would at times stream out our shot-line and buoy to twenty feet below the surface, making decompression stages at ten feet difficult to maintain. The peculiarly low 53° water temperature made these stages even more uncomfortable, as we jostled together, chilled and shivering, clutching our bags of coins. On the third dive of the day, as the sun slipped down into the sea with us, seething shoals of trevally and kingfish would move closer and closer around us as the light diminished. After the vital decompression minutes had ticked by, protecting us from the "bends" symptoms which had killed our predecessor, Harper, sixty years earlier, it was a deliverance to bob to the surface. A vigorous swim against the rip and we would drag ourselves up to the *Ahiki's* ladder and cruise back to our anchorage, three quarters of an hour away, at the Great King.

With each descent to the wreck we felt a keen edge of excitement. This time we might lay our hands on the gold. In the vicinity of our initial finds we discovered numerous pockets of coins. The fifty-two wooden bullion boxes must have crashed together and split in this area. As the wreckage crumbled and settled, fierce undersea currents plucked up coins and lodged them in crevices and holes; or else they remained buried under the corroding debris.

Our two airlifts like giant vacuum cleaners, would suck away the sand overburden and expose the coins, imbedded in black seams of oxidised steel plate. The exhaust from our scuba regulators, rattling up the alkathene pipe of the airlift, created a powerful vortex at the intake. Speed is essential when working at depth.

These airlifts certainly put us in the jet-set! The cascades of bubbles rumbling in plumes over our heads, flecked with golden sand particles, attracted hordes of fish so dense that at times it became difficult to see. With picks, crowbars, screwdrivers and knives we levered out silver coins. Nearly stacked in vertical seams, they could be chipped out one by one.

Others came off in great black chunks of tumbled half-crowns, florins and shillings. The immense pressure of the collapsing wreck had flattened some coins to wafer thinness, or doubled them around plates. Some coins were found adhering by their edges to the roof of a cave. At some time they would have rested on piled wreckage which had later disintegrated leaving them welded in place by corrosion and coral growth. As we toiled, each diver imagined that the next handful would reveal gold coins lying in a thick bed just like the silver he was tearing away. Somewhere, very close to us, under the wreckage, the gold must be heaped, still shiny, not corroded into great lumps like this silver. Perhaps beneath a bright blue sponge or a patch of lolly-pink coral. We were finding coins everywhere in the vicinity among the litter of broken champagne bottles, twisted lead pipes, encrusted portholes, eroded girders and porcelain bathroom tiles. Each shift some divers would mine coins while one prospected for fresh deposits.

Without our decompression meters, buoyancy compensators and contents gauges, so many descents in such hellish conditions could hardly have failed to produce an accident. Since recompression facilities were twenty-four hours away in Auckland there could be no mistakes. Conventional diving tables involve human error. This risk would be too great when five divers would be using them for repetitive dives under difficult sea conditions.

Our five automatic decompression meters offered the safest means of calculating our repetitive diving pattern. While there is a potential for mechanical failure, we dived in pairs, the possibility of both meters failing being rather slim. Also we avoided entering decompression time. As any error in a meter would be amplified with repetitive dives, we always made routine decompression stops on our second and third dives.

A spare scuba set and relief diver were always ready on the *Ahiki*, patrolling as close in as possible.

In all our fifty odd descents not the least trouble occurred. All we suffered were cut hands from the broken glass everywhere.

On the fourth day morale was sagging. The one half-sovereign aboard the *Ahiki* was scarcely enough to overcome the cold and fatigue down below. It was hard to feel wretched when £60 lumps of silver were being dragged up on ropes, but we were beginning to doubt whether the gold really existed. The reasonable weather could not last much longer.

To dive on the wreck site involved a paradox: very exposed to the south-westerly winds, it had a strong swell smashing against the cliffs, and the back surge rolled us round even at 150 feet. While a north-easterly would produce calmer conditions over the site (except for the seething rip tides) this wind is the worst of all in the Three Kings area.

There is no safe anchorage or shelter from this wind, and our skipper, Peter Sheehan, a veteran fisherman in this locality, would head for North Cape when north-east conditions were imminent. The first signs of such a weather change were already appearing.

I was working on a deep sand excavation on the second dive of the day, shovelling coins out and tossing them on to the rock sill to be gathered later. John Pettit had discovered this deposit earlier in the morning and he said he had a hunch it would yield gold. Being the sole diver to find gold so far, "Goldfinger" Pettit's optimism made me feel a little warmer as I tossed out the coins and groped deeper. Through a flurry of sand and silver a gleam of gold flashed. Fever-ishly I snatched up the sixpence-sized disc. St George and the dragon shone through the light covering of reddish algae. Suddenly all consciousness of numbing cold and depth vanished. I finned over to where Kelvin was fossicking nearby. I grabbed him by the leg, waving the coin at him doing a crazy haka and gushing bubbles.

We had prearranged that should any diver find gold the others were to be informed at once to boost morale. I tore back into my diggings and soon found five more gold coins. Too precious to entrust to the sack, I slipped them into my face mask where I could keep an eye on them as I worked.

But this was not the mother lode. Bedrock soon appeared. The main bulk of the gold must be under the wreckage nearby. Powerful currents and surges down here had obviously swept coins into all sorts of niches.

This day we dived until the last light. After the final shift had surfaced in the sunflecked tide-race we had eleven golden coins in the wheel house: still shiny after sixty years of immersion which had reduced a steel ship to ruin, they evoked a new respect for gold. Man's idolization of it in a changing universe seemed more understandable. Each was a tangible link with the disaster: dated 1902 they would have been in mint condition when the *Elingamite* sank.

Next morning a north-west wind was howling around the wreck site. A swing to the north-east was coming. We tried one more dive in a desperate bid to locate the rest of the gold, but plunging seas and rising winds cut this short. Our air supplies and food were virtually exhausted anyway.

We had not expected to be able to stay so long in those exposed waters. Rather than join the *Elingamite* or the *Kaitawa* a few miles away, we stowed our gear and set out for the shelter of North Cape. With huge swells looming up over our stern we prepared to count our haul. In a half circle on the compass under Peter's watchful eye, our eleven gold coins winked in the sun. By his seabooted feet were two nail boxes piled high with silver. Unfortunately the gold was no trouble to tally. Each of us would have one piece as a reminder of our resolution to return as soon as possible for the rest of the *Elingamite*'s golden cargo. These half-sovereigns had been lovingly fingered until their thin reddish coating had worn off, except around the rims. We did not want to clean them any more or their wreck value would be destroyed.

As the others dragged the heavy nail boxes of coin out on deck Kelly and I busied ourselves photographing the gold coins. We wanted good news-shots of them before we reached land and split them up among our team. I teetered on the edge of the deck the eleven precious discs spread in my palm while Kelly focused on my cheesy grin. It vanished with John Pettit's warning: "Remember, Doakie, if you lose one, it was yours." The coins suddenly felt too hot to handle, too prone to jump out of my hand and skip lightly down through the sea to the white sand where they had lain for the past sixty years. I think everyone breathed more easily when Kelly put his camera away, and I placed those tokens of the next year's treasure hunt back on the compass.

We crouched in a circle on the rolling deck with a mound of money between us. As we sorted shillings, half-crowns and florins, counting them into plastic bags, we chewed over the expedition and replanned it for next time.

Each of us tossed in new chunks of anecdote which made me realize how isolated a diver is in his own sphere of vision with a unique set of impressions even after diving close to others.

As Kelly split up black slugs of half-crowns with his diving knife he recalled that he must have been partly narcosed at one stage on the fourth day's diving. He had finished photographing me perched on the coral encrusted lavatory pan, an object of great beauty after half a century of sea life had colonized it. Swimming over the debris with his camera he had been looking for some coin to pose me beside. I had pointed to a patch of blue rock, which at second glance I had recognized as a huge compressed conglomerate of coin filling the gap between two rocks. Kelly now told us that he had glanced at it and dismissed it as too unphotogenic! So much for his inebriated mind. On his next dive it had suddenly hit him: this was a massive reef of coin. This time he had attacked it with spike and crowbar, prying loose ten pounds weight of silver before it became too tightly compacted to chip any more off.

Through it a steel shaft ran, so affected by the action of the sea that I always swore it was a weathered wooden spar. Had we been able to move this it would have broken open the reef. That was when the next shift of divers had taken a strong proplon rope down from the *Ahiki* and attached it to the shaft. Peter had backed off, his vessel shuddering under full power. The rope had drawn as tight as a steel band. It stretched, the shaft quivered and water rumbled around the *Ahiki*'s stern, as her propeller rattled and shook.

Topside we had clustered around the bow. Jag had an axe poised to sever the line if a heavy swell broke over the wreck site and threatened to swing our tethered ship on to the rocks. Suddenly the line slackened. The ship surged backwards and Peter closed his throttle down, leaning expectantly from the wheelhouse. We showed him the end of the rope. There was still enough strength in that part of the *Elingamite* to resist all the power we could muster.

As our piles of counted coin grew we determined to come back with heavier gear next time. "Just wait till we can poke a bit of gelignite into that reef," Kelly drooled. He had a personal grievance against that lode of silver which had deceived him when he was narcosed. Trying to take good photos as well as work had placed an extra strain on him, yet he was loath to lose any opportunity to both work and record the activity when each dive might produce the Eldorado: a bed of gold coin greater than the stack of silver we were now counting.

Jag sipped a can of beer and bemoaned our lack of heavy equipment to excavate deeper into the wreck. As we sat back from our task and sipped too, he told us he had seen the rudder near where we were working. This fitted Mr Harper's description; "in the turret head" was where he had said his father found the bullion.

"That's near the rudder," Jag concluded. "It was invisible on the bottom, but as I rose I made out the outline from fifty feet above."

We no longer had any doubts. We *were* on to the treasure. On our journey homeward all sorts of schemes were devised to enable us to tear into the wreckage, to comb the sea floor, to detect precious metal among the tons of crumbling steel, and to lay bare our gold hoard. Many excellent proposals involved an enormous capital outlay and none of us could afford that type of risk.

Kelly would be away all year in Dunedin, working for the Underwater Construction Company of which he was a joint director. In those cold southern waters they had contracted for the installation of a new wharf at Port Chalmers. He undertook to work in spare time on the design of a range of new equipment for our next assault. John and Jag would arrange air supplies and boat charter, Jeff would look after wine and food supplies in his usual thoughtful manner, and I would personally take care of the recovered bullion, clean it, deposit it in bank vaults and pursue the legal aspects.

As the *Ahiki* moved upstream we stowed the last of the coin, washed the black corrosion off the decks and prepared for the reception on the wharf. In my note book I had tallied our loot: 1,000 half-crowns, 400 florins and 3,000 shillings totalling over £300 in face value and some eighty pounds weight of sterling silver.

When we rounded the last bend in the mangrove-lined river, our mouths went dry. A large throng of people was waiting for the treasure hunters to arrive.

After the small haul of our previous trip a fortnight earlier, we had found all sections of the press clamouring for our story. It had burst at the "silly season" for the newspapers, when world-wide news services slow down over the holiday period. At this time journalists are sent up in aircraft to count school sharks off the beaches and generate "shark scare" headlines and the front page news features bikini girls blistering on beaches.

So before setting out again we had decided that since our story was so keenly sought after it must be worth paying for. First, however, we needed the help of the press's research facilities. We had no idea what the legal situation was with regard to our treasure. Nor did we have the time while preparing for this major expedition, to chase around seeking information.

I had had a brainwave: "Whichever newspaper can give us a firm lead as to who the legal owners of the bullion are, gets our story," I had suggested. All that the press knew at that stage was that we had recovered some *Elingamite* treasure. We were not admitting that we had only fifteen pounds worth in face value from our first haul.

Eventually one truly enterprising chief reporter had rung me to say he had traced the owners. The Northern and Employers Assurance Group had taken over the Mutual Indemnity Marine Company, original insurers of the specie consignment for the Bank of New South Wales. They had paid out on the loss. The coin was now theirs, but we could make a hefty salvage claim.

Our conditions satisfied we had released our photos and our initial story went all over New Zealand and Australia and as far as Berlin, Paris, London and Bangkok. Kelvin and I had then signed an attractive contract for the story and pictures from this latest expedition.

But now we eyed the mob on the wharf with dread. We had to protect our story from news photographers or we would lose our contract. How could we unload our tons of gear and protect the bullion from people swarming all over the ship?

Peter had it all worked out. He intended to put into this wharf only long enough for us to unload the lolly-pink coral-encrusted lavatory

57

pan, some portholes and wreck souvenirs. The heavy storage cylinders would be winched off and some divers would leap into their waiting cars and drive around to Peter's private little jetty further up the narrowing tidal creek, in a dense patch of mangroves.

As we neared the wharf cries floated across: "How did it go? Get any more? Any luck?" But this crowd was mostly friendly Northlanders. Not the host of Christmas holiday-makers we had anticipated. No newsmen seemed to be there. Almost half of them were Peter's relatives, a warm genuine group of families: his daughters, their husbands and excited children waiting to see what their seafaring grandad had got.

Still we were cautious and carried out our scheme. The lavatory pan aroused intense interest.

"The only bit of the *Elingamite* to complete the trip from Aussie," was one comment. To these Northland people the ship was part of local history, and her name a household word for years. One told me that card-playing Northlanders with three kings in their hand, would triumphantly say "Elingamite!"

Peter embarked his relatives and we cruised upstream. In a ferment of interest we dragged out our treasure for them. We could never have had a more appreciative audience. Coins which we had partially cleaned flashed from palm to palm.

"Hey, look at this one. The Queen's all squashed flat."

"Here's a shiny one. Eighteen seventy-three. Let's see the gold. Is this all the gold ones you got?"

That last one made those of us divers still aboard wince, but we were all the more determined to raise more.

Peter's eldest daughter explained why there had been no huge crowds on the wharf. Mrs Walker, the fishing fleet radio operator at Awanui, had kept up a daily schedule with Peter, to ensure the safety of our ship. She had kept the story to herself. We learnt that she and Peter had even developed their own code to deter radio eavesdroppers. Had the story got out its news value to us would have been ruined. Newspaper publicity would have brought down on us hordes of city folk on holiday at the popular beaches around Kaitaia and we feared for the security of our treasure.

As we quietly loaded our bullion into the waiting cars, and set off for Auckland and our deserted families, we were thankful that it was from friendly Northland we had sailed and not the big city.

This time the press really had a picnic. Kelly had some excellent photos for them, both black and white and colour. There was no newspaper duel now as everything was pre-arranged and our story was published just as I had written it without any distortions or inaccuracies. The *Weekly News* made a special feature of it with a colour cover and centre section. These same colour shots were later published in several overseas magazines, a credit to Kelly's camera work under rugged conditions.

The treasure-hunting weather was all over now for the year and the expedition members had to split up and resume normal lives and humdrum jobs. At least our families were glad of this after two lengthy absences right at the height of the Christmas holiday period.

Chapter 5

ALMOST AT ONCE Kelly had to set off south for Dunedin to start his diving job. For the whole of 1967 he would have to work six days a week, three hours a day in the icy water of Port Chalmers. The work site was at fifty feet. Down there he and his fellow professional divers had to prepare a bed of billiard-table smooth shingle, compacted hard enough to support each of thirty huge 1,000 ton concrete caissons. These were to be locked together and backfilled to form the new export wharf.

As Kelly shivered in the southern summer, I baked in the northern heat, cleaning our 5,000 silver coins. Each required a particular treatment, depending on the adhering metallic or coralline covering. Some coins, exposed to the electrolysis set up in sea water, had been eaten away smoothly to wafer thinness. Only a vestige of Queen Victoria's stately head remained. Others, having lain in close proximity to other metals, had been protected from this electrolytic action, which eats away the baser metals first. Such coins had a thin black sulphide coating which, after a soaking in vinegar, fell off to leave a discoloured but flawless coin. Rubbing with a paste of ammonia and baking soda and cleaning with silver polish brought these coins back to a brilliant lustre unknown in modern coinage and rare in the finest silver-ware. Our *Elingamite* coins, we learnt, are of a purer silver than is available to New Zealand jewellers.

Many coins were encrusted with a stubborn coralline growth, studded with broken glass, sea shell fragments and chips of coal. This resisted all efforts at removal until I dipped them in strong hydrochloric acid. I was very careful to clean only a small portion, revealing the nature of the coin, while preserving it as an authentic wreck souvenir.

There were coins which resisted even this treatment. I tried nitric acid. It worked frighteningly well, but to my horror the silver nitrate from the reaction stained my hands jet black. Nothing would remove this and I suffered acute embarrassment with my midnight hands, for over a month, until it wore off.

Then I built a makeshift rumbler, such as lapidarists use to polish gemstones. Two wringer rollers powered by a washing machine motor tumbled tins full of coins for hours and hours with a deafening racket. This saved me from black hands, but I nearly had a horrible accident. Pressure from chemical reactions built up in one tin, until it exploded. A black vapour of corrosion and silver shrapnel sprayed all around the section, and when it cleared I had to start coin hunting all over again. It was some days before the tin lid turned up in a neighbour's flower bed. It had vanished with such velocity I had been afraid to start looking for it.

As Jan, my wife, was sorting and grading coins she started to notice that the shillings covered a considerable period of time. Gradually she built up complete sets of each decade, from 1900 back to 1860. Beyond that point there were partial sets. Going back over the years Queen Victoria changed from a stern old lady to a stout, crown-bearing matron, until in 1837 the coins showed a graceful young woman, her hair piled high. The older coins were worn so thin the details were often barely discernible. It was a thrill for Jan when she found a coin stamped with a different likeness. Dated 1835, it bore the head of King William IV.

One day late in the summer I was pleased to see a friend, Neil Robinson, arriving at the gate. He had come to bring me some very valuable news.

Some years before, Neil had written a magazine article about the *Elingamite*, as one of the most famous of New Zealand shipwrecks. With our adventures he had recalled the sources of his own research —some very old copies of the *Weekly News*—and had had photo copies made of these pages for me. I glanced with growing excitement through this stack of photostats.

"But this is fantastic!" I burst out. "There's enough material here for a book." He nodded. An author himself, that was his idea in helping me.

There was also a wealth of valuable data for the treasure hunter. "Wait till the boys read this," I said. "The complete cargo manifest!"

I was kicking myself for not having the foresight to research old newspaper files the moment we had become involved with the *Elingamite*. We were reluctant treasure hunters, who had not really been looking for the wreck, and when it was found, were not really expecting to discover the bullion. Now we had been infected by the most virulent gold bug imaginable.

The photostats cured that. To my utter dismay I read that the specie consignment was mostly silver: "It has now been ascertained that the *Elingamite*'s total specie is valued at £17,320, apportioned as follows: £4,000 silver for Lyttelton; £3,000 gold, £10,300 silver and £20 copper for Dunedin."

So there were only 6,000 gold half-sovereigns aboard—about the same quantity of coins as we had already raised in silver. They would fill no more than four small wooden boxes. Why had we been so sure it was all gold? For a long time I could not understand what had misled us so badly until one day I found several erroneous references in books and newspapers, such as the following: "She carried gold bullion to the value of £17,320, of which £4,000 was later recovered." From here the distortion had grown unchecked, until after our very first treasure find in 1967, the newspaper reporter did a little arithmetic and came up with the calculation: "The coins remaining in the wreck are worth £37,000 at official prices."

This explained our gold bug. But the new facts would cure forever a lurking suspicion in all our minds. While we were raising so much silver and so little gold we often wondered if this really was the *Elingamite* bullion we were working. Now there was no doubt.

Next I read of the earlier salvage attempts, six failures culminating in diver Harper's fatal descent after raising only a small part of the bullion, mostly silver.

My hopes soared again when I did a little rapid calculating! £13,000 in silver coin would weigh the same whether the denominations were shillings, half-crowns or florins, since, the weight of each coin was proportional to its value. Using scales I found that five shilling pieces balanced two half-crowns. Each half-crown weighed half an ounce, and I discovered, was ninety-five per cent pure silver. At the prevailing world price for silver such a coin would be worth N.Z. 75 cents. Therefore, regardless of denomination, the entire silver consignment would weigh over one and a half tons and be worth—my mathematics boggled at this one.

My friend had given me material to start research for this book but also as a consequence of these facts, the whole purpose of our next expedition was redirected. Quickly I got a letter off to Kelvin in Dunedin. He replied: "Pity about the amount of gold. Actually I suspected as much but hoped I was wrong. Not to worry, it is still money and £13,000 of silver should be reasonably easy to find. It will be a heap as big as a car." I calculated that since the bullion was in fifty-two boxes, allowing for the gold occupying four (enough space for 6,000 coins), each box would weigh roughly sixty pounds, which seemed a reasonable weight for easy handling. In fact each box would be about the size of the nail boxes we had used on the *Ahiki* for storage: 18"×9"×9".

Kelvin wrote again in February: "I envy news of the heat up there. It's damned cold here. Yesterday it hailed nearly all day. When we surface from a dive the wind is an icy blast straight off the ice cap. Too lazy to go round you, it whistles clean through. I bought a thick pair of corduroy trousers and a gorilla jersey yesterday. I wear about six layers of woollens at work and still shiver all day. Occasionally we get a day that's hot as hell but they're far apart.

"I've been thinking over our approach to the wreck, now I know what we're after. We will need a three-inch airlift driven by a piston-type compressor. My theory is to anchor a boat firmly over the site if we can get perfect weather. We lift off all the heavy rubble, loosen the whole area with explosives, airlift it to the boat and put it through chicken-net screens.

"This diving job has made me pretty proficient with explosives underwater. I've got the advice of the best tunnellers in New Zealand and I've learnt all the things in the book and lots of things the books don't tell you. I've learnt how to tie the correct knots in cordtex explosive fuse so that it won't sever itself on firing. They've told me how to boil a billy by lighting a fire of gelignite underneath it. 'Perfectly safe,' they said. 'It won't explode. Just burns with a really hot, white flame.' Nobody offered to give me a demonstration. When blasting at the work site they even showed me how to blast shags out of the water. Wait till they dive down near the caisson to catch a fish. Then set off the charge. They surface like a missile and feet going like tornadoes, they disappear over the horizon."

I continued my research into the *Elingamite* history in newspaper files and libraries. My letters to newspapers in New Zealand and Australia steadily brought a deluge of exciting mail. Best of all I received first-person accounts from survivors like Norm Cassrels in Auckland, Ellen Doorty in Matamata and Wally Perkins in Newcastle, while Sir Douglas Robb, the Auckland surgeon, gave me two accounts by his mother and father who were involved in the disaster.

Meanwhile Kelvin helped me by his frequent visits to the Dunedin Public Library. In late autumn he wrote: "I took a day off diving yesterday to go through the 'Old New Zealand' section of the library. Very interesting. I dropped my electronic flash gear, breaking the battery. Acid oozed all over their gleaming mahogany floor. The lady who looks after this room is extremely particular about its upkeep. The acid fizzled and hissed until I managed to borrow a rag from another lady and wipe it up unseen. But the mark is indelible.

"I fixed up a temporary small battery but the flash is not firing reliably so some of these photo copies of *Elingamite* reports may not turn out."

All winter poor Kelly visited the library night after night and was regularly last to be ejected at closing time. However, the librarians took a personal interest in his quest and could not have been more helpful. In Auckland I received great help from the *Herald* and *Weekly News* people.

I was also increasingly occupied with the legal aspects of our treasure ship. The story of the search for legal claimants to the *Elingamite* bullion and to her hull dates right back to 1963 when our

63

diving friend Dr John Kramer, an American veterinarian, started the ball rolling. Like us he was interested in wrecks and wrote to Lloyd's of London seeking details of the *Elingamite* wreck and asking if there was any truth in the rumour that her cargo was gold dust and not gold bullion.

Their reply simply quoted the book *New Zealand Shipwrecks* by Ingram and Wheatly, saying that she sank in fifty-five fathoms and advising John to contact the Salvage Association. John duly wrote to them seeking who the underwriters were, how much coin remained, and querying the fifty-five fathom depth. He knew there had been early salvage attempts of limited success, and such a depth was tremendous for those days. He received no answer. The quest was dropped until 1967 when Kelvin had again written to them, asking the same questions.

Meanwhile I learnt the exact records of the specie from the archivist of the Bank of New South Wales in Sydney, original consignees of the bullion. Then the Salvage Association verified what the news reporter had told us: The specie was insured by the Indemnity Mutual Marine Company, today associated with the Northern and Employers Assurance Group.

There followed a long impasse while we tried to get this group to acknowledge their claim, since they had already paid out on the loss. We understood that provided they accepted ownership and would appoint us as their salvage agents our treasure would not have to be passed into the hands of the Receiver of Wrecks, according to the Shipping and Seamen's Act 1932, section 348.

Kelvin in the meantime initiated a similar quest for the owners of the hull, since we wished to purchase this to be free to raise any scrap we found, including the huge propeller.

After a lengthy exchange of letters with London, Liverpool, Sydney and Melbourne, we eventually established that although the Maritime Insurance Company of Liverpool had paid out on the ship, they had not accepted abandonment. Therefore the wreck still remained the property of the now defunct Huddart Parker Company. At length we contacted a Mr Perkins, former accountant for the old shipping line, who still heads a holding company for its assets. For $50 we were able to purchase the hull and received a signed and sealed document which establishes our syndicate as owners of the *Elingamite*. There is one catch: we are legally responsible for any damage her hull might cause to shipping!

From Dunedin Kelvin wrote: "It would be great if we were living closer together during this expedition planning. I feel I'm at the other end of the earth down here. When it was bitterly cold, with a half-inch of snow blanketing the diving barge I climbed out of the sea into the diving cabin to read your letter about suntan and marvellous dives at the Poor Knights, in crystal clear water. As I quivered and shook, peeling off layers of suit and clothing, huddling over the oil heater, I recalled I had not seen the sun for a week. Sometimes I wish I had never come south. The *Elingamite* seems an insubstantial fairy dream down here."

Some days later he mourned: "This working six days a week, daylight till dark, on uninspiring work, just pouring stones out on the bottom through a sieve and grading them flat, gets very monotonous. What say we part for the Kings straight after New Year's Day?

"I have now got a small detector working but it is not water-proofed yet. I have to finalize the radio receiver part. I want it to be workable entirely by the diver, not requiring anybody on the surface. I hope I can make it differentiate between ferrous and non-ferrous metals at the *Elingamite* site. The detector will indicate coins but will also indicate iron. A mixed reading would be useless, since we know where the ship is. I hope to be able to make it ignore iron readings and pick up non-ferrous."

Throughout 1967 Kelvin Tarlton wrote to me about his constant experimentation and rethinking on the problems of locating and raising our car-size mound of silver. Such devices as he planned belong to a field of technology where theory just won't do. In the ocean world too many unforeseeable factors intervene and render absurd the best of plans; the only way such devices for underwater use may be developed is by active, realistic experiment. For this Kelly was in an ideal situation with his diving job at Port Chalmers. Here he had strong currents and plenty of mud, if not the great depths and a real treasure ship.

I edited all his letters and handed them to him for comment. To my delight he offered instead to write a personal account of his work:

"The problem of how to extract the coins from the corroding wreckage was one that had been worrying me for some time. Our light portable airlifts using regulator exhaust had been ideally trouble-free and handy but this system just could not provide the powerful action we needed to recover one and a half tons of coin. At first glance the obvious thing to do was to loosen the bottom with explosives, then use an airlift suction pump to take it all to the surface where it could be sieved and sorted. However it soon became apparent that there would be a number of difficulties in this.

A surface airlift is the most simple and effective method for divers to lift a mixture of sand, stones and water. It consists simply of a pipe into which air is injected at the bottom. The air-bubbles, rushing up the pipe, take with them water, stones, your hand, or anything that comes near the intake. The further the pipe extends upwards and the more air injected the better it will work.

"Blockages are the main problem with airlifts. If a stone larger than the diameter of the pipe gets picked up and jams across the intake the pipe will fill with air. Suddenly buoyant it takes off for the surface dragging the diver and everything else with it. To prevent this the diver has an instant cut-off tap to stop the air in the event of a blockage. He must then wait precisely the right length of time for the suction to stop before switching on the air again. The rush of air will then blow out the stone and set the lift working again. If he waits too long and the pipe is full of heavy material such as sand, stones and mud, it will lose upward momentum and come roaring back down the pipe blowing up great clouds of mud and sand which quickly engulf the hapless diver. At other times a blockage may occur inside the pipe which will take hours to clear.

"Nevertheless the simplicity of this system would, in calmer waters, make it worth the trouble. At the Three Kings where we would have to contend with heavy wave action and strong currents, the difficulties would be multiplied. The pipe would have to be able to bend and flex with the movement of the water yet be rigid enough not to collapse under the suction when it was working. Wire-reinforced flexible rubber hose looked ideal but the cost was going to prove prohibitive. PVC semi-rigid plastic pipe was cheap enough but I felt it would perhaps fracture with the constant bending. Added to this was the probability that we would not be able to anchor the mother ship very close to the cliffs and would therefore need a small boat or raft equipped with screens to sieve the debris that came to the surface. Such a rig incorporating a heavy air compressor, screens and crew would probably not be seaworthy enough. We knew it would have to resist overturning on the occasional cresting wave that was bound to come along every now and then, even in the best weather.

"Considering the inherent difficulties of large surface airlifts with those added by our exposed wreck site, my mind turned to self-contained airlifts, which do not raise material right to the surface but either spew out their load onto a floating underwater screen or carry their own screen attached to the top of the pipe. I settled for the latter design and to be even more self-contained I decided to try one that ran off its own air tank.

"In my lunch hours and whenever I had a spare moment I made up experimental models on the Port Chalmers diving barge out of a length of three-inch plastic pipe that had served as the lavatory outlet on the wharf labourers' hut. A storm had broken it off and it

66

lay in twenty feet of water some hundred yards from our barge. Not wishing to be spotted by the foreman I donned my lung and swam along the bottom groping around in two feet visibility to find the pipe. After losing my bearing several times I eventually located the right area by the number of streamers of white paper draped on the weeds, and soon found the pipe half buried. The trip back along the bottom was uneventful but when I pushed off the bottom to surface under the barge the current caught the pipe and started dragging me off down the harbour. I was forty feet from the barge when I surfaced, and despite my frantic efforts to best the current, I was losing ground. Fortunately one of the boys saw my plight and threw me a rope. The pipe trailed behind me with the elbow poking into the air like some gigantic periscope drawing much laughter from the crew who had assembled to see what was going on. I now had the basic materials to start building experimental self-contained airlifts.

"The first model had a chicken mesh net at the top to catch the coins that rained back down after travelling up the thirty-foot length of pipe. Armed with seventeen two-cent pieces to represent half-sovereigns, I disappeared into the bottom of the trench towing the thirty-foot airlift and its attached net behind me. I turned on the air and like some hungry monster it started devouring the bottom. I switched it off quite pleased with its first trial run. Now was the big test. If I could bury the two-cent pieces in the bottom over a few square yards then recover them from the net after airlifting the area, success would be in sight. With the coins suitably buried I started the airlift sucking up the mud, sand and stones. Suddenly I was aware that something was going wrong. Peering up through the gloom I could see the pipe rapidly angling over me. I slid out from underneath just as it thudded to the bottom. The net, as well as catching the coins, had been catching all the stones which had built up until it overbalanced. In the net along with several hundredweight of stones were seventeen two-cent pieces: a hundred per cent recovery! If this rig was going to be used it would need a large float and guide wire to hold it upright which would be rather an encumbrance. Sorting the coins from the stones was going to be a lengthy task so I started redesigning.

"The next model would have another pipe leading from the net sending all the stones and coins back down to the bottom alongside the diver while the lighter sand and mud carried on with the air towards the surface. This would overcome the overbalancing effect. Before this one was off the drawing board the inspiration struck me that if I could harness the counter-effect of the falling stones I would only need half the amount of air to make it work. By utilizing the bend from the lavatory system I made a double 'up-and-down' airlift. A hole in the top allowed the air to escape, letting the stones fall down the return pipe displacing water and creating additional suction.

"I jumped off the diving barge towing my 'up-and-down' airlift behind me. I switched it on and as before the sand, mud and stones roared up the intake. Hopefully I watched the outlet beside me waiting for the stones to start pouring out. Nothing happened, so leaving it running I swam to the top of the pipe. All the sand and stones were roaring out the air exhaust hole, not getting time to separate. Suddenly the whole thing took off for the surface. I dodged to one side and grabbed for the shut-off tap as the bottom whistled past me. The trailing scuba tank clouted me behind the ear and I and thirty feet of PVC pipe arrived amidst a welter of bubbles on the surface. The intake had blocked, allowing the pipe to fill with air.

"To overcome this problem I decided to lengthen the top horizontal piece to allow the air and stones to separate more before coming to the exhaust hole. It was better, but still many stones and coins went out the exhaust with the air and many small bubbles and much mud and sand carried on down the return pipe. Added to this, the whole thing leaned at a horrible angle when the air collected in the top pipe, putting it off balance. The matter was finally settled when I surfaced beside the barge with the unwieldy contraption as the diving tender was coming alongside. With a crunch the spinning propeller hit the plastic pipe, chewing it up into small chunks.

"With that I decided that airlifts were out. A water jet or a water-driven gold sucker would have to be the answer.

"I made acquaintances with old 'Ned' a weather-beaten Otago goldminer who, with no knowledge of diving techniques, had bought himself a diving suit, compressor and other gear and with his long-suffering wife had built himself a shack away up in Skippers Canyon, far from the nearest human habitation and there set about to 'make his fortune' by diving for gold. Over a few pints of beer in the local hotel I learned the finer points of making a gold sucker dredge: how to make riffles in the back of the dredge so that all the gold dust would get caught yet stones and sand would fall out the back. Whereas the airlift depends on a stream of compressed air the dredge works on the principle of a water venturi. From the surface a powerful pump sends water down a one and a half inch hose to the dredge. By firing a jet of water into the dredge pipe, a suction at the main nozzle is created which picks up the gold-bearing sand and blows it across the deeply corrugated riffle box. There the gold dust lodges, allowing the rest to blow out the back.

"At the wreck we would use this same principle of dredging to move the sand and stones overburden though it seemed doubtful that we would be able to separate the coins from the stones. I tried a water jet and found that I could blow light sand and mud away leaving heavier stones and two cent pieces still on the bottom to be sorted by hand. The blockages which plague the airlift system were no trouble now. The big problem was the amount of mud stirred up. However when the tide was running in the bottom of the trench the mud was quickly carried away. This I reasoned would be the simplest system for use at the Kings, where we expected strong currents would quickly carry away any sediment stirred up in dredging.

"Next I became absorbed by the possibility of locating the treasure electronically. In an American skindiving magazine I read how a converted army mine detector had been altered to indicate whether a ferrous or non-ferrous object had been detected. Perhaps I could make a metal detector that would differentiate between the gold or silver coins and the pieces of iron ship at the Three Kings? If this could be done what easier way could there be to find the deposits of coins under the tons of corroded wreckage, sand and rock? I again haunted the library reading every electronics magazine I could lay my hands on in search of articles on metal detectors. After several weeks of searching and burning the midnight oil I had located four articles and technical papers on metal detection. It seemed that the only type of locator that I could possibly make without a well-equipped laboratory was the beat frequency capacitance loop type. This is a simple radio transmitter that sends out a set frequency radio signal from a large wire loop. Whenever the loop comes near a metal object the capacitance of the loop alters the frequency of the signal. With a simple device fitted to a small transistor radio it is possible to tune into this and listen to a squeal in the receiver alter in tone as the loop is brought near a metal object. By the addition of another circuit I would be able to tell if the object was iron or treasure. It seemed simple enough. Although one of the more authoritative articles mentioned that this system was not as sensitive as the more sophisticated methods of metal detection none of them quoted just how sensitive it really was.

"Flushed with enthusiasm I spent long hours and a number of dollars building the transistorized transmitter and its waterproof housing. Finally I had it working and only needed a transistor radio in the underwater housing on which to receive my treasure signal.

"A cargo boat with a Chinese crew arrived in port and I heard the whisper that the crew had transistor radios for sale. I asked those on the wharf who were in the know and they pointed out to me a gang of Chinese sailors painting the side of the ship as they dangled on a plank near the water line. Back on the diving barge I armed myself with a pocket full of notes, jumped into our diving boat, cranked it into life and chugged across to the paint gang. They seemed rather surprised to see me, bristling beard, clad in my diving suit and piloting a smoke-belching iron can.

" 'I want to buy a transistor radio', I shouted above the noise of the motor. They went into a huddle jabbering away to each other in Chinese and casting suspicious glances in my direction.

"Eventually one of their number straightened up and said: 'Velly solly we good sailors no got transistor', and turned to start painting again. I waved a handful of notes at them. 'Me not customs man. Me not police man. Me only diver who want a transistor!' But they were not impressed by my plea and repeated their declaration of virtue. I gave up and chugged back to the barge. Next day I learned that one of the boys on the wharf had bought a dozen radios off the same gang an hour afterwards and was now offering me one at a considerably inflated price. Our barge winchman had a broken transistor that had seen better days and was now beyond economical repair. So armed with a soldering iron and another broken transistor radio I combined the best parts of both and managed to get one to work. Soon the whole contraption was housed in the waterproof case and trials could begin.

"The article in the electronics magazine had said that it was not extremely sensitive but they had not said it would only detect an object the size of a dustbin at three feet! They also had not mentioned that when you immerse it in salt water the range is shortened dramatically so that you nearly have to hold it against the object to get a reading. Added to this was the fact that while it could detect either treasure or iron, if you mixed them, as at the wreck site, the whole machine was thrown into confusion and all it would emit was meaningless squawks.

"Disheartened I swam over to the Union Company ship repair wharf to check on the propeller of the *Wairata*, a coaster of similar size to the *Elingamite*, that was tied up there. To my surprise the propeller looked to be practically identical to that of the *Elingamite*. Enquiries to the chief engineer soon produced the facts: a four-bladed one-piece bronze casting weighing eight and a half tons and eighteen feet in diameter. It was held on with a key and one big nut locked by a ring of smaller bolts. A letter to the explosives advisors of I.C.I. Ltd. produced the dampening reply that they doubted if it could be blown apart unless the boss was hollow and even then they were not hopeful. As it turned out I was wrong in assuming that the *Elingamite*'s propeller was a one-piece bronze casting. In actual fact the bronze blades were each bolted to the boss separately and the whole thing streamlined by the addition of a cement plaster over the bolts to give the appearance of a one-piece casting.

"Wade had meanwhile contacted an Australian marine historian, Peter Williams of Victoria. To our joy Peter had in his collection a scale model and plans of the *Elingamite*, and when asked for help he went to enormous lengths to assist us. We pored over his photo copies of the plans and the model, trying to pinpoint our treasure site with some relation to the actual layout of the ship. However, the battered *Elingamite* had lost her form so entirely that we achieved little of value.

"Now that the wreck belonged to us our syndicate felt it would be wise to prepare for the recovery of the huge propeller as a form of insurance; our expenses were very heavy and this would give us an immediate return. Accordingly Peter was asked what he knew about the propeller, since its construction was vital to our chances of salvage. If it was cast in one piece we could never raise it without a large, specially equipped ship. Even if such a ship would venture close enough into the West King, the expense would be excessive. Our only hope was to blast the blades off and haul them up individually. But this might prove impossible: propellers are often cast from special malleable alloys. If a rock is hit the blades would bend but not break off, leaving the ship with some propulsion. Such a a propeller would be impossible to break up with explosives.

"Peter wrote to Wade: 'In answer to your question about the prop. I can only suggest it could be any of several metals: gun metal, another bronze alloy, or even iron or steel! Unfortunately my old records of the *Elingamite* make no mention of the type of propeller used. Up until the 1880s the largest propeller cast in one piece was a sixteen-tonner, but this was for the Admiralty. Most marine engineering manuals of the period suggest that naval props were usually bronze while the greater numbers of merchant ships had cast iron or steel props. However, instead of a one-piece casting a large vessel like the *Elingamite* just might have four highly pitched blades bolted on to a bronze boss. Bolted blades were very popular as a blade was cheaper and easier to replace than a fully cast propeller should the ship hit a rock. Even in 1887 cost was a major factor. I think the Huddart Parker Company would have chosen this cheaper alternative. Of course the blades could be bronze, or just iron. While bronze blades were two and a half times the cost of iron they lasted longer and did not shatter on impact.'

"Peter made us hopeful! I then went to see a Dunedin scrap metal firm who showed great interest. They considered that the prop would be of manganese bronze. The manager raised an interesting

71

point: The shaft on steamers of that period was often bronze too. If this was so the shaft would be of more value than the prop. Allowing ten per cent loss from corrosion he calculated that the propeller would be worth £3,000 conservatively. Copper prices were soaring at the time, but some fall was inevitable. They were very keen to get the *Elingamite* propeller. So were we, if it were feasible. Besides, Wade was very keen to study the propeller closely to see if it had struck the rocks while still spinning. This would throw fresh light on the issues raised at the Court of Inquiry.

"Preparing for the explosive tasks ahead I tested some electric detonators in my small perspex pressure chamber, to depths of 160 feet, and then test fired them to ensure that none leaked. Time was fast running out and I had further experiments before leaving for the north. Our syndicate had decided to invest heavily in the making of a colour documentary film. If we hit the jackpot, this film would be an added treasure. At this stage I was working frantically night and day on my 16 mm Pathe movie camera fitting it to an underwater housing. The last few days ticked by as I tried packing house, buying tickets and running final pressure tests on the camera equipment in our one man diver's recompression chamber at the port. Then final farewells to the other divers and their families and we were on our way back to the north, the car bulging with underwater cameras, baby's clothes, sun hats, and even a box of Christmas spirits which we had been warned was in short supply in the north."

Chapter 6

THE YEAR OF research and preparation was drawing to a close now and John Pettit and Jag were chasing after a suitable charter boat. We were saddened to learn that we could no longer use the *Ahiki*. Peter Sheehan had collided with a Marine Department regulation which makes it illegal for a commercial fishing boat to have scuba diving apparatus aboard. It was originally designed to halt the commercial fishing of crayfish with breathing apparatus, an extremely efficient method. Time and again I have run up against this loosely framed legislation which ties up all sorts of diving activities in its meshes. When mooring a sonar buoy for an Auckland University physics experiment our volunteer diving team had been forced to rendezvous at sea with the trawler, taking our valuable scuba gear out to meet it in a small open boat. I was bitter with the frustration at this absurd rigmarole and now this same red tape was upsetting our treasure hunt. Finding another skipper prepared to risk his boat at Three Kings would be no easy matter.

Early in December John Pettit wrote Kelly: "Jag and I have just returned from a 500-mile tour of the north looking at boats and talking to skippers. It is now fairly certain we will be taking Larry Walker's scow, *Lady Gwen*. Larry is most co-operative and willing. I offered him $20 a day for the days we were unable to dive and $50 a day for those we do. We will supply all the food etc., and sail from Awanui straight after Christmas.

"This scow is perfect to work from: stable, tons of deck space, low freeboard, power winch and spanking new twin diesel engines— 100 h.p. Fordson. One real snag is accommodation. If we take two extra divers there will be nine aboard and only four bunks. I have calculated that four more safari beds could be fitted on deck under an awning. The galley is quite good but the plumbing is primitive. . . . Believe me, we have tried for a lot of boats but this is the only one available for our purposes.

"I have calculated conservatively that the expedition will cost us $1,200 for fourteen days' charter, food, air, gear, explosives, movie film and insurance. This is pretty tough with the four of us bearing all the expense. If we strike a storm most will be lost. Jag and I feel we should make a real effort to get the propeller as soon as we get there."

73

Things were starting to move at last! All that remained was that solid chunk of time, as we waited for Kelly to finish off his diving contract in the south and join us at Christmas. The weather was ideal now and the days dragged by painfully.

By this stage I had immersed myself into the *Elingamite* story so thoroughly I knew the whole episode by heart. Somehow the hours of research, peering at photostats and microfilm, had saturated my mind with every tiny detail. The names of survivors were like people I had met. I was burning to return to the Three Kings now I knew so well the events that had occurred there at the turn of the century. But the disaster had gradually come to mean more to me than simply a series of happenings. From today's viewpoint there is some pattern or meaning to it all, but I was puzzled by the distorting Victorian prism I was forced to view the *Elingamite* through. The reality of that cold, grey ship's skeleton under my hands was so immediate to my mind.

First it was just the Victorian flavour of the original accounts that worried me. This style of writing was so peculiarly stagey and florid. People seemed to have had a stereotyped education and a great class-consciousness. This left them with a stock of appropriate cliches and genteel metaphors, so that the expression of real emotions was carefully insulated by conventional patterns of speech. It would have beeen too indiscreet to say what you really felt. The worst excesses of my favourite author, Thomas Hardy, of the Victorian pot boiler, and the melodramatic villain all seemed to people the *Elingamite* story.

I tried rewriting such statements in modern idiom but found this was impossible. Then I realized that my problem lay in the very attitudes which this language conveyed. A man like Steven Neil, who viewed foreigners with contempt, as cowards less virile than himself, who placed such a tremendous emphasis on his British blood, who believed so firmly in the traditional courage of all Britons in sea disasters embodies the very spirit of those times. Such attitudes could only be expressed in the original word patterns. Translate Neil into modern speech and his very concepts and reactions seem absurd for a modern man. About the decision not to accompany his wife in the first lifeboat, Steven Neil said: "Today, after all the trials I have passed through, I praise Almighty God with all my heart for enabling me to decide aright. By remaining I preserved my manhood and was by God's grace the means of saving some of the unfortunates around me from their terrible predicament." In my story Neil describes how he felled an Austrian making a dash for a lifeboat, with a blow on the jaw. Of the captain who rescued him: "Hurrah for the British Navy who tracked us over the pathless sea

74

with the astuteness of a bloodhound following a path on shore."

As British novelist Evelyn Waugh said: "It took the Second World War to disillusion men from the old British code and make them more aware of the courage of humanity in general."

I had to remember that this was a time when New Zealanders were colonials, when the British Empire was seemingly by divine right the fittest power on earth to control the destinies of all others. The myth of racial superiority coupled with the social barriers of class was all too evident in the *Titanic* sinking in 1912 with a loss of 1,500 lives. The survivors included a great proportion of first-class passengers while the list of those lost was proportionately mostly steerage passengers and foreigners. The ideal of British fair play and honour took a thorough thrashing. British men disguised themselves as women to get into a lifeboat. While the last of the big spending Edwardian generation, over one hundred gentlemen, tossed in the lifeboats, nearly two hundred women and twenty-three children on the liner waited for it to sink. There was courage, true courage, but those who "cracked up" were often the ones who afterwards were the most outspoken about the cowardice of the foreigners and who loudly praised the courage of the men with whom they hoped to identify themselves. At the U.S. enquiry a steward from the *Titanic* stated: "There were various men passengers of Italian or some foreign nationality other than English or American who attempted to rush the boats." To the survivors all stowaways in the lifeboats were Chinese or Japanese. There was a firm and loudly voiced opinion of the superiority of Anglo-Saxon courage. At the enquiry things finally grew so bad that the Italian Ambassador demanded and got an apology from the fifth officer who was using Italian as a sort of a synonym for "coward".

Newspapers at the time of the *Elingamite* disaster said: "The weakness of those foreigners was lost sight of in the heroism and self-forgetfulness of the men of our own race"; "In the hour of sudden danger British seamanship and British passengers are implicitly to be relied on. The ship's company met disaster with unquestioning discipline. There was no panic or selfish folly." It went on to say that while the Austrian passengers swarmed around the lifeboat like bees this disaster was not like other sinkings as it was a British ship. Yet another columnist wrote: "I really don't think that there is any of the races of mankind who are so heroic as ourselves in facing the perils of the sea. I have as little national or racial prejudice as any man but the verdict of guilty goes against those Austrians." However, a British major at Kaitaia replied: "It is mean and un-British to slur whole nations. There is good and bad in each. I can say a certain English survivor who was landed at Houhora acted like a hog, taking two blankets for himself when there was not enough to go around. We have to share this country with foreign immigrants."

After reading such opinions I realized that a thorough anatomy of the *Elingamite* disaster would reveal many fascinating things about human nature at the turn of the century. It would also show that in a catastrophe it is not always possible to make the wisest decisions. When a lifeboat is crammed to capacity it may seem most prudent to club with oars those struggling survivors who threaten to overwhelm it and drown everyone. Cool reasoning might say that either some survive and some drown or all drown together. In a disaster like this one sees the true meaning of tragedy as the Greeks conceived it: The series of events which, once set in motion by human folly, must unfold relentlessly; which no human agency can check; and of which the outcome produces consequences far out-weighing the blame that might be attached to the original error. Like the stone rolled down the hillside in a moment's thoughtless play which threatens to smash on to a busy highway.

To allow all this to come to the surface, I have decided to leave the accounts of the passengers in their raw state, much as if I was actually interviewing them. Initially material was gleaned from newspaper files all over New Zealand, which Kelly photographed and reproduced postcard size for me to squint over. Then I started receiving countless letters carrying snippets of useful information and new leads to follow up. My greatest ambition was to obtain some first-hand impressions from living survivors. I tried but seemed to be working over the horizon of living remembrance. After much effort I did hunt down some survivors but few could remember very much until I met Norman Cassrels, who as a little seven-year-old lost his pet magpie when the *Elingamite* sank.

Book 2

Chapter 7

SUNDAY, 9 NOVEMBER 1902 dawned misty and calm at the Three Kings. It was King Edward's birthday in London and Auckland but, screamed over only by gulls, this remote part of the colony of New Zealand knew no loyal inhabitants.

In Sydney four days earlier the S.S. *Elingamite* had embarked 136 passengers, ready to leave for Auckland on her regular five-day trans-Tasman voyage. Now she was a few hours away in the fog.

A vast island-dotted submarine mound rises steeply from the 13,000-foot ocean depths to within 200 feet of the surface. Over its shoaling bottom and sunken ledges the Tasman Sea and Pacific Ocean meet, in a seething rebellion of tidal forces. Here, forty miles above the northernmost tip of New Zealand, Antartcic swells flexing up the long Tasman sea corridor clash with surges from Pacific storms. The moon-tugged tides, a barely perceptible movement in the deep Pacific, must quicken as they meet the upthrusting plateau, and roil furiously over its surface to keep pace with the surrounding ocean.

In this confusion of forces the tides become unpredictable. Currents and sets change at random, sweeping the flanks of the steep-faced island chain with roaring tide rips, whirlpools and huge surges.

Westernmost in this chain, rearing up from the plateau like a drowned mountain, is the West King, its weathered tip 350 feet above the swirling surface waters. On this morning a dense pall of mist writhed above its black summit, shrouded the neighbouring islands and pinnacles scattered in line nine miles to the north-east and blanketed some 200 miles out into the Tasman towards Australia.

At 5.30 on the evening of November 5, the farewells on the Sydneyside quay had faded as the *Elingamite* untied from Australia and moved off down the bridgeless Sydney Harbour, passengers thronging the rails. On the foredeck among the steerage passengers were Arthur Robinson and his mate Jordan, two sturdy young Australians off to try their luck farming in the Canterbury high country.

From Newcastle eleven motormen were setting out for Auckland where they would drive the city's new electric trams, the first in the colony, to be inaugurated a week after their arrival. Eleven rugged Austrians were completing a long voyage from Europe to join their countrymen on the Northland kauri gumfields. There were already many men from the Dalmatian coast, now Yugoslavia, working on the gumfields. In those days they were known as Austrians. Hardy men, these passengers understood only a smattering of English, which was to lead to some serious misunderstandings.

A cabin passenger, young Hallamore, waved farewell to his father, general manager of the Union Bank, Melbourne. After a holiday with his parents he was returning to his shipping clerk job in Napier, and his new position as a rugby selector. His strong frame bent over the rail as the sun burnt red in the Sydney sky, copper-tinged in the haze from recent bush fires. And still the Sydney kids piled high their bonfires. He would be lighting bonfires too before the voyage ended.

For his health's sake Fred Doidge, travelling representative of the *Cootamundra Liberal*, was setting out for New Zealand where his fortunes would flourish as a Liberal Party MP and he would eventually receive a knighthood. Mr Leifson, a keen angler, was taking his wife and child for a New Zealand holiday. Pert, pretty Miss Maybee of Balmain, Sydney, was going to visit her brother in Dix's Gaiety Company. She wore a fine feather boa, her feet like tiny clappers in her great bell-shaped dress. With a taste for fashion and a cheery temperament, in the face of hardship her high spirits were a buoy to others.

Homeward bound, six-year-old Connal Robb sat on deck by his mother. Mrs Robb had taken him to see a Melbourne doctor, hopeful of treatment for his crippling spinal caries. Connal loved the voyage along the harbour foreshores and remembering the rough crossing to Australia he said "Mother, I wish we might have land about us all the way to Auckland."

Annie Hugo had arranged her wedding trousseau in the cabin, aided by her mother, who was accompanying her excited daughter to her Whangarei wedding. Her daughter would wed without her father. Returning to Dunedin was the widowed Mrs Scotting with her fourteen-year-old daughter Winnie.

With the first motion of the ship Mrs Scotting became ill and remained in her cabin for the rest of the voyage. Winnie would arrive in Auckland motherless but Miss Maybee would take care of the orphan. Of the Chadwick couple from Kaipara, only Mrs Chadwick would arrive, a widow with a badly crushed leg. Their daughter had cancelled her ticket at the last minute and would for a time be posted missing.

Little Miss Greenwood stood by the rail with her father and mother, who owned the A.1. Hotel in Wellington. She would arrive alone, to be comforted and taken in by the kindly Mayor of Auckland, Mr Alfred Kidd. There was seven-year-old Norman Cassrels with his pet magpie and his mother; the girl Ellen Doorty, travelling steerage with her friends the Hankinsons and helping with their two children; and Mrs Berry with her three children, Eva, Albert and Dorothy, and their granny Mrs Sully. Neither six-year-old Dorothy nor her granny would reach Auckland.

Among another chatting group of saloon passengers was Mr Gunther, inspector of the Colonial Sugar Company, Parramatta, who had never done much boating in his life, let alone paddle a raft for eight hours. And Mr Peter Jones of Sydney who would eat nothing but crabs and whisky for two days. Dr Goldie had just had a month's health holiday in the Blue Mountains. Before he would return to his position administering the Auckland Asylum, he would scale cliffs with a rope and an oar, and be mistaken for a dirty-faced stoker. Captain Reid, Mercantile Marine Superintendent and Henry Wetherilt, Government Inspector of Marine Machinery, found conversation easy. Before Steven Rabone Neil of Sydney would arrive in Auckland he would watch his wife and little daughter vanish into the fog and see eight people die.

Exactly 1,054 miles away along the route to Auckland the tides were ripping and buffeting around West Island. The usual southern set of the current was swinging to the north.

As the *Elingamite* was steaming down the harbour a fortunate stowaway was discovered and put ashore at Garden Island just inside the heads. "Goodbye," he cried. "I'll see you no more." Then with good weather and a following wind the *Elingamite* set out across the Tasman. Powered by a single eighteen foot six inch screw her slim 310-foot hull averaged twelve and a half knots. Only forty feet in beam and drawing nineteen feet she was much lighter than modern ships of the same length. Her 2,585 tons had been assembled at Newcastle-on-Tyne in 1887 by Messrs Swan and Hunter. As she was a reserve cruiser for the British Admiralty her decks had been specially strengthened for the mounting of guns.

Captain Attwood had until recently been chief mate of her sister ship the *Zealandia* with whom she shared a regular run: Dunedin, Lyttelton, Wellington, Napier, Gisborne, Auckland, Sydney, Newcastle. From Newcastle (Australia) she carried 850 tons of coal, railway sleepers, timber, twenty bags of mail destined for Auckland and Gisborne, apples, loquats, oranges, cases and cases of gin, schnapps, brandy and whisky, Sunlight soap and straw hats. In a steel tank near her stern were locked fifty-two wooden boxes containing £17,000 of gold and silver coins, consigned by the Bank of New South Wales to its branches in Lyttelton and Dunedin: freshly minted gold half-sovereigns and pennies bearing the head of King Edward the Seventh whose birthday it would be on Sunday; shillings of all dates, back to

1839, marked the ageing of Queen Victoria, who had died the year before; half-crowns, florins, sixpences and threepences dated 1900 gleaming in the wooden boxes.

As Sydney Heads fell behind in the twilight the helmsman steered a course for the northern tip of New Zealand: south 88° east. This was to be maintained until a landfall was made.

"Outside the Heads it was rather rough," Mrs Robb recalled, "but nothing to speak of. Indeed there was very little of the *Elingamite*'s favourite roll thanks to the 850 tons of coal that had been shipped. Connal and I were both a bit sick on Thursday morning but once on deck we remained there and gradually picked up. Captain Attwood, with his usual consideration, arranged that we should have our meals on deck, as on the voyage over to avoid carrying Connal down to the saloon and up again."

At noon each day the chief officer Mr Burkitt would take a fix on the sun, read the distance run from the patent log trailing over the stern and determine latitude and longitude. By Thursday at noon the ship was 200 miles out into the calm November Tasman, and by Friday noon another 285 miles had fallen behind her.

At 3.25 that Friday afternoon the crew was mustered for a rather circumspect boat drill. Henry Wetherilt, as a ship's surveyor, eyed the procedure critically. The small ship's dinghy on the starboard side aft was swung out and in. No effort was made to check that the falls on the aft lifeboats would lower freely. The lifeboat covers were not lifted to see that each contained the regulation equipment: oars, rowlocks, sails, water cask, vegetable oil to calm the seas, a tin of oil for the lamp, rudder, tiller, two painters and hatchets. Although by regulation each boat should have contained a compass, these were kept in a box on the bridge. Lashed to the after-deck were two rafts. There were no knives to cut them free. Each raft should have had water, oars, rowlocks and sails, but Captain Attwood had not seen them moved since he took command in July, four months earlier.

Ted Allen, the donkeyman, had not seen the lifeboats lowered more than three times in six months, although boat drill was supposed to take place twice each trip. None of the officers had had any experience of boat handling while on the *Elingamite*. Under ordinary circumstances it would be possible to have the boats out in four minutes, an officer being allotted to each boat, at which time the boats would be provisioned. Mr Burkitt, the chief officer, had checked the boats and rafts two months earlier. The boatswain was to have examined the boats when the ship was in Auckland on her previous voyage, testing the chocks with levers and seeing that everything ran freely.

In the mate's log the Friday boat drill was recorded and the voyage continued, engines turning seventy-four revolutions per minute. At noon on Saturday Mr Burkitt took their position. He found that the ship had covered 780 miles but was three miles off course. This was ascribed to bad steering rather than the influence of any current. However, that was the last time he was to get a sighting of the sun.

During the afternoon the ship gradually entered a haze, reducing visibility to two miles. Navigation would now have to rely upon an accurate knowledge of the distance run and the speed of the ship. Then, allowing for the light north-easterly wind and any currents, the *Elingamite* would steam the remaining 260 miles, pass the Three Kings Islands to port and round North Cape for Auckland. But at 4 p.m. that Saturday, the patent log was found to have fouled. It had registered only forty miles since noon instead of the forty-eight which, at the speed of twelve knots, would have been covered in those four misty hours. Although the mate corrected the log, reliable navigation could no longer be based upon distance run.

At 6 a.m. on Sunday morning the captain was awakened, as he had ordered. Since the ship was nearing land and visibility was reduced he felt his place should be on the bridge.

Mrs Robb and Connal had watched the days sail by and the ship speed on her way. They were congratulating themselves on an exceptionally fine passage. This Sunday morning they were supposed to sight the New Zealand coast, but the fog spoilt that thrill for Connal. This would be his last day at sea. Early on Monday his father would meet them with the carriage on the wharf at the foot of Queen Street.

At 10 o'clock the haze thickened suddenly, closing down to two ship's lengths in a few minutes. Captain Attwood decided to slacken speed. From dead reckoning the ship ought to be six or seven miles south of the south-west King. He could have ordered a reduction in speed with the engine telegraph, but this would mean an instant response. The roar of excess steam vented from the boilers would blot out the sounds of breakers and the fog whistle reverberations he was straining to hear. So he sent for the chief engineer Mr Fraser.

On watch below and in charge of the engine room since 8 a.m. that morning was Jim Morrison, the fourth engineer. He slowed the engines down to forty revs a minute. At the same time Captain Attwood altered course to east-north-east,which would take him slightly further north. On a previous voyage he had encountered a southward running current in this area. This would counteract it, he thought.

Beside him on the bridge Captain Attwood had a copy of the *New Zealand Pilot* which showed that over the shallow plateau between Three Kings, Cape Maria Van Diemen and North Cape there was a three- to five-knot current. Within five miles of the islands, its influence would be even greater. But on his new course he would have a clear run.

His charts were wrong: the Three Kings were incorrectly surveyed and their true position was one and a quarter miles south. His assumption about the currents was wrong: on that Sunday the current was setting to the north-east. Even worse he had already veered to the north to counteract the assumed southerly set. Her true position uncertain the *Elingamite* was creeping through the dense whiteness towards a misplaced dot on the chart, unaware that her keel was being tugged ever closer by a moving stream of water, a current which equalled her own four-knot speed.

Most mornings Captain Attwood would have breakfast at eight with his saloon passengers: Captain Reid, Henry Wetherilt, Fred Doidge, Dr Goldie, Mr and Mrs Chadwick. Steven Neil had noticed his absence from the table on Sunday morning: "The chief mate told me the captain had had his breakfast taken to him, as he could not leave his post, the weather being so thick and foggy."

Steven went on deck at 9.30 a.m. taking his small daughter with him, to leave his wife in peace as she wrote letters in their cabin. On deck he noticed that the ship was creeping along at about four knots. Groups of passengers thronged the foredeck and amidships, straining their eyes into the fog. The ship would have passed the Three Kings about an hour earlier and for the last two hours she had been going dead slow through the whiteness, her foghorn blowing. Most of the passengers had got up in good time, including the sprightly Miss Maybee: "The captain had promised us that we would see land if we were early."

John Ralph was standing with others on the foredeck: "It was almost as black as night. We could not see a ship's length ahead. We had not long before had breakfast and I was standing with others chatting on the for'ard deck."

Mr Gunther, the Sugar Refinery man was also wondering when they would sight land: "We had had very fair weather all the way from Sydney. Saturday night set in a thick mist, and on Sunday morning when we got up we found it very murky. We thought we had passed the Three Kings, and were having an after-breakfast chat."

Mrs Robb and her little son still awaited the first sight of the New Zealand coast. "We were sitting on deck as usual, Connal and I, on Sunday morning about 10.30 a.m. Connal had been unhappy and was stopping his ears that he might not hear the foghorn."

Soon the *Elingamite* would round the North Cape and sail down the east coast of Northland to Auckland.

Mrs Perkins had packed her luggage in the cabin ready for the end of the voyage. Even the baby's bottle was packed away and she was standing on deck looking into the fog. A friendly sailor came up, chucked the little boy under the chin, and took him in his arms to show him the new country, when it burst through the mist.

Captain Reid had made far too many landfalls to be interested in this one. In the smoking-room he was chatting with Dr Goldie and Henry Wetherilt.

As the ship had moved in close to land, her keel no longer thousands of feet from the floor of the Tasman Sea, Mr Leifson, the keen angler, began to think about fishing. With his wife and child he had been looking over the stern as the single screw quietly thrummed in the dark blue water. "A line over the stern might produce some results," he had thought. Leaving his wife and child on the stern, he went below to get some fishing gear.

Strolling around the decks Steven Neil and his daughter met Captain Attwood at the corner of the bridge where he was pacing up and down. "We are going rather slow, captain," he remarked.

The reply, "Yes we have to go slow in weather like this. I have her going dead slow."

"When are we going to see land?"

"Very shortly. As you can see I am taking all possible precautionary measures." The captain walked back to his place on the bridge. (He had had prepared "Sir William Thompson's patent sounding apparatus," and intended to start using it at 11 o'clock. A reading of less than 100 fathoms would mean danger.)

In the steerage cabin twenty-year-old Annie Hugo was examining her wedding frock, excited at the approach of Auckland and the thought of her husband-to-be awaiting her arrival. Her mother was examining a lifebelt. Unable to read she asked Annie about the instructions on the cabin wall telling how they should be adjusted. "There's no need for that," said Annie. "We won't require them".

Mr Burkitt, the chief officer, was writing up his log in his cabin before turning in after his watch. The sound of the fog whistle came muted to his ears. He recorded that for the last two hours it had been sounding and the ship had been going dead slow since 10 a.m.

After breakfast Mr Vine, the chief steward, was in the lazarette getting out stores: "I heard a bumping, thumping sort of noise and rushed on deck to see what was up. It was a thick fog but just then it lifted and I could see the rocks towering above. I immediately rushed below, and calling a steward and stewardess, stationed them at the head of the companionway and furnished everyone with a lifebelt.

85

I had hardly commenced when I got a message from the captain, but I had anticipated his orders."

Looking around Steven Neil saw a man stationed on the lookout at the forecastle head: "Soon after speaking to the captain I quite casually walked to the skylight of the engine room and looked down. The piston rods of the engine were moving very slowly. I then walked to the side of the vessel and gazed through a thick bank of fog. I saw one of the most beautiful sights my eyes have ever witnessed. It is not easy to describe, but it reminded me of a transformation scene in a theatre. A thick, heavy bank of fog had come down the side of a hill. It did not touch the water and was clear enough for twenty or thirty yards high. The scene very much resembled a snow-clad mountain. Charmed I stood looking at it for some seconds. Then it struck me we were making straight for it. As I gazed in awe the cry 'Breakers ahead' from the forecastle was followed by the alarm signal to the engine room: 'Full speed astern'."

Amidships in Mr Gunther's group, one of the passengers shouted: "Look!"

"Ahead I saw a great green mass with white on the foreground. Another moment we saw breakers and realized we were running into a big cliff."

On the foredeck, for the sake of something to do, Mr Ralph had been timing the foghorn blowing every two minutes: "Glancing up, quick as a flash there burst upon us a sight that struck terror in all who saw it. White breakers were foaming and heaping not two hundred yards ahead. We simply stood horrified for the moment and watched the vessel going on to destruction. A scene like a panorama opened out of the darkness. A shining blue light puzzled us moment-arily—this being the phosphorus shining in the breakers. I looked towards the bridge and saw the captain ring the telegraph three times, which I believe means 'Full speed astern'."

Miss Maybee was playing with little Teddy Hankinson: "We peered for a sight of the promised land. By and by the expected cry of 'Land ahead' was heard. All that could be seen however was a dense white fog bank, but on drawing a little closer a rift in the fog revealed a horizontal line of the reef on a level with the vessel's side. At this time the fog was so thick that on looking upward we could not see higher than the steamer's funnel. Then as the rock suddenly sprang out of the dense cloud it formed one of the most beautiful sights I have ever seen."

The sailor holding Mrs Perkins' baby took one look at the onrush-ing wall, handed her the baby and leapt into the sea forever.

Mr Burkitt had completed writing his log. He was just lying down when suddenly he heard the telegraph sound to stop the vessel. He sprang up from his bunk. Looking out his porthole he saw the face of a great rock close up against the ship's side. As he rushed on deck the vessel grounded on the rocks and became pinned up, apparently on a ledge.

When the ship struck Mr Leifson was in his cabin getting some fishing lines and did not hear any shock: "Just as I was about to step from the saloon on deck, with my gear, Miss Adamson came up and told me we were *on* the Three Kings. The first thing I noticed was a great cliff towering high above the masts, partly obscured by fog. The water on the starboard side was fairly smooth, but on the port (landward) side there was a heavy swell and no visible landing place. Most of the passengers and crew were up forward, but my wife and child were at the stern. I swiftly joined them, and as the ship was jolting vigorously, I told them to cling to the netting on the deck cargo while I dashed below for lifebelts. When I returned they were already supplied so I handed those I had to other passengers. I went below for more to hand around. The stewardess and stewards were very calm and tried to furnish everyone with a belt. The former got me one."

Mrs Robb was chatting to Dr Beattie about her boy's illness: "The ship was creeping along as if feeling her way and we were leaving the captain and officers to their business. Suddenly Dr Beattie rose to his feet saying: 'I wonder if they really do know where they are going?' With that the fog drifted apart, and lo, towering rocks above and ahead, and a line of breakers below! A great ringing of the captain's bell to reverse the engines, a grating on the rocks, then a crash as if the bottom of the ship had been knocked in, followed by a scraping and grinding as of the keel on the rocks. Then ensued a running to and fro, and next minute, as it seemed, the passengers were fastening on their lifebelts. I ran to our cabin for ours—they were gone. When I got back to Connal our faithful steward Pratt was putting one on Connal and turned to fasten mine, saying: 'I have been thinking of this all morning. Now stay where you are,' he said."

Sitting in the smoking-room beneath the bridge, and beside the steering gear with Captain Reid and Dr Goldie, Henry Wetherilt heard the ring of the telegraph to the engine room and the sudden grating sound of the rudder being moved hard to port. He and the others immediately rushed to the side of the ship and saw the rocks ahead. The lookout man's cry rang in their ears.

"Engines taking a while to reverse," Henry remarked to Captain Reid. The propeller had stopped turning. They all knew something must be wrong and waited anxiously for the propeller to start thrashing. Wetherilt stepped back to the engine room skylight. Below the gleaming pistons were motionless. A clatter of anxious feet on the steel decking. Some commotion followed by a flogging sound like a heavy hammer. Several people were moving around, beyond his sight. Impatiently the telegraph from the bridge rang out again. Wetherilt darted to the rail. "If he gets his engines going it will be all right even now," he said to Captain Reid. He had not felt the ship strike. As he looked again down the skylight he heard a thud like a hammer being thrown down. Back at the rail, he and Captain Reid leant over to see that the bow was resting on the rocks and the stern, still moving in response to the rudder, helped by the wind and sea, was swinging broadside onto the rocks.

On the bridge Captain Attwood saw the breakers seconds before the lookout man's warning. At once he rang "Full speed astern". The wheel spokes flew hard over to port, swinging the bow to starboard. The engine room repeated the captain's order. The engines stopped, as was necessary before reversing. Nothing happened. "Full speed astern," Captain Attwood repeated. No movement came from the engines and the ship glided forward. The third engineer rushed up onto the bridge to blurt out that for some strange reason the engines would not respond.

"It's too late," Attwood replied as his ship shook beneath their feet, not more than two minutes from the time the danger was first seen.

The *Elingamite* hit bow first on West King at 10.40 a.m. There was a light north-westerly wind, a moderate swell and a south-easterly current.

From this point the passengers' accounts offer a fascinating conflict depending on where they were at the time. Some were shocked, felt a huge concussion, and ensuing confusion and terror. Others felt nothing, like Mr Leifson, and acted coolly: "Now we had no doubt; the ship was mortally wounded, sinking rapidly, and had to be abandoned."

Chapter 8

AT THE TIME of writing Norman Cassrels is the only living man who has vivid memories of the disaster.

"I was between the age of seven and eight and travelling with my mother on the way from Sydney to Auckland. I was playing around on the ship at the time. It was a very, very dense fog, so thick you could hardly see more than a few yards in front of you. Occasionally it would rise a bit forward of the bridge where the officers with their sextants were trying to take a shot of the sun but there was no sun for them to see. The foghorn was going continuously. There were a number of people around, I think mostly womenfolk. All of a sudden there was an all-out cry. The bell rang. I remember hearing the bell ringing; apparently it was a bell for the ship to go full speed astern. The fog lifted just at that moment when before us were the rocks. There wasn't any possible hope. I can't remember any severe impact but a ripping noise seemed to go through the ship. There was a tremendous scream from the womenfolk and others in which I joined. Asked later on why I screamed I said: 'Well everybody else screamed,' which was quite a reasonable thing to say.

"However, the next thing was a rushing around, everyone clearing off and apparently my mother and myself were left on the foredeck. I was frightened and crying. Mother took me up to the port side of the ship. The ship had swung right round from head on, against the rocks and the two of us looked over the side. She said: 'There you are boy, it's quite all right it's only a wharf we have come into. Don't be frightened.' And if my mother said it was only a wharf we had come into, well I was quite satisfied and I wasn't frightened any more.

"I can remember also while looking over, the water dripping from beetling cliffs which were right over the top of us and coming down onto my head. We were right up close in and directly under the rocks and I am sure that the tide was well out because there seemed to be nothing else but the serrated flat rock on which the ship was grinding itself to death. All boats on that particular side, the port side, were useless. They could never have got them off. We came around to the starboard side where there was a big whirl. The people flying around and rushing. I didn't understand it. I can't tell you of any panic. I think there was talk of panic."

Another of the few survivors still alive is Ellen Doorty, then an eighteen-year-old girl. "I was sitting on the deck talking to my friend Mr Hankinson and minding the children. I was peeling an orange when the ship gave a big bump throwing us out of our seats. All we could see was a large grey curtain. Then the order came: 'All women and children to the boats,' which was very difficult as the ship had tilted on her side. Mrs Hankinson decided to stay with her husband and she put her little son Teddy in my care. We were put in the first boat to leave."

Halmond Hankinson's first knowledge of the wreck had been when his wife came running down from the forecastle deck saying they were close to the rocks: "I ran and looked. There was excitement as passengers dashed from their cabins. Alice McGuirk, the forecabin stewardess told me there was no cause for alarm and handed out lifebelts. I got two, one for my wife and one for my little daughter. I got my boy into the boat with Ellen, but it pushed off before I could persuade my wife to leave me."

Steven Neil had watched the ship bear down on the rocks: "At that moment I knew I had to keep a cool head. My wife was down below writing. My little child was playing about on deck. I told her to stand quiet until Dada got back. I ran down to the cabin and called my wife to come up and look at the most beautiful of sights. We stood together the three of us and watched ahead. She was remarking on how beautiful it was when the ship gently glided up on to the rock. There was no concussion, we just skidded up."

To James McGeorge of Dunedin the vessel seemed to slide on. "Lifting up on the swell she thumped down and the forward hatch blew right out. The third cook, Tom Regges, jumped over the side with a life line, when a huge sea lifted him high into the air and crash he came down onto a ledge of rock and we saw no more of him."

Mr Gunther felt a bump: "The port side of the ship began to work gradually towards the shore, and she started to crunch up amongst the rocks. There was no excitement. Everyone seemed to keep remarkably steady and cool. The captain gave the order to man the boats and the crew at once moved up to the boat deck and proceeded to lower the boats down to the level of the passenger deck. It was very difficult to work on the port side, in fact only one boat was got out there, but on the starboard side the work was easier. So far as I could see most of the women and children got in first. Some got over the ship's side and some got into the boats off the rail, the boats coming up that high on the swells. I went down below and got myself a lifebelt."

Fred Doidge, (the MP to be) saw a quite different scene: "At twenty minutes to eleven the lookout man on the forecastle signalled 'breakers ahead'. The engines were at once stopped and there, two ships' lengths ahead, looming 350 feet up into the fog, was a solid mass of perpendicular rock; but to everyone's amazement instead of the ship backwatering she was being carried straight on to the rock. The deck was soon crowded with passengers, women kneeling in prayer, others in faints or hysterics and men were in some cases crying like children. It was a heartrending scene, the most terrifying of all being the sickening deadly crashes made as the rocks stove great holes in the ship's bottom.

"Considerable difficulty was experienced in keeping some of the more timid from rushing the first boat being loaded with women and children. As it was lowered past the main deck two men made a most desperate jump for it, but missed and fell into the water beneath and were washed out to sea. In lowering the next boat one of the stewards had five of his fingers broken. The second and third boats (boats 3 and 5) were successfully floated and most of the women and children were safely got into these next two, one of the crew keeping some terror-stricken men back with an axe.

"Both the rafts on the after boat deck were then sent off—one was seen to contain one of the stewardesses, Mrs Alice McGuirk, to the horror of all left on deck; a woman who throughout had displayed great courage. Then Boat 6 was lowered and I got into this."

Miss Maybee, waiting for a sign of land, definitely felt the crash: "She grated mightily on the reef. This was followed by a great crash and then all knew that the vessel was doomed. For a moment everyone seemed stricken dumb and unable to do anything, but recovering themselves the passengers began to get their lifebelts and prepared to leave the ship. Captain Reid, from first to last a man among men, called: 'Come along ladies and get into the boat' (Boat 2)."

The two nautical experts, Henry Wetherilt and Captain Reid, had watched the ship glide up on to the rocks as they waited for the engines to go astern. They now felt that there was little cause for excitement. Henry asked Reid what he thought best.

" 'I'm going in no boat in this fog. She'll bilge herself soon and lay over against the rocks. She'll last all day here.'

"We then went to see how they were getting out the boats. They tried to get the port boats out first as that side was next to the cliffs and more sheltered. There was ample room between the ship and the rocks to get them out. The ship was then on an even keel although rolling gently with the rise and fall of the sea. I started to help with Boat 2 but owing to the shocking way it was being handled I turned away, saying: 'I'm not going to be mixed up in this. Here's where the loss of life is going to be.' When the list developed I called to

Captain Attwood: 'Would it not be better to launch the starboard boats and pass the port ones over?'

"I don't know whether he heard me on the bridge. They went on putting out the port boats.

"Leaving Boat 2, I went further aft. Mr Ralph and others came running up, saying: 'Reid, you know this place? Are there no landings here?'

" 'Yes—I know all the landings here.'

"Someone said: 'I wonder if the captain knows?'

" 'Perhaps he doesn't. If we're on the Great King there's a place just around the point where we could all land and there would be no need to get flurried. We could then send a boat across to the mainland.' I called to the captain: 'Have you hit the Big King?'

" ' Yes.'

" 'Oh, it's all right, there are plenty of landings here. I know them. If you give me a boat I'll go away, find the landing, and come back.'

" 'All right. Take number 1 boat.' "

Somewhere in that middle ground between Reid and Attwood, a tragic error was compounded. If this was the western face of the Great King, Reid was right; the eastern side does have a good landing. Attwood probably thought Reid, because of his professed knowledge of the region, could tell where they were. But the opposite side of the West King is more precipitous than the side the *Elingamite* had hit; this area has the worst currents and tide-races and it was nine miles from the Great King in the thick mist.

From the boat deck above John Ralph aided Captain Reid to lower number 1 lifeboat to the rail of the promenade deck. It was a struggle. "All the running gear was foul and the tackle was so tight we had to cut it with knives. The falls jammed when we tried to lower away, the tackle being more like a stick than a rope and appeared as if it had not been used for ten years. Having lowered the boat to the level of the passenger deck, Captain Reid and I, assisted by Mr Leslie of West Australia, filled it with women and children. There were motherless children and mothers looking for children. Most were provided with lifebelts. As the vessel was now pitching and rolling, bundles and gear were flying in all directions. Our boat was swinging wildly ten feet up and down. In getting in, Mrs Chadwick of Kaipara had one of her legs badly hurt, being crushed between the ship's side and the boat. Mr Wrigglesworth had his hand badly cut and Miss Maybee was also severely bruised."

Aboard number 1 boat Miss Maybee was not frightened: "The sensation was awful; you could not imagine it really. Yet all the time I had no fear of anything. It is a most peculiar thing. I seemed to be dreaming and at the same time feeling that I would not drown. When I got into the boat I felt all right, and said to myself 'Nothing can happen to me now.' I have been in two or three tight pinches but I've always managed to come out on top. As we were getting in the boat there was a lady (Mrs Perkins) standing on the deck with a baby in her arms. She seemed incapable of making any effort to save herself so I caught hold of the child and literally dragged it from her, and got into the boat. The mother of course followed quickly. There was great difficulty in getting the boat out as the davits did not work freely."

Eventually Captain Reid had to cut some of the ropes:

"I then told the men to lower away as I did not consider that the falls could support the weight of more passengers in the boat. The Austrians on board tried to rush the boat and we kept them back, shouting out that the women must go first. The boat was then lowered towards the water. Some men got into her, while others had already jumped, as the ship was settling down. When the boat was three parts down the lifeline jammed in the block of the after fall. I called out for them to clear it. As they could not I slid down the line and pulled it out. The after fall was not fast and it went down suddenly. The second mate let go the forward fall. As the disengaging gear would not work the falls had to be cut. Afterwards I found this was not a fault of the gear, which had broken in the sudden snap. I looked for the axe. I couldn't see it although it was in the boat. We were smashing against the side. I managed to cut the falls with a penknife. Most of the passengers had by then left this side of the ship, except Wetherilt. Fending off the boat I told my men to shove off.

"Just then Mr Chadwick, a passenger, came along and I called on him to help. His wife was in the boat. I also asked Mr Neil and others to come down and pull on the oars. None of them came. I'd intended to go and find a landing and return. The captain called out to do this 'and return as quick as you can'. As I was going Wetherilt yelled: 'Come back as soon as you can. I'll wait for you.' I replied: 'All right. Save the money and my commission papers.' 'All right, old man.'

"By the appearance of the vessel when I left her I reckoned that she would last all day. Within three minutes we had lost sight of her in the mist but could still hear a grinding sound."

Miss Maybee also refers to the Austrians: "A number of Austrians rushed the boat, but most of them were promptly pushed off. I felt calm and collected and that I had to do something. I grasped a pole and was keeping the boat from smashing up against the ship when the pole broke in half and sent me sprawling into the bottom of the boat."

Mrs Robb saw that the boats could not be lowered on the port side owing to the rocks, so carried Connal round to the starboard where they were lowering the first boat: "When it was level with the rails two men dragged me up into it, and a third handed Connal to me. The boat was filled with what women and children were handy, and Captain Reid (the Auckland shipping master who happened to be a passenger), with some passengers and two sailors to help, took command. In all we were twenty souls. When lowered there was great difficulty in getting it free. In the long run the ropes were cut with pocket knives. Mrs Chadwick's husband was there with agonized face. Captain Reid called to him to come down by rope, perhaps he did not understand—anyway he came not. He was afterwards seen on the raft, that was all. Captain Attwood called out that he thought we were on the Great King—the largest island of the Three Kings—Captain Reid said he knew of a landing place, and promised to return to the ship as soon as possible."

Steven Neil placed his wife and child in the boat: " 'Oh daddy, please come,' my child was crying. It was a terrible moment. An officer seeing us parting advised me to get into the boat. As the boat was being lowered, (see Appendix 2) under the cool command of Captain Reid a number of Austrians made a rush for it. I said to them: 'If you are men, for God's sake let the women go first.' One of them replied 'I vants the boat,' and he dived into it from the side of the vessel. I inwardly resolved that the next man who attempted to do a thing like that would get the punishment he deserved. The opportunity soon came. I was about to pass a woman (Mrs Robb) and a poor little cripple into the boat when an Austrian forced his way between us. I hit him mighty hard on the point of the chin, felling him to the deck. I said, "If there is a further rush slaughter them like you would sheep.' When the next boat (number 3) was being loaded we did our best to place all the women in safety. This done, I walked amidships and saw a raft being prepared at the aft part of the vessel. I went down to assist."

In Boat 3, crashing against the side of the ship while men struggled to lower it, were Norman Cassrels and his mother:

"One hero of the sinking whom I heard of after in the papers, was Mr Neil. He was rescued from the big life raft. There were sixteen on that raft and all but eight were drowned or jumped overboard through drinking salt water. I was rather lucky that I didn't end up on that raft. My mother took me down by the companionway where the magpie, that she had bought for me in Sydney, was hanging up. She told me to stay there by the magpie until she came back. She wanted to go down below to pick up a coat for me. I suppose she may have been gone a long time to me, but I was too interested in everything so left my position there and off I went. I climbed up over some cases and the next thing I was on the poop of the ship watching the men undoing the life raft. This was the craft that Neil and company were going to throw off. The ship was rolling, the seas were coming up pretty heavily on the stern. It was a greasy swell more than anything: not what you would call a rough sea. I think I must have been chased away by these men because the next thing I am coming back over the cases of fruit that I had to climb up on, piled upper deck high when a voice called out 'My boy! My boy! Where's my boy?' and I called out 'I'm here, Mater.' She was always 'Mater' to us all. I climbed down to her. If she scolded me I couldn't tell you. It's too long ago. But she put an overcoat on me. She also put a lifebelt on me but it was rather large. I think if I had fallen in the water I would have been upside down rather than the right way up. My mother, when she had gone below to get things for me, had also picked up a purse which she thought had some money in it. She might need some money where-ever she landed, if she ever landed anywhere. She also apparently took a rug as well which I still have or what's left of it. She had a sister on board with the sister's husband and their daughter. She went down into her cabin, collected the things she wanted, and when she went to get out of the door it had locked itself. It was completely jammed with the roll of the ship. She could hear the water down below coming in the lower decks and there was nothing she could do. My mother never panicked. She sat down and said: 'Well I can't get out, that's the end of it.' The ship rolled the other way. The door opened and mother flew out and up the companionway as fast as she could go. When she got up her sister called out that her husband hadn't got his lifebelt, nor had some old man and I can see him now with a long beard. He was about eighty-odd I understand. He said to mother: 'For God's sake get me a lifebelt,' and mother tackled a steward who was coming up from the companionway with a whole swag of them and dragged two or three of them from him and she helped to put them on the old man and her sister's husband as well. This was just a little incident that happened during that panic on board the ship.

"The ship was rolling from side to side and there didn't seem to be very much chance of anyone getting into the boats. The last boat was at the rail and there was the purser, Mr Chambers. Mother had helped him. He had been very sick on board ship coming over, 'flu or something of the sort. Mother always carried a medicine chest and she had dosed him up. He considered, and he always did con-sider in the years after, that he owed his life to her: 'You've saved my life and I will try to save yours.'

"Well, the first person to be saved was me. He picked me up. With the roll of the ship the lifeboats, hanging in the davits, had swung right away out and he had to wait until the boats came in again. When they smashed alongside the side of the ship was the time for people to try and get in. I was thrown into boat 3 by Mr Chambers and caught by one of the crew. I can't remember Mother getting in but one of the horrible accidents I do remember. It was not horrible to me then because I wasn't old enough to understand. A man followed me. He was a shortish chap with a moustache. In retrospect he reminds me of a cartoon figure, 'Old Bill'. As he got in he took hold of the gunwale of the lifeboat. The lifeboat was swinging out, the ship was swinging over and he went out with the lifeboat dangling from the gunwale. I was standing looking right down into this man's face when he let go and I saw him sucked under the vortex of the ship as she was swinging back the other way. I will never forget his face. I will never forget the incident. It is something that is written indelibly on my mind from now till the day I die.

"Well eventually we got down into the water. I don't remember my mother being there. All I do remember is a tremendous crowd of people. We had no sooner struck the water than it was pouring into the lifeboat. She had a gaping hole in the side and everyone was stuffing in bags—anything at all. If it hadn't been for the buoyancy tanks we would have sunk. Everyone had to set to work bailing. I had a little sailor cap on. Someone dragged it off my head and was using that. The womenfolk were using shawls, anything at all, helping to bail and apparently they had a certain control. The men on the boat were pulling away from the wreck. The ship was going down.

"We lost sight of the ship in the fog. Next thing we picked up Captain Attwood who was standing on a lot of the flotsam around about in the water. There was a girl picked up, Winnie Scotting, a youngster of about fourteen. She was pulled in by one of the men on the boat, one called Luke Lunevich. He lived up in Kaitaia until recently. Later there was a romance about that. His first wife died and he advertised to see if he could find this girl. He wanted to marry her but unfortunately she had passed on.

"One thing I did see was rather upsetting. It has lasted with me all my life. When we were in the vicinity of the wreck, I remember hearing a boom. It was the blowing up of the boilers on board the ship. The fog had lifted at that time and I said to Mother: 'Is that another boat over there?' And she said: 'No, boy, that's the same boat,' and then the *Elingamite* heaved herself up bow first and slid under the water. It affects me even today to see pictures of ships sinking. There is something so alive with them, something almost greater than human with these things. As I say I shall always see that ship going down. It was an experience.

"Going through the wreckage I remember seeing a hand come up and grab an oar. A last dying action I suppose because they couldn't pull the person in. I remember seeing the old man floating in the water dead, the old man my mother had put the lifebelt on. I also remember our magpie, but he wasn't singing. He used to say: 'There is no luck about the house, there is no luck whatever.' He was pretty well right. He wasn't saying it then. All he was doing was saying 'Caw, Caw!' in a very weary voice. Poor little thing!"

At this point the sequence of events is far from clear. After a close study and comparisons of all accounts, this seems to be what really happened.

By the time Boat 1 had been launched and Boat 3 had been lowered away from the promenade deck rail, "the crashing had become appalling," said Dr Beattie. "We were fairly waist high in water on the deck and remained there only with difficulty. Miss Cora Anderson, my daughter-in-law, and I got into the dinghy which we believed was the last boat capable of leaving, the list having rendered the port side boats useless." At the same time as the dinghy was going down the starboard side aft with nine on board, the mysterious Boat 4 was also being lowered. As she hit the water very near the rocks the third officer and two seamen took her around the stern to the starboard side. Among the thirty-three occupants was a large proportion of the crew including the chief engineer, Mr Fraser. In the confusion she was the only lifeboat to be provisioned.

Fred Chambers the purser saved the ship's papers. He had to descend a ladder to the aft well deck and rush along the alleyway 100 feet long past the engine room to his cabin amidships. He risked his life every moment he was in the alleyway or cabin as at any moment the ship might sink. When he reached the deck again the water was shooting through the hatches. He leapt into the dinghy.

Boat 3 was stove in, either during the lowering or by contact with some wreckage in the water. Peter Jones of Sydney was one of the forty-five aboard: "Four of the men took off their shirts and stopped the breach as well as possible. The leakage was checked sufficiently to enable the boat to be kept afloat by means of constant bailing."

Jim Donaldson, his hand badly injured, was one of the last to leave: "As that boat was getting away two passengers, a young lady and a gentleman, who appeared to make no effort to secure their safety, were washed overboard clasped in each other's arms. The gentleman, who is supposed to have been her husband, endeavoured to comfort her, but he also appeared content to accept his fate."

G   97

At this stage all the starboard boats were launched. On the port side, near the stern, Mr Leifson had arrived at Boat 6 with his wife and child. "The ship was bumping and rolling heavily. I told my wife and daughter not to go in the first boat, which was surrounded by a large number of passengers, as I feared a rush. It was successfully launched with only a few people in it, but I saw them pick some more out of the water. The captain was on the listing bridge, giving orders and appeared to be calm. The officers and crew, including the stewards were behaving nobly and worked like Trojans, doing their utmost to launch the boats and get the women and children in. There did not appear to be any possibility of launching the port boats, which meant that many people would be left out of the others. I tried to get my wife into Boat 3 but she refused to go without me.

"The ship then commenced to settle down forward and the other boats excepting the port lifeboat (Boat 2) which would not move from the chocks having been launched in the meantime, we were left with no means of getting away from the wreck. The position was very critical. I decided to stand by the wreck. We tightened up our lifebelts and took off our boots and shoes. The seas then commenced to break over us and carried us off our feet once or twice. I told my wife to hang on to the skylight while I went up to the boat deck to reconnoitre. I spoke to the captain on the bridge. I saw four or five men struggling hard to launch number 2 lifeboat but she would not move. I also saw that Boat 6 was successfully launched on the port side and although it looked ugly I decided to tell my wife to jump for it. As I got back to her a big sea had just carried her off her feet and nearly overboard but a lurch to port carried her back again. I was just in time to clutch her and drag her to the port side. I snatched the child from her, lifted her on to the rail, put the falls into her hands and swung her out just as the roll brought the boat to her and she slid in nicely. Then I threw the child in after her, and succeeded after a time in getting in myself."

When the impact came anxious, illiterate Mrs Hugo, the lifebelt instructions unread, collapsed on deck. She was eventually placed in ill-fated Boat 4. Meanwhile Annie, having managed to get into a lifeboat just had time to kiss her mother goodbye forever and jump overboard, to be picked up by Boat 6.

But Dr Beattie, Miss Hugo and the other forty odd passengers in Boat 6 were not to stay dry for long.

Aboard the sinking ship Allen the donkeyman was struggling with the obstinate Boat 2 on the listing starboard side of the boat deck, near the bridge. Bags of mail were bobbing around, released from the mailroom when the pressure from the influx of water burst up through the decks, where the waves were now breaking. He toiled at cutting all the falls. He had the conviction that as the ship sank the lifeboat would be floated off.

Between the ship and the towering cliffs, Boat 6 rowed up and down, buffeted by the backwash, picking up others floating among the debris. Cases of schnapps, oranges, trunks, hatches, all tossed madly in the confused water.

Miss Greenwood of Wellington, whose father and mother were lost, was rescued by the purser's boat: "When the boats had all been launched, though generally a coward as regards the water, I took the advice offered and jumped from the side of the steamer, about twelve feet, into the sea. I sank but soon came to the surface, confused and struggling, and was pulled aboard the purser's boat, and later changed to another boat containing ladies." All around the sea was strewn with wreckage and fruit. She saw the body of an old gentleman, who had been in the steerage at the beginning of the voyage but later transferred to the saloon. He had been crushed between a boat and the steamer.

Mr Leifson's boat was crammed full of people and although in a very awkward position, between the fast sinking ship and the rocks, they continued picking up people out of the water and clinging to wreckage. Then the boat, having struck some wreckage or a rock, filled and capsized.

"We were all thrown into the water. I caught my wife in one arm and child in the other. They were both face downwards but I managed to turn them over. Their lifejackets held them above water but the backsurge, rebounding between the wreck and the shore and the swell running up between, produced a very confused sea. My wife then held the child's face upwards. She was very brave and did all I told her. Supporting them I made for the rocks to try and land but found it impossible. A brave passenger named Passy also tried to swim ashore with a line in his teeth. I then swam towards a mass of heaving wreckage and got hold of a trunk with a round top. This broke away from my grasp several times, until I succeeded in catching the iron handle, to which I clung with one hand, supporting my wife and child with the other. I did not find it so very hard to sustain them but the cold immersion began to tell upon my wife. She told me to let her go and try to save the baby and myself."

Fred Doidge was also in Boat 6: "We got off successfully with about twenty passengers, including half a dozen women and children. We pulled towards the rocks, hoping to find a landing and when within a few yards of what we saw was a hopeless chance, a heavy piece of wreckage struck our boat and we capsized. Everyone sank beneath the surface and we all expected to be dashed to pieces against the rocks or drowned before coming to the surface again. Luckily we were carried out towards the wreck by the backwash, choking with salt water, and struggling with the aid of our lifebelts through scores of cases of fruit and other debris. We clung to boards, ladders and temporary rafts, but there seemed to be little hope."

After this capsize Fredrigo Passy, a Portuguese cook, had swum inshore to seek a landing as there was no means of saving all those struggling in the water. He must have been a very strong swimmer: "I made it to a flat ledge under the cliffs. It was quite dry and would have held one hundred people who could have got up there through the surf had I managed to take a line from the wreck. I tried to help another man up there but he pulled me down."

Meanwhile the seas were breaking right over the sinking ship. On the steeply canted port side Ted Allen the donkeyman was still wrestling to free Boat 2. His foresight in cutting the falls was fully justified. A wave of just the right force came, lifted the boat out of the chocks and floated her off. She took to the water stern first as though she had been launched in the ordinary way. Four men at the oars and two at each end guided her off the rocks and negotiated her through the jumbling wreckage and the struggling and drowning passengers. Passy dived several times for a woman who had sunk and managed to get her to the boat.

To Leifson it seemed as if a miracle had happened: "Number 2 lifeboat came round towards us, after much difficulty on account of all the debris." Miss Anderson was the first to be picked up, then Dr Beattie, then the Leifsons, clinging to the waterlogged trunk: "The boat had been steered clear of the wreckage and the rocks; the capsized boat was bumping her and the sinking ship threatened to engulf her. The men in that boat behaved like heroes. We grabbed the lifelines, thoroughly exhausted, quite unable to heave ourselves aboard. The donkeyman and the cook helped my wife and child. I owe my life to Dr Middleton. I had let go the lifeline with one hand and was about to let go with the other. My family safe aboard all I wanted to do was to relax into oblivion. Dr Middleton pulled me aboard. Mr Waters, having stepped from the boat deck into Boat 2 as it slid off, was still dry and warm. He held me to him to warm me. Some of the crew rubbed me to restore circulation and I soon recovered."

By this time all the other boats had disappeared into the mist. Only Boat 2 remained to pick up all the passengers floating among the wreckage. Mrs Sully died soon after being pulled aboard. The long exposure and wild waters were too much for her. The second mate, Mr Renaut, was hauled aboard. He and the captain had been clinging to the funnel guys as the ship had listed so far to starboard that the upper bridge was half submerged. They were swept away and swam to the sun deck, where they found temporary safety.

Mr Burkitt, the chief mate, was pulled in almost naked, but he took the tiller at once. As the ship sank he had taken to the water from the upper bridge, where he had raced to get the lifeboat compasses stored there. He swam out to some wreckage. Eventually the captain and second mate hailed him and he swam to them. Near them clinging to the wreckage, were a little girl and boy whom they immediately placed in Boat 2 when it arrived. (The captain was picked up by Boat 3, later to be transferred to the jolly boat.)

Mr Burkitt's account states that Boat 2 was immovable "because someone had cut the falls, making it impossible to move out of the chocks." Was he covering for the faulty state of the boats? The "someone" was Allen the donkeyman, and had he not cut the falls the boat would not have floated free. Mr Burkitt said later: "I was most annoyed at the time but I realize it was the best thing the donkeyman ever did in his life."

The chief steward, William Vine, having seen to the distribution of lifebelts, sought to provision the lifeboats: "I brought up a lot of biscuits but I don't know which boat they were placed in, (Boat 4) if any. The whole thing was over in about twenty-five minutes. I helped the quartermaster to lower the port quarter boat. She was the last. After she had left I ran round and saw three men trying to lower number 2 lifeboat. Seeing it was hopeless I called to them to dive from the seaward side and make for the other boats, which they did. By now I was clinging to the funnel. I slid down the guy and got a grating off the boat, which I made into a raft. On this I picked up two children and a man. I saw the captain and mate and second mate all floating near me in the water. Eventually Boat 2 picked us all up."

Eva Berry, aged eleven, was one of the children Vine had saved: "My mother was holding on to ropes on the deck when a wave washed her, Dorothy and grandmother overboard. Chief Steward Vine put me on some wreckage with Winnie Scotting, and we were later picked up by a lifeboat carrying my mother and brother. We had lost Dorothy and grandmother (Mrs Sully) died soon after she was brought aboard."

Last man taken into Boat 2 was Bill Lennox the "brassboy", who had drifted about perched on a large case, with his arms around a recovered case of schnapps. On being told to come aboard he replied: "Never mind me, pick up the others first. I've got enough here to keep me going for a week." In the photos of the survivors he is easily recognized by the mischievous twinkle in his eyes and his comical moustache.

Now crammed with fifty-two people, Boat 2 had recovered every living person from the sea. Seeing no hope of recovering any more they pulled some distance away from the wreckage and prepared the boat for sailing.

At half past one they set sail for the North Cape of New Zealand, to the south-east.

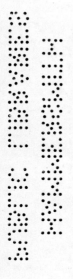

Chapter 9

DURING THE LOWERING of the lifeboats, the attention of some of the men passengers had turned to the two liferafts. One of the first to reach them was Dr Goldie of Auckland: "When the steamer struck I saw that nearly all the passengers were rushing to the boats and that no one appeared to be paying any attention to the two rafts which were carried on the special boat deck above the saloon. I considered, however, that the rafts were safer than the boats and whilst the crew were busily engaged in getting out the latter, I went to the rafts and attempted to untie the ropes with which they were secured. Finding it impossible to untie the ropes I went down to the saloon and obtained six table knives, which I distributed amongst a number of male passengers. In a few minutes we had the rafts free and the vessel, giving a lurch, shot the smaller raft overboard.

"I noticed that the raft was being rapidly washed astern and I dived after it and got aboard. Very soon afterwards several passengers and members of the crew swam out to the raft and I helped them aboard, thus making a total of nine on the raft. By this time the second and larger raft had been launched and a keg of water placed on board of her. We were now some distance away, no other passengers were attempting to reach us and it was impossible for us to render any further assistance. We started to drift with a strong south-east current.

"As we drifted away from the wreck we saw the steamer gradually settle down, her bridge being underwater when we last saw her. The captain had been washed overboard and we saw him floating on some wreckage. The boats were then standing by the vessel picking up the people who were in the water. The second raft came along and we started to drift in company with it. There was a thick mist and we were soon out of sight of land. We rowed up to the other raft and transferred two of her nineteen passengers to our raft, thus increasing our party to eleven and leaving sixteen on the other raft including one lady Mrs McGuirk, the forecabin stewardess. The large raft was provided with rough seats (none appear in photos) ours having none and also a keg of water (empty!) and on this account it was thought that the stewardess would be more comfortable there. We drifted and rowed alternately until about two o'clock in the afternoon.

The other raft having a weaker crew (only one oar) than ours, were unable to keep up with us and drifted out of sight."

When Mr Gunther arrived at the stern, "the ship was bumping very heavily and leaning over to starboard. The smallest raft had been got clear of the ship. I saw Dr Goldie and Hallamore and others jump from the stern of the ship and swim for the raft. I did the same and got on the raft. There were eight of us on the raft and we found she was gradually floating away from the ship. We watched for a little while, in the hope of picking up one or two more. Then the big raft came floating towards us. There were nineteen on her, and we took three off, making eleven on ours and sixteen on the other raft.

"We were gradually drifting all the time. All on the raft were amateurs. There was a fireman and two men who were working their passages, all the others, passengers. At first we seemed to be watching for somebody to give us a lead what to do, then we decided to keep clear of the island and try to get round the back of it. There was not much sea although there was a break at the foot of the cliffs. We had two oars and we pulled for a good while but the current seemed to take us out and we lost sight of the land. We tried for a time to follow the boats but we got out of sight of them and of everybody. At last we sighted the other raft and we kept company for some little time. Then one of the boats came past us and told us they were looking for a landing on the island. Then we drifted away altogether and could neither see nor hear any signs of the breakers. We decided that nothing could be done but to keep the raft's head to the wind."

The accounts of two of the survivors on the "large" raft contain some striking conflicts with those on the smaller one.

Steven Neil, having dispatched his wife and child in Boat 1 and felled an Austrian to the deck, had swum out to the larger raft from which he could watch the struggling passengers being picked out of the water by lifeboats. In the midst of the wreckage he saw Captain Attwood: "Standing on floating wreckage out in the open seas, he was as much a captain as when he stood up on his own bridge. Poor unfortunates were struggling in the water and Captain Attwood gave his attention to each. It did one good to see his whistle go up to his mouth ordering boats to pick up lives. He seemed to rise to the occasion in every way and the boats obeyed his orders implicitly. You would have thought it was a sham fight instead of a wreck. (Obviously Mr Neil had a pugilistic outlook!) No man in the world could have been cooler or nobler or braver."

The waves were breaking over the nineteen in the larger raft which was half submerged. "The other raft," said Mr Neil, "which had left earlier, was above water. Its deck was dry, the cylinders appeared to be built higher and it was not so crowded. I called to this raft and asked the men upon it to find room among them for the forecabin stewardess. Whether they thought there was a danger of swamping if they approached too close I don't know, but they did not take the poor woman. Some time later this raft came nearer and three of our men jumped out to her and were taken aboard. The jolly boat then came along with the purser, Mr Fred Chambers, to whom I had been introduced, in command. I could see at a glance that there was not to be much room in the boat for those that were there, but we called out and asked if it were possible for them to take one or two from us. One of them remarked that the boat was leaking and I learned that the purser had been ordered by the captain to make as quickly as possible for the lee side of the island and find a place where they could camp.

"After the first excitement was over we made an examination of our craft and found that we were in a worse predicament than we had supposed. There was a water keg on the raft and we had looked upon it as full. It did not, as a matter of fact, contain a single drop of water. We had two sculls but only one rowlock which left us with one scull to propel us. Within a few minutes Danielson, who was a quartermaster on the *Elingamite*, improvized a rope rowlock. Using both oars we then struggled to get to the leeward of the island, but the current was too strong for us, and we realized that we were at the mercy of the winds and the waves. Plenty of fruit in cases was at the time floating amongst the wreckage, with which the sea was covered. Not expecting any such dreadful experiences as we were doomed to pass through, we did not make any great effort to secure the fruit and it was by good fortune more than anything else that one of our number picked up two small apples. Instead of getting to the lee of the island we gradually drifted out for probably twenty miles, When we looked around us at daybreak there was only the open sea around and the sky overhead."

Arthur Robinson, who had been sleeping in the men's steerage cabin, had awoken to the shouting and "hurrahs", as he thought. The other men in the cabin imagined that land had been sighted. At that moment nobody in the cabin realized there was any danger. Arthur was on his way to Lyttelton with his friend Jordan; "We booked for Lyttelton and intended to go up country."

On deck he and Jordan took one look at the rocks through the fog: "I remarked to my mate Jordan that it was all up and he agreed with me. I took matters coolly, knowing that the worst thing that could happen would be to get excited. I tried to inquire from some of the officers what was the best thing to do. One officer said the ship was evidently on the rocks and could not get off and that we must get the boats out. I then, with others, assisted the crew to get the boats down from the davits and to get the women and children into them. After that had been done one of the officers suggested that the rafts should be got off the main aft deck. The lashings of the rafts were thereupon cut and the last raft was shot out from the main deck. I looked around and saw only a few of the men were remaining. As the time had evidently come to look after number one, I jumped into the sea and got out to the raft, along with Jordan. There were nineteen on the raft. We had two oars, but only one rowlock. We were immersed in the water, the raft being much too heavily laden and it was hard work to do anything. About half an hour later we came across the other raft and asked them to take two or three off our raft and so lighten it. Mrs McGuirk, the stewardess, appealed to them to take her off and the men on our raft supported her appeal knowing that we were in a terrible condition owing to being half immersed in water. The other raft did not come close enough just then but soon after it came pretty close and three of our number jumped off, swam to the other raft and were pulled aboard.

"We had a keg aboard which would have held about thirty gallons of water. Unfortunately it was empty and the only use we got of it was to give it to the stewardess to sit upon—it kept her dry. After a time, however, the raft being very deep in the water, and weight being a great consideration we decided to dispense with it and we threw it overboard."

Twelve feet long and nine feet in breadth the raft was constructed on the gridiron principle with airdrums on either side for floats. The main construction was of nine by two planks over which four by two battens were nailed, with four inches between each. A few side ropes provided the only handholds.

The raft drifted on through the night borne by the current right past the Kings and away to the east, its sixteen occupants sitting with water up to their waists, the wash of the sea continually breaking over them.

Through the mist and without compasses, Boat 2 steered for where its occupants thought North Cape would be; they peered into the mist hoping to catch a glimpse of Cape Maria Van Diemen light. Burkitt steered for the first two hours; then Passy, the man who had tried to swim ashore with a line, relieved him, while the second mate navigated, maintained a lookout and encouraged the passengers.

"Late in the afternoon," Dr Beattie said, "we sighted a boat believed to be the captain's, apparently making for Cape Maria, but soon lost sight of her again in the fog." This boat carried a sail and was the only other boat sighted by Boat 2. It could very well have been the mysterious Boat 4 which alone carried a compass, and some provisions (three tins of biscuits weighing sixty pounds). Many days after the shipwreck this lifeboat was found far to the north, upside down.

Throughout the bitterly cold night the second mate cheered up the fifty-two passengers. In the 22-foot boat there was no room to move and nothing to eat except a few oranges and loquats, a case of schnapps, picked up out of the water and a beaker of water. "We suffered more from cold and wet than from hunger," said Mr Leifson, "and we had, of course, no chance to dry our clothes. My little child almost collapsed but my wife and I kept up her circulation by constant rubbing. Some sang chorus songs during most of the night; fruit and schnapps were distributed at intervals." As they sailed in an easterly direction, light intermittent rain fell through the night, and at first light the chilled passengers hoped the mist would have lifted to give them a sight of the cape light. By 8 a.m. it cleared and course was altered to south-east on which haul they sighted Mt Camel by early morning.

Nearly twenty-four hours later they arrived at a small sandy beach where, exhausted and stiff, they clambered ashore to be found by a group of Maoris who took them to Houhora and treated them with great kindness.

Not all the others were faring as well. Hauled into Boat 3, Captain Attwood tried to keep everyone together, but in the fog the rafts were soon lost from sight. For some time blasts from his whistle kept near him Boat 5, the purser's dinghy and Boat 2, in the first mate's command. He told the third mate, in Boat 4, to set sail for the mainland and give the alarm. Boat 2 also left, once prepared for sail.

As Attwood sought a landing the occupants of his boat were kept busy bailing. Rising up to the thwarts water was pouring through the gap in the stoved planks and there was a danger of swamping. Some cases found floating in the wreckage supplemented the boat's bailers and held it in check.

Further off in the mist, at the mercy of the tide, those on the heavily laden raft struggled with one oar, and a paddle. Mr Wetherilt and his companions sighted the purser's boat, and hailed him to take the stewardess on board. The purser said their 10-foot boat was crowded and could not take her. Wetherilt could see it was a small boat, but could not understand why the passengers should have all been crowded in the forepart.

When later on in the afternoon they drifted together again, the purser told them the captain was around in the lee of the islands and everyone was to make for there. Wetherilt was furious: "All very well to say go around to the lee of the island with a thing like a raft."

He shouted to the purser's boat that they had a rope on the raft. If the boat would tow them they would hang clear and make no attempt to board the boat. The purser said he could not do it and went on. They then asked him to take the stewardess. The purser replied that he must go on and tell the others. Wetherilt was sure the purser heard him speak about towing and that they had a line.

This whole incident is typical of the confusion and misunderstandings that arise at times of crisis. Under duress decisions are made and later regretted. In sea disasters it all seems to hinge on the painful choice of those in command; whether to save some, or risk losing all.

Questioned later at the inquiry Wetherilt said: "I am not sure the purser heard everything I said, but he ought to have heard. I am quite positive I did *not* ask the purser to go and look for land and come back, nor did anyone on our raft. All our cries were to take the rope from us or stand by us or take the stewardess off. There was a bit of sea on and the purser said he could not get close enough."

When his boat first came upon them, Chambers the purser said the rafts were together. Mr Wetherilt had asked that the stewardess be taken off. "It is untrue that I personally objected. My reason was that our boat was leaking and shipping water. I called out: 'Mrs Mac, will you come with us?' I don't know whether she heard or not but she seemed to shake her head. Tom McColgan, the carpenter, really in charge of the boat, then said: 'The girl will be just as safe there as here for the time being.' We were unsure of our position and looking for land. The boat was crowded and six or seven people were bailing continuously. If we had taken one from the raft we would have had to put one man out of the boat on to the raft. We had seven aboard, and the boat would not have lived in the sea with more."

Asked why no hero offered to change places, Chambers said he did not think there was any danger. He denied speaking to the raft more than once or hearing Mr Wetherilt ask him to take a line. When they had left the raft Mr Wetherilt was agreeable that they should go away, look for land and return for them. "At the time," he said, "I felt we had acted for the best, but I now see that we have done wrong. I thought the raft had more chance than the boat, as the boat might have capsized. Mr Wetherilt saw we were all in the bow: our boat was down in the stern and there was only one plank between the gunwale and the water. The boat's head could not be kept to the sea and she was leaking all over."

Andrew Rossie, one of the sixteen on the raft, said that they had

108

seen one of the boats and signalled it to tow them: "Wetherilt stood up holding a rope while everyone shouted. No notice was taken. Possibly we were not seen. For the next hour or two we lost sight of all the boats. Then we drifted back with the current towards the wreck where seven feet of funnel still showed above the water. With difficulty we kept the raft off the rocks.

"Towards night, out of sight of land we again sighted the purser's boat and the other raft. Mr Wetherilt asked the purser to take the stewardess. He replied that his boat was leaking and therefore he was unable to take her. He said he had been sent to tell us to try to make for the lee of the island. When Mr Wetherilt complained that this could not be done, the purser told us: 'Keep the two rafts together, and I will come back for you.' This was clearly impossible as evening was closing in. I did not hear the purser say: 'Will you come with us Mrs Mac?'

"At this time Mrs McGuirk was not exhausted or in any distress. In fact, after we were left by the purser's boat she had called to the other raft: 'Take me on your raft. I shall have a better chance.' We tried to bring the rafts together, but there was a danger of collision damaging the floats. The stewardess was afraid to make the effort to reach the other raft unless it came much closer, for fear of drowning. I did not hear Mr Wetherilt ask the purser's boat to take us in tow."

The state of confusion is even more evident with the words of raft survivor Arthur Robinson. He heard the purser reply to Mr Wetherilt's request to take the stewardess: "She's safer on the raft because our boat is leaking." Robinson could recall no conversation between the purser and the stewardess, or the request by Mr Wetherilt for a tow. He said that Mr Wetherilt appealed a second time to the purser to take the stewardess, but they had only met his boat once. There seemed to be room enough in it for Mrs McGuirk. At the inquiry it was said that there clearly was room for the stewardess in the purser's boat, which should have taken the raft in tow. The defence replied that in that case both craft would have been found together after four and a half days.

Chapter 10

SURE THE *Elingamite* would last all day, Captain Reid had set out to find a landing place. Boat 1 had pulled out around the reef and skirted the two small islands, until she came around the back of West Island, opposite to where the ship lay. Even in the dense mist his error was obvious: he could not identify the place at all with his idea of the Great King. Hopeful of a landing place, he pulled on and found some more islands. He then knew he was not in the Great King area. For a time they lost sight of land.

In his boat Miss Maybee felt good-humoured and helpful: "When the fog lifted a little I judged from the sun that we had got out of our course about a mile. I informed Captain Reid of this and he followed my advice, saying: 'Very well, that is the best of having a good bump of locality.' By following the course I had set we got back to our course again and sighted land. Captain Reid struck a place which, though a bad landing, he thought he would attempt. He prepared to swim ashore while the others backed the boat in, but the passengers objected to his leaving."

Miss Maybee felt that the men all worked splendidly during the voyage: "Several of the women were suffering from seasickness, but I felt that I had no time to be sick. I got hold of an oar and started to pull. One of the men said: 'Never mind that, missus, you have a rest.' I jokingly answered: 'I am not a missus yet, but I am missing at present.' We found an Austrian curled up in the bottom of the stern of the boat, where he had been lying unobserved. We thought the Austrians had all been thrown out of our boat when they rushed it as we were getting away. He was soon pulled out of his nest and Captain Reid, by means of threats at last induced him to assist in bailing, though he was not much good at it."

Another deeply laden boat appeared out of the fog. All hands started shrieking to attract it. Those aboard were bailing freely, so they ran down to stand by it, passing Boat 4 on the way, with its sails hoisted about to take off for help.

As they were standing by Boat 3, another boat approached. It was the dinghy, Boat 5, to which Captain Attwood had now transferred in order to find a landing. Despite the leaks it was much more manoeuvrable. Captain Attwood pointed out a likely landing place and led them all in.

Holding the boats off with oars, they landed the women and children first.

"As we got the chance we jumped and scrambled on the rocks," Miss Maybee related. "The children were dragged ashore somehow, some having almost all their clothes torn off them in the process. By this time it was almost dark—between 6 and 7 p.m. and a drizzling rain was falling. It was very cold on the sharp rocks—spikes I would call them. We were wet, cold and hungry. The children had been very good until this time. We each took a little brandy and huddled down among the spikes using our lifebelts for pillows. A rough tent was rigged out of sails against the cliff face. This gave some protection for the women and children. We were on a narrow ledge of rock, only the size of an average room, surrounded on three sides by water. All night the spray kept coming over us at intervals. All night the two remaining boats were fended off the rocks, and some men stayed in them."

Mr Ralph the racehorse owner, said: "It was after six o'clock when we landed on what turned out to be the Middle King. After a search we found we were unable to light a fire, there being nothing in the way of firewood. Fortunately a stream of water was found trickling down a rock face. All hands were wet through and very miserable, but did their best for the women and children."

The chief steward, William Vine, was ready to return to the wreck site with Captain Attwood, Captain Reid and others, but it was decided that it was too dark and foggy and they would have to wait until morning. The ladies protested strongly at being left alone.

Mrs Robb and her son were among those landed on the Middle King: "Once clear of the ship the men pulled round the rocks in search of a landing place, but none could be found. There was no compass to guide us and there were no provisions but a keg of water and a box with the ship's papers. Now and again the fog lifted and we would see another boat and then lose sight of it again, as the fog closed around us. After rowing about and resting by turns, when we lost sight of land, Captain Reid found a sheltered place where we might remain till the fog lifted, for it was impossible to land. We had made up our minds to spend the night there when two other boats came in sight. The fog had lifted and sun shone out, showing an island opposite [also wrongly supposed to be the Great King] with a good landing place. The other boats were making for it so Captain Reid decided to run up a sail and join them. We were all but beaten getting round the outlying reef—the men were rowing by this time, sudden squalls came upon us—when we heard Captain Attwood's whistle and we took it to mean that he had found a landing. With this hope our men pulled on and so it was. There were some people scrabbling on the ledge of rock as we approached.

III

"Imagine a narrow inlet, the sea having broken through the cliffs on one side, a ledge as hard and sharp as rocks are made, some twenty feet above sea level, the sea roaring on three sides, the spray dashing up on the ledge and the seabirds screaming and screeching all night long, with the fog and rain in addition. Ah me! I never wish to hear those sounds again, dreary, cruel, desolate, eerie. But to return. Some seventy-three souls in all from the three boats took shelter there. The men rigged up a kind of tent from some sails for the women and children. We had landed about 5 p.m. and by 10 p.m. we thought it must be morning. Alas, there was an eternity to be gone through ere that. I thought this surely was our opportunity to follow Mark Tapley's advice, but Captain Reid was the only one who evinced the jollity he did not feel. Good soul! He had given Connal his waistcoat and an orphaned girl his jersey, and he had had a bruised ankle on board. I had not a halfpenny of my own to mind, but I managed to hold on to his watch and chain and money—I was able to return the latter. All I saved from the wreck were a few raisins from dinner on Saturday—they were Connal's food on Sunday."

Ellen Doorty settled down in the tent for the night, singing little Teddy Hankinson to sleep. Next day he awoke crying so they ate some orange peel: "I tried to comfort him, telling him Mummy and Dada and sister Gladys would soon be coming."

In the leaking Boat 3, Mrs Cassrels had clung to her boy as they approached the Middle King: "I remember asking Mother did it hurt to get drowned. And she said: 'No boy. You hold on to me and I will hold on to you and then we will be with God.' I was quite satisfied. There was singing of hymns on board. I believe they asked Mother to sing but she said she was saying her prayers within herself. She didn't want to bother singing. We went along in Boat 3 till at long last we drifted to a shelf of rock somewhere round seven o'clock, and we struggled ashore.

"Life on the rocks was a pretty arduous one. On that tiny flat area the sailors slept nearest the sea. I laughed when that night I heard the words: 'Hey Bill—get your nose out of my ear'ole.' And in the morning I asked mother: Couldn't I have my podgie (porridge)?

"Winnie Scotting the fourteen-year-old had a red petticoat which she had taken off and that was used for a distress flag in the daytime. One of the lifeboats was badly smashed up. They had got the bits and pieces ashore for firewood. They dried some matches—they had a few wax vestas and I can see those wax vestas on a little wedge of rock being dried with the warmth of the air. How they got the rest of the fire going I can't remember. I know that once they got a fire going they were able to cook some food for us, the food being to my

The Huddart-Parker single screw steamer *Elingamite*, 2,585 tons

Elingamite on the rocks at West King: a newspaper artist's impression in 1902

The schooner *Greyhound* (Captain Subritzky) passing West King as she searched for victims of the disaster

Fifty-two people who crammed No. 1 lifeboat reached Houhora and brought
first word of the disaster

The whaleboat from Houhora which intercepted the *Zealandia*

Captain E. Attwood (master)

Miss Maybee

Key figures in the shipwr

Captain Reid

Henry Wetherilt

William Vine (chief steward)

Fourteen-year-old Winnie Scotting

Steven Neil reunited with his family

Ted Allen (donkeyman) and Bill Lennox
(brassboy)

Six ships searched for four days until the *Penguin* found the raft. Only eight of the original sixteen on board remained alive

Artist's impression of the raft, 1902

H.M.S. *Penguin* finds the raft

A contemporary painting of some of the seventy-nine who found a precarious refuge on the Middle King

On the calmest day the divers ever experienced at the Kings, a landing was made on the rocks into which the *Elingamite*'s bow had crunched. After sixty-six years, wreckage still lodged some forty feet above the sea

memory a limpet. Mother chewed the limpet and I swallowed what she chewed, which is a very wonderful act for a mother to do I think. Any mother would do it I think under the circumstances. I always think of those limpets when I see them on the rocks today.

"Near where we were marooned on this little triangle of rock, all seventy-odd of us, was another little island. When the tide was out there was just one mass of moving kelp with long arms sticking out of the water—absolutely terrifying and nightmarish. Even to this day I have a very wholesome respect for any water that is filled with kelp. The men tried to climb the rock above us to get the seabirds' eggs that could be seen but that was an impossible task. We also saw a four-master sailing ship. It sailed right past us. The moan and the disappointment that a ship, apparently looking for us, should pass like that with all the flares that we had and the fire we had and the smoke from lifejackets, the petticoat flag flying: all to no effect."

When Monday dawned Captain Reid took Boat 1, Captain Attwood the jolly boat and they put off to the scene of the wreck.

"The boats were manned by the crew," Mr Ralph said, "as the officers absolutely refused to allow any of the passengers who volunteered, to go." As the sea was too rough Captain Attwood did not get to the wreck area, and he had to return. With a fresh crew he made a second attempt but failed.

Next morning at four o'clock Captain Reid left to go to the wreck: "It was then blowing hard and a nasty sea was running. The fog was as dense as ever. I pulled till eleven. One of the crew told me that the forecabin steward had swum ashore from the captain's dinghy to see if he could find a landing. The men said they could tell the rock when they saw it. We pulled down and sighted him. There was a big sea and the spray was going right over the man, who was crouched on the rock. We rescued him with great difficulty, backing into the breakers, and he swam them to grab a line we threw and was hauled clear. We then went on to the place where the *Elingamite* had been. The sea was running heavily and the wind increasing. I could see no trace of the ship nor any food floating. The fog was just as dense as ever. We decided to pull on a little further in hope of finding some drifting food for those back on the rocks. We saw plenty of whisky and grog of which we took two cases aboard. Also some oranges and onions.

"Plenty of dead bodies could be seen floating by. I could not go far without a compass and as the men had been two days without food, continuously at the oars, I was afraid they would go to pieces. We tried to get back to Middle Island where the people were, but could not pull up to them against the wind and current. The men were thoroughly beaten, their wrists giving way and their hands were bleeding. The fog lifted for a moment. I saw another island that we had not seen before and which I recognized as the Big King. I told the men there were goats on it and if we could not make the island the people were on, we must make the Big King. We toiled and pulled and beached there at 7 p.m. Someone shouted that it was fairly sheltered but as there was a heavy sea running round the inlet, I could see no safe landing place.

"As there was no anchor in the boat I told the men that they would have to go ashore and get stones for the purpose. While the others went ashore, I stayed with two sailors in the boat. We lay down without any covering, I having given all my clothing but my coat and pants to the women and children. During the night, which was very foggy and raining, the wind shifted and the sea came right in on our sheltered cove. We were continually shaken with cramps and had only a little gin to drink.

"I knew then that the boat back at the landing would be smashed by the wind change, so ours must be saved. We rode the gale out all night. In the morning the wind decreased and the weather improved a little. I dropped the boat inshore and sent my companions on shore telling them to go and tell the other hands to catch goats and rabbits for provisions and that I would wait for them until 4 o'clock. My idea was to go back to the Middle King with what food we had found for the women and children, and shift the whole party to where we were on the Big King."

On the Middle King Mr Ralph and the others had watched closely as Captain Reid made four attempts to reach the cape where they were huddled, hoping he had recovered some food. Eventually they saw his boat bear off towards the big island just becoming visible to them through the clearing mist. "It was pitiful to hear the children calling out from hunger. We had one case of brandy in our boat which was placed in my charge and served out to the women and children only. The men did not get a drop, nor did they grumble. The nights were terrible."

During the day two sailing ships passed the island and although the men scaled the mountain and made a signal fire by lighting dried vegetation and frantically waved the women's skirts and petticoats they attracted no attention. The men left on the island began to search for food. They got a few limpets and crabs. Miss Maybee did not like the crabs: "One claw was enough for me. The children were crying bitterly for food. 'Biscuit Mammy,' one little fellow cried. His mother was deeply distressed at being so helpless to supply his needs.

"We had some wet matches. After drying them on the rocks we

managed to light a fire and boiled our limpets and crabs in a bailer. Firewood was too scarce to build a fire large enough to dry our clothes. There was not even enough room on the rock to light one. A sailor tied a rope around his body and dived in to recover some of the wreckage of our boats, which were breaking up.

"On Monday night heavy rain fell at first, then the stars came out and Tuesday morning broke forth fine. The sun came out very strong and scorched our skin, but it enabled us to dry our clothing, sodden since Sunday. During Monday night I was seized by cramp, but felt better in the sun on Tuesday. That day we decided to make an effort to catch some fish, and a line was made out of a corset lace, with a bent hat pin as a hook. Using limpet for bait we caught three fish. When the first was hauled in I felt tremendously happy. We boiled the fish in the same old pan, and the repast was greatly enjoyed, especially by the children."

Mrs Robb said: "One of the boats had a case of brandy and brackish water was found on the rocks. These were jealously guarded and doled out at intervals, and so the first night passed. Captain Reid kept the men and boats well in hand: the women folk missed him the following day when at daybreak he and Captain Attwood left in two boats to return to the wreck if possible. Captain Attwood put back unsuccessfully some hours later, his men utterly exhausted warring with tides and currents. He made a second attempt later in the day with the same result. Captain Reid got near enough to the scene of the wreck to rescue one of the crew who had been left on a rock all night, and to pick up a case each of onions and oranges and some gin but his men grew sick at the sight of dead bodies floating about.

"He made four gallant attempts to get round the reef to return to us but was beaten back. We saw no more of him till he came in the *Zealandia*'s boat to our rescue. Towards evening he had run across to the real Great King where the occupants of one raft had already landed, Captain Reid, with one sailor, remaining in the boat all night.

"But to return to the rocks. The fog continued all Monday with roaring seas, due, I believe, to tides and currents. Many attempts were made to scale the cliffs in hope of finding birds' eggs, but in vain. A few sticks were found, and one or two dry matches, and a fire kindled. In the bailer we boiled such shellfish as could be picked from the rocks and all the crabs that could be found. Connal and I let the crabs pass that day—by Tuesday we were ready for our share. About 5 p.m. we settled down for another night. We thought of the other boats and the rafts. Our hope lay with the first mate's boat with fifty-two on board which was to make for the mainland—Cape Maria Van Diemen—whence word might be sent to Auckland and we reckoned how soon we might look for rescue. Would the *Zealandia* get word before leaving for Sydney, so that she might look out for us, or would she go on her way knowing nothing? And when would a special boat reach the scene of the wreck? Could the mate's boat by any chance have failed to effect a landing, and was our only hope a passing vessel? Our discomfort from overcrowding in the tent had been so great on Monday night, I thought to spend Tuesday night outside in a hollow between two rocks, but I was no sooner settled there with Connal in my arms than the wind changed and rain came on, so we were forced to seek such shelter as could be had.

"We lost our two boats that night; they broke from their moorings and drifted away. There was a good deal of fainting and hysteria on the part of some women that night and much wailing on the part of children for the food that might not be had. But when darkness gave place to daylight the fog had lifted and the sun shone in a clear blue sky. I can hardly describe the effect of this on our faces after the exposure to sprays and fog."

Hunting food on the Big King, Captain Reid's men saw a fire and came upon two huts and a camp set up by the eleven survivors of the smaller raft. Their appreciation of these comforts was immense. Said one old sailor: "This is the 'otel de Parry orlright."

As they gratefully dried their clothes and nibbled titbits of food, Dr Goldie told them what had happened to them after they found themselves alone on the raft in the fog on Sunday night.

"We had no idea of our whereabouts, not knowing where New Zealand or the Three Kings were. About this time a high gale sprang up, with a strong wind—I think it was a nor'wester—and heavy seas, which kept washing over us and drenching us to the skin. About four o'clock the fog lifted for about a quarter of an hour and we saw the Big King. We started to pull up towards the leeward of the island. A few minutes later the mist came on again and we lost our bearings. Occasionally we could hear the breakers dashing on the rocks of the island and we then pulled vigorously for about an hour in the direction of the sound so far as we could judge.

"By this time we were able to discern in the distance a line of heavy breakers, and, later on, two large rocks which formed a promontory on the Big King. We then made violent struggles in pulling against a very strong tide and high seas to get to the leeward of these rocks, hoping thereby to get into calmer water and find a landing place. All the men rowed the sluggish raft with courage and determination, as we felt sure that unless we rounded the point before dark we would be washed out to sea and have very little hope of recovery. Of course by this time we were all very much exhausted being soaked to the skin through the seas constantly washing over us, and stiff with the intense cold. Still we cheered one another and kept on pulling, four men to each oar. The tide was very strong and we made very little headway for some time.

"Towards dusk we rounded the point and got into calmer water but owing to the strong current we were still unable to make much progress. We were now about half a mile from the landing place in Tasman Bay. We pulled at the oars with all our might, and as one man fell exhausted another would take his place. As each recovered sufficiently he grasped an oar and pulled again. For about an hour and a half we battled thus against the tide, but making very slow progress. Finally we rounded two smaller islets but owing to the force of the current we could not get to land. At this point we were in great danger of being wrecked on a submerged rock, but we narrowly escaped it and we pulled on.

"Eventually, after dark, we escaped from the current and reached a landing place, which we have since found is one of four landings marked on the charts. So exhausted were we by this time that we could hardly jump from the raft on to the reef. The rocks were covered with seaweed, and by grasping this we were able to scramble up. We were too exhausted to make any attempt to secure the raft. We let it go after removing its painter and the oars."

Hallamore told Captain Reid: "One of us wrote on the raft 'S.S. *Elingamite*, wrecked on the Three Kings; send help' and sent it adrift. We found ourselves on a narrow ledge of rock, with high cliffs at the back which we could not attempt to climb at night. Our first act was to stand together and give three loud cheers, so relieved were we to know that we were safe from immediate danger. We then divested ourselves of our cumbrous lifejackets and took off our outer garments to wring the water out of them. Huddled together in a vain attempt to keep warm we spent a miserable night, suffering very much from the cold and tormented greatly by enormous mosquitoes.

"We were totally without food and our only nourishment was a teaspoonful of brandy, served out to each man from partially filled flasks with which two members of the party had provided themselves before leaving the wreck. We found a few stagnant pools of brackish water, full of decayed vegetation and larvae with which we quenched our thirst. In addition to the cold and the mosquitoes, the hard and sharp rocks, and the dripping of water from the overhanging cliffs added to our discomfort. The terrors of the night were increased by the fear that the incoming tide would come up and wash us off the rocks, but fortunately the tide did not come up as high as we expected.

"At daybreak on Monday morning we prepared to ascend the

precipitous cliff at the back of the ledge of rock. First we placed an oar upright against the cliff, with a lifebelt at the top and the bottom, as a signal to any vessels which might pass. The ascent of the cliff proved to be by no means an easy matter. Tying our rope to my arm I managed, with the aid of an oar, to climb up to a higher ledge of rock where I secured the rope to a crag. The others then ascended and we found ourselves at the foot of another very steep cliff, covered with dense teatree scrub. A number of the men, who were without boots, found it impossible to walk any further on the rough ground. Rough sandals were made by cutting open some of the lifebelts. Handkerchiefs were used to tie them on. Rough hats were made from the canvas of the belts. All day Monday the fog was thick, with a drizzling cold rain.

"When we climbed the hill, hauling ourselves up by the teatree and resting our starved bodies frequently, we found ourselves on a small plateau about 300 feet above the sea. Here we decided to build a camp. While the others prepared it, myself and another set out to locate a Government food depot which we thought was established on the island. We have since learned it does not exist. We climbed to the highest point, some 900 feet high, expecting it to be there. On our return to the camp we found some of the men rubbing sticks together to light a fire. Others were drying three matches. We also tried to start a fire with a watch glass, when the sun struggled out for a few minutes, periodically.

"When sticks and watch glass failed we combined both methods. After some five hours the matches seemed to be drying satisfactorily. On attempting to light them, the heads fell off two of them. After drying the only remaining match a little more, a similar attempt was made with it, the result being half the head broke off. Further drying, and then the crucial test. Success now fortunately awaited our efforts. A shout of joy rang out on the island when the remaining portion of the match suddenly blazed into fire and fell into a heap of dry leaves. With shouts and cheers we piled on dry teatree which was abundant, and dry leaves. We soon had a big, blazing bonfire. We quickly took off our wet clothes and draped them around the fire, while we tried to warm ourselves, getting a little scorched in the process. After shivering in wet clothes for thirty-two hours, the fire was a delight. Once our clothes were dry we built a teatree hut to shelter us from the cold night winds. Our second night was more comfortable and some of us managed to sleep.

"During Monday morning some members of the party driven by hunger climbed down to the shore to hunt shellfish. They managed to find enough crabs for each of us to have three, and some limpets, which were rather unpalatable. Each crab contained a good spoonful of nourishment and after thirty-two hours hunger we dined royally. Some of us ate the succulent portions of rush stems. I was fortunate in catching a lizard, which once roasted was most tasty. While down near the shore that Monday morning Captain Reid's men came upon us, exhausted after their long rowing since four that morning. We were overjoyed to learn of the survivors from the three boats reaching Middle Island.

"On Tuesday a sharp lookout was kept for a rescue ship. We knew the *Zealandia* was scheduled to pass our island, but they would not know of the shipwreck. A large bonfire was prepared in readiness should she appear. Further searches were being made for a food cache, when the mist cleared and we saw for the first time the captain's camp, huddled on the island opposite ours. An excellent stream of water was also discovered. Anxiety was growing. Half a dozen more crabs and a few limpets did little to allay our hunger. We were too weak to catch the goats. We sat around the fire, peering out to sea for a sign of hope. It did not seem possible to last another day."

The survival of those Three Kings castaways depended on a slender chain of coincidence. Had not Ted Allen the donkeyman used his initiative, broken standing orders and cut the falls, lifeboat 2 would not have floated free from the sinking ship, rescued the occupants of the capsized Boat 6 and, conned by the first mate, sailed down to Houhora to tell the world of the disaster.

Fifty-two survivors had landed on a sandy beach near Houhora. Mr Leifson said: "We lit driftwood fires and rigged up a sail to shelter the four women and two children at night. A group of us set out to seek help and we came across a young Maori girl but she couldn't understand English. She ran away and brought an old Maori woman who could speak a little English and we made her understand who we were and what had happened. The Maoris offered us some bread and led us to their settlement, the women and children on ponies and the men on foot. Most of us were barefooted and this made the three-mile journey through scrub country a trial. However the Maoris were like angels to us. After getting the women and children safely home they returned with the ponies for the stragglers. Soon after, tea and scones and clothes were provided for us and we spent the night at their settlement, journeying on to Houhora on Tuesday afternoon."

Meanwhile the news had been relayed on and telegraphed to Auckland on Monday the 10th, the day on which the King's Birthday was celebrated. This caused a stupid delay. The Auckland agents for Huddart Parker, L. D. Nathan, immediately telegraphed a northern township, Helensville, where they knew the tug *Sterling* lay, 100 miles closer to the Three Kings than any Auckland vessel. But it was a holiday. The telegraph operators, while in contact with each other, stuck rigidly to regulations and refused to relay the message. Had the *Sterling* left the Kaipara Harbour on Monday night she would have reached the Three Kings by Tuesday afternoon.

Next Nathan's decided to try to divert the *Zealandia*, which was due to pass the Three Kings on Wednesday the 12th, bound for Sydney. Wireless did not exist on the New Zealand coast. A telegraph to Awanui sent the schooner *Greyhound* off at three on the Wednesday morning to try to intercept the *Zealandia*. The lighthouse keeper at Cape Maria Van Diemen was also contacted and asked to try to signal the news to the *Zealandia*. All hopes were dashed when he later advised that for some reason the *Zealandia* had passed by further out than usual, beyond communication. Great relief was felt at the Auckland telegraph office when on Wednesday morning news was received from the far north that the *Zealandia* had picked up eighty-five survivors from the Three Kings and was returning to Auckland. A large anxious crowd at the telegraph office eagerly sought further news, but the officials had none to give. When later a list of names began to come through the wires from Houhora there were scenes of joy and intense disappointment. All through the night carriages and cabs were pulling up outside the office as relatives and friends clamoured for news.

And how did the *Zealandia* learn of the shipwreck? A passenger from New York, bound for Sydney, Mr MacMurran said: "At about 6 o'clock on Tuesday morning I was strolling on deck when a whale-boat appeared off the beam waving a distress signal and hailing the ship. Since the steamer was making good speed, a sudden stop meant venting the boilers and through the deafening roar of escaping steam the words drifted up: '*Elingamite* wrecked Three Kings'. Without waiting a moment to pick up the whaleboat the *Zealandia* sped to the rescue."

On their own initiative the whaleboat crew, skippered by Ian MacIntosh, had raced from Houhora, thirty miles out to sea in four hours, using oars and sail in a desperate attempt to divert the *Zealandia*. Now, successful and absolutely exhausted, blown by an offshore wind, they lay on their oars bewildered to find themselves suddenly alone and far from land. (See Appendix 1.)

When his big adventure on the Middle King ended young Norman Cassrels was not sorry: "So at long last the day came when *Zealandia* found us. The lifeboats came in; there were two or three lifeboats. I remember us getting into one of the lifeboats and there were tins, big biscuit tins, full of bread and butter. Wonderful, beautiful bread and butter. I had one piece in one hand and one in the other hand and the next thing one was stolen from me. I yelled but whether I got it back or not I don't remember. At long last we got over to the *Zealandia*. Little Eva Berry had butter on her hands and when being helped aboard her hands slipped and she fell back into the lifeboat, cutting her leg badly. Mother was too sick and overcome with it all to eat. She was carried up to the deck in a dead faint and she didn't come round out of that for a long time after. I was taken into the music room and given a piano stool to lie on. The rug that mother had still hung on to covered over me. I went to sleep there.

"There is nothing very much I can remember about coming down from the Kings to Auckland. I do remember having a little handkerchief for a cap with knots on either side and the overcoat that mother had saved and that someone was taking photographs on board the ship and I'd got into the wrong group. I was sitting there as large as life in front of the photograph but I am in Boat 1 with a Mrs Neil in that picture. Mother had a heavy sort of woven scarf and she had torn this apart and Mrs Neil had part of it and Mother had the other part. We eventually got back to Auckland and I can remember standing on the deck looking to see if I could see anybody and then I suddenly saw my brother and sister and my father but mother was too overcome to see them or to even get out on the deck."

Auckland was unaware of the success of the *Zealandia* until Wednesday the 12th, so the Northern Steamship Company's *Clansman* was hastily provisioned and sent to sea at two on Tuesday morning.

Calling in at Opua for extra coal after a rapid, fuel-consuming trip, Captain Farquhar telegraphed ahead to Houhora, requesting that Mr Burkitt, first mate of the *Elingamite*, accompany them on the search. By nine on Tuesday night the *Clansman* was off Houhora Bay, and Mr Burkitt came out to meet them in a boat. As they steamed off for the North Cape in the dark he told them how McIntosh had set out early that morning to try to divert the *Zealandia*, and that he must have been successful as she had passed Cape Maria Van Diemen so far out she must have been heading for the Three Kings.

There was a very anxious man among those on the *Clansman*— Mr John Robb, manager of the Kauri Timber Company, whose wife and six-year-old son were among the missing. A keen lookout was kept as it was now likely that they would meet the *Zealandia* returning from the wreck. Near midnight a ship was sighted ablaze with electric lights, rare in those days. "The *Zealandia*," said Burkitt, and blue signal lights were flashed, answered by three dynamite bombs. From the *Clansman*'s bridge, Burkitt hailed Captain Wylie on the *Zealandia*. He replied that he had picked up eighty-nine survivors but the third mate's boat and one raft were still missing. A boat was lowered from the *Clansman* for a better exchange of news, and an overjoyed Mr Robb found his wife and son among the survivors.

On Monday, 10 November, John Robb had left home at 7 a.m. to meet the *Elingamite*: "I was hoping to bring Agnes and Connal back with me in time for breakfast, but on reaching the end of Queen Street wharf found the steamer was not in the harbour, and was not even signalled which meant she could not reach the wharf for at least two hours. I then walked along to the office and spent about an hour there. Mr White, manager of the Auckland mill joined me, it being a holiday and the mill closed. He came back to the wharf with me and said he would wait till the steamer came in and help to get the travellers ashore. We met Dr Sharman, health officer, driving towards the wharf, stopped him and asked if he would take us off to the anchorage in his boat. He told us there was still no word of the steamer but promised to take us when she arrived if we cared to go. All day long we marched up and down the wharf watching the signal station, half an hour at dinner being the longest time we were away. Shortly before six we got the customs people to telephone to Tiri Tiri (an island with a lighthouse some miles down the harbour) and asked if the steamer was in sight. On learning that there was no word of her I decided to go home to tea and report the non-arrival, and come back to town again.

"On getting back about 8.30 p.m. I asked the telephone exchange to connect me to Tiri Tiri. They asked if it was the *Elingamite* I was enquiring about; she was not yet reported from any point along the coast. Though I was now getting a little anxious I could not see that anything more could be done that night. Even if the steamer did come in shortly the doctor would not go aboard till morning. Until he had been there she could not come alongside the wharf, so there was no chance of the passengers landing until the morning. I got home about 9.30 p.m. and had not been much over half an hour in the house when a cab came tearing along and stopped at the door. It was Mr White bringing news of the wreck. Dr Sharman was among the first to get information and he, knowing I was on the lookout for the steamer, telephoned to Mr White who came post-haste to me.

"We immediately set off back to town again to get what news we could, and learned that the steamer had been totally wrecked on the Three Kings Islands on Sunday morning at 10.30 a.m. and that one boat with fifty-two on board had reached Houhora, on the mainland. No word of the others but the message ran they were supposed to have got landed on the Three Kings. Shortly after we got to the telegraph office the names of those at Houhora came through and when Agnes and Connal were not among them, my anxiety was of course greatly increased. We got into the telegraph operating room and found Mr Saunderson, the agent's manager there. He informed us that word had been sent all along the coast to try and intercept the *Zealandia* (which had left for Sydney a couple of hours before the news of the disaster came) and get her to go and search the Three Kings, and also that the *Clansman* and other boats would be despatched from Auckland on the search as soon as ever the crews could be got together and steam got up.

"The *Clansman* was the first to go and the fastest boat so I got a passage on her. We got under weigh at 1.30 a.m. on Tuesday morning and about mid-day reached Opua where eighty tons of coal were dumped on board in double quick time and off we went again. Word was sent from Opua to Houhora for one of the *Elingamite*'s officers to be ready to join us at 9 p.m. Up to time we were there and picked up the first mate of the *Elingamite* from whom I learned that Agnes and Connal had got safely away from the wreck in one of the boats and he had no doubt but what they were safely landed on one of the Kings, the weather though very foggy, not being stormy at the time of the wreck. This was a ray of hope, but though the captain, engineers, firemen and everyone on board the *Clansman* were doing every mortal thing to push her along, we could not possibly reach the Three Kings till at least 3 a.m. Wednesday morning, and could not do much till daylight, which meant three nights and nearly three days exposure for those on the rocks.

"I was fearful of the consequences. Our great hope was that the *Zealandia* had by some means been intercepted and got the news, in which case she would reach the Kings in plenty of time to get the people off before dark on Tuesday. After leaving Houhora a sharp lookout was kept and shortly before midnight just off the North Cape a steamer was sighted, which proved to be the one we were looking for. On getting within hailing distance we learned that she had been to the Kings and taken off eighty-nine people. A boat was lowered from the *Clansman* and we were soon alongside the *Zealandia* and in answer to my enquiry I got the joyful news that both Agnes and Connal were safe and well. When I saw them I could hardly believe it was possible they could have come through such ordeal with so little trace of suffering.

"Then so far as we were concerned the troubles ended. The *Zealandia* headed for Auckland and the *Clansman* went off on her search for those that were still missing.

"On deck the next morning the cause we had for thankfulness became more than ever apparent: there I found children whose

123

parents were missing, fathers and mothers whose children were missing, wives whose husbands were missing, and though some of these turned up later on there are still many aching hearts, for those lost on the raft and number 4 lifeboat. When the *Zealandia* steamed up the harbour all Auckland seemed to be on the wharf and the welcome our party got was I think as hearty as any. It remained for cablegrams, telegrams, letters and visitors to take the tale of congratulations in the next week, of how Connal, small hero in charge of the black skirt, holland blouse and red hat is fast becoming an ordinary boy again."

Chapter 11

SUNDAY WAS PASSING now and the wind blowing from the sunset was driving raft 2 and its sixteen occupants further and further out into a darkening Pacific.

"At night the sea became choppy," Steven Neil related. "Tom Mallins, the fireman, Ellis the second steward, and stewardess Alice McGuirk, all being thinly clad, began to suffer greatly from exposure. We clung together, the sixteen of us, for warmth. The shivering fireman was pressed to my chest. At about half past seven o'clock that evening we decided to appoint one of our number as commander. The choice fell unanimously upon Henry Wetherilt, who at once took up his role.

"All night long we looked for lights, hoping to see a fire on the island, little thinking we were drifting far out to sea. The new commander was given the two apples that had been picked up among the flotsam. These were divided, each into sixteen parts and we had one part each. Not much, a sixteenth part of an apple but I munched the rind of mine several times over. There was no water or food on the raft. When we looked about us at daybreak there was only the open sea around and the sky overhead. We had drifted out for probably twenty miles."

"It was a miserable night," Andrew Rossie recalled, "raining and a very heavy sea. We kept hoping we might meet some of the lifeboats. Anyway, we planned to make for land east by south. We did not know at the time we were in the grip of the current which runs between the mainland and the Kings, and which was bearing us eastward."

Arthur Robinson said he felt no thirst or hunger for the first two days: "I attribute that to being continuously saturated with salt water. Every time I sat down to take my turn at the oars the waves and spray came dashing over me every minute, keeping me thoroughly drenched. It was just the same when we lay down to rest. Water was flying over us all the time and we never had a chance to get dry. In the initial stages of our ordeal we were drifting along with a ten-acre patch of wreckage: cases of oranges, apples and such things, which were part of the *Elingamite*'s deck cargo. But unable to direct our raft in any direction, it was terrible to see it all beyond our reach in the strong current. As for the two apples we divided, I wished I had not had my share because a piece got stuck in my teeth and the wretched thing tormented me."

"About nine o'clock on Monday night, "Neil related, "I found that Dickson was dead beside me. I was horror-struck. He was an old friend of mine in Sydney and had been selected by the new Auckland Electric Tramways Company to take up a position as driver. We agreed to let his body remain on the raft until morning, hoping to make land by then and give him a decent burial. But when Tuesday morning came there was no land in sight. Two more of our number lay dead alongside Dickson. The exposure of that dreadful night had been too much for them. As there were already signs of putrefaction and our heavily laden raft made existence harder for those still alive, we agreed to put the bodies overboard. I kept Dickson's watch, knife and a few trinkets to give to his wife.

"Our sufferings throughout that Tuesday, our third day adrift, were very great. One of our number insisted on drinking salt water, and soon another began to follow suit. We pointed out the consequences of such a mad act but they seemed to be losing their reason. To us all it was maddening to gaze around on water extending on all sides as far as the eye could reach and know that we were perishing of thirst in the midst of it all. From time to time we became aware of sharks following us. Whether the bodies we had slid overboard had been eaten or had sunk straight down, we dared not think. We could never bring ourselves to look back for fear of seeing a horrible sight. Albatrosses, too, hovered around us. Several times we tried to kill one with an oar for food. As the day wore on our misery became more acute. We were troubled with illusions. Land, green and sloping invitingly down to fresh water lakes, came before us. It was always unreality despite our rising hopes.

"Ellis the steward had only recently got over a serious illness. Typhoid, I believe, and he was in a weak state to begin with. The poor fellow bore up pluckily but he knew his chances were small. Gradually that day he became a near lunatic. While many of us were deteriorating, our commander, Henry Wetherilt, Danielson the quartermaster, Mallins the fireman, Andrew Rossie and others, stuck doggedly to the oars."

Rossie said: "We pulled for hours thinking we might be able to make land. We kept on pulling but the current beat us and we kept drifting backwards and forwards with the swing of the current and tide, while the sea was sweeping over us all the time. The first two days had not been so bad but now even those at the oars were beginning to get maddened. Danielson, Robinson, Wetherilt, Jobson and myself all pulled as long as we could every day. We often felt like despairing but we continued to ply the oars."

Throughout the day Mr Wetherilt sat beside the stewardess, who bore the rigors gamely. "The scorching heat," said Wetherilt, "and its glare on the water produced acute agony. Thirst caused our tongues to protrude like pieces of leather. The terrible strain on the eyes of the blinding sunlight caused us to keep imagining we could see things. From the desperate efforts at the oars, the rowlocks were greatly worn. One oar had snapped in two. By frantically paddling we had managed to recover the blade and lash it to the handle. The blistering heat and sudden immersion when the raft took a sudden dip had a painful effect on our skin, which became chafed and swollen and blistered especially on the feet and legs."

As time passed, delusion and fact blended into an endless nightmare. Neil put it this way: "It was, as far as my memory serves me, on the Tuesday night that we saw the flashing light of what seemed to be a lighthouse, on the left-hand side of the raft. Henry Wetherilt said we had better make for it, and we tried. Struggle as we might, however, we could make no headway against the power of the current and the choppy seas which kept breaking over us. While pulling, we broke one rope rowlock, and this had to be repeatedly repaired. When we looked up again towards the light we found we were no nearer than at the start. It may well have been a star we were chasing.

"Just then a scream went up from the crew. We could see the masthead light of a steamer bearing down on us. The steamer appeared to hear us. We prayed fervently. She came to a full stop—our hearts beat faster—and lowered a boat. There was a light in the bows of the boat and we watched it advance with anxious eyes. The big ship seemed to anchor there while the boat made practically a beeline in our direction. Rescue any moment. We stood up and screamed: 'Ship ahoy! Help us for God's sake. We're starving!' Our voices sounded strange, even to ourselves as these cries went out tremulously over the dark waters. We had no means of signalling. The boat came, to all appearance within 100 yards of us. It could not have been further than 200 yards off. Then the boat seemed to be encircling us. Her lights approached nearer to the first light we had seen. Then the boat became lost for a while and seemed to be returning to the ship. Our screams became frantic, but they were not heard and 'God help us' we pleaded, as the boat disappeared and we lost sight altogether of the ship. Robbed of hope of immediate rescue we hoped that the ship might lie by until morning."

Rossie said: "We thought we saw a boat lowered, but I doubt it very much now. Soon after that we got into another current and our raft seemed to be going right round and round, the light appearing first on the one side of us and then on the other. There was a fearful sea running. As pulling was so hard we dropped the sea anchor and let her drift a little, then hauled it up again and had another turn at the oars for an hour or two trying to make for the light. Then Mr Wetherilt asked us what we thought about it. He said: 'I think we had better let her drift. No doubt a boat has been sent to pick us up and they may get us in the morning.' So we decided to let her drift and during that night we must have drifted a vast number of miles."

"During that Tuesday night," said Neil, "Muirhead became very ill. He was a comrade of mine, on his way to take up a position as a tram driver in Auckland. I cheered him up as well as I knew how, reminding him of his friends at home and his good old mother out in New South Wales, bidding him to bear up for their sakes. Muirhead promised me to keep a brave heart and later in the night he said: 'It is all right, old boy, we'll be saved yet.' Then he lay down alongside me and we fell asleep from exhaustion.

"Presently I was awakened by a kind of monotone. I listened and I made out the words to be: 'I'm gone, I'm gone. Good-bye. I'm gone.' Raising myself into a sitting position. I gazed around and there, a few yards out from the raft, was Muirhead, floating on his back with his hands lifted upwards, singing: 'Good-bye, good-bye.' Snatching my lifebelt from under my head, I threw it to Muirhead, shouting to him: 'For God's sake catch this, man.'

"The poor fellow seemed to be unconscious of what was going on around him. He touched the lifebelt with his hand and thrust it aside. Rossie, who was watching this sad episode with me, then threw another lifebelt to Muirhead, asking him to catch hold of it, but this he served in the same way. The last we saw of the poor fellow was when he was floating away from us, singing his mournful good-bye. The moonlight was shining on his upturned face and he never ceased his monotone."

During Wednesday, the fourth day adrift, the temptation to drink salt water was too great for many. Ellis the steward, half crazed, kept flopping his head over the side. Four times he was pulled out of the water, but he must have swallowed a considerable amount. Weakened from the outset it was strange that he clung to a wisp of life so long. Steven Neil sucked a threepenny bit to stave off his thirst, but Alice McGuirk could not resist any longer. To Neil's horror she began to trail her hand over the side and scoop up handfuls of seawater. Having shared some of her clothing among those who had very little, exhaustion and exposure brought her to a final collapse during that day. Hopeful of rescue they kept her body aboard.

The stronger men, taking turns at the oars, pleaded with the weaker ones to leave the sea water alone. Rossie, Wetherilt and Neil kept a close eye on them to discourage it, for if they thought they were not being watched down would go a hand. On one occasion Rossie savagely tore a salt-soaked handkerchief from Jordan's hands. Of those who drank salt water, he alone survived.

Two more men died on Wednesday night. Young Jack Pretty from Melbourne had asked Rossie several times during the day to keep him safe: "Tom Mallins and I were doing our best to look after him. In the night he was lying beside Tom, and when water began washing over the raft I asked Tom: 'Where's Jack?' At half light we looked for him but he was missing, as well as another man who had jumped overboard in the dark."

The body of Alice McGuirk was slid into the sea.

By Thursday morning the raft was riding much more lightly relieved of the seven dead. Still the survivors kept sighting imaginary land, unaware that the nearest point was sixty-three miles away over the horizon. Completely insane, making repeated attempts to leave the raft, Ellis died in the arms of Neil who, after restraining him for so long, slipped him overboard.

The *Clansman*, having left the *Zealandia* to return to Auckland, raced on in search of the missing boat and raft. They had not rounded the North Cape when a seaman directed Captain Farquhar's attention to an open boat he had seen away on the port bow in the silver track of the moon. The *Clansman* soon drew alongside. It was the whaleboat from Houhora which had dashed so bravely to divert the *Zealandia*. Besides the skipper McIntosh, she was manned by E. Wagner, A. and N. F. Thomas, and C. and R. Northwood. Chick Northwood had a camera on board and it was his waving camera cloth that hove to the *Zealandia*. As the whaleboat was hauled aboard Captain Farquhar praised the tired men, for it was clear that if the survivors on the exposed rocks had had to wait for the *Clansman* a number of people would have died.

The *Clansman* headed east of north that Wednesday morning so that the Three Kings could be approached after daylight along the line of drifting wreckage, where the raft might be expected to be seen.

While searching east and west the *Clansman* met H.M.S. *Penguin*, which ran up a signal asking if they had any news. They sent a boat across to negotiate a shared search pattern. Each ship would approach the Three Kings from the opposite direction.

At 10.30 a.m. the *Clansman* sighted the first wreckage: a lifeboat cover painted white. By noon, having passed other wreckage the ship was off Morton Jones Island, easternmost of the group. She then steamed west past the Great King, blowing her whistle to attract anyone who had made it to shore. Not a sign of life nor wreckage was seen.

Away to the south-west a small schooner was beating towards them. This eventually proved to be the *Greyhound* from Awanui skippered by Captain Subritzky. Still searching the shore with telescopes, the *Clansman* drew towards the schooner. No sign of life or wreckage. Meeting off the south-west corner of the Great King, Captain Subritzky came across in a boat to tell them he had systematically searched all the islands close in by rowing-boat and was positive that there was no living soul there. In a bight to the south of the Great King he had picked up three bodies still wearing life-jackets. One, a young man with a slight sandy moustache who had a bill in his pocket from a Sydney tradesman; the second, an old man of about sixty, stoutly built, bald, and with grey whiskers; the third, a sandy whiskered man of about forty. Mr Burkitt went across and identified the first as a fireman. The other two were steerage passengers. Captain Subritzky reported that wreckage was drifting in a north-easterly direction, most having come ashore on the Middle Island. He had picked up a lifebuoy, several cases of schnapps, and a case of Sunlight soap among other articles. The two vessels parted and the *Clansman* continued past the bleak Pinnacle Rocks to the south-western island where the ship had struck.

"There seemed to be no possible hope of any landing on the island," said one sailor. "Its walls ran precipitously up to a towering height and the swell sent the waves swirling into its base and up for several feet. Racing rivulets of water dashed back down the cliff faces after the receding waves, in a fury of beaten foam and froth. Even in the bright sunlight the place looked fearsome enough. God help those who were at the sea's mercy in such a place with fog all around them."

Near the fatal island they fell in with the *Penguin* again, coming around from the opposite side: "Her news, like ours, was blank and she left us with the intimation from her commander that he intended running up north-east for sixty miles on a zig-zag course."

The *Clansman* carried on, completing her circle of the Kings, keeping a sharp lookout with glasses and from the masthead. About two miles off the north-east corner of the Great King they again fell in with the wreckage and with some excitement came upon an up-turned boat. This turned out to be the *Elingamite*'s dinghy in which the purser and carpenter had got ashore. Her stern was badly torn but otherwise she showed no damage. A little further on a large piece of wreckage was passed—probably a portion of decking. For several miles they sailed through debris of all kinds: straw hats, cases of wine and schnapps, hatches, railway sleepers, planks, the rudder of a lifeboat and an enormous quantity of fruit. There was no sign of the *Elingamite*'s mailbags.

At dusk the search was abandoned. Low on coal after her fast dash to the north, the *Clansman* put back to Houhora, where she picked up fifty-two survivors waiting there. On her way back she fell in with the Union Steam Ship Company's steamer *Omapere*, sent from Auckland to join in the search.

With advice from the *Clansman*, the *Omapere* decided to search in a north-easterly direction too, helping the *Penguin* with her zig-zag sixty-mile search. As the *Clansman* sailed southwards on Thursday morning she hunted around the Cavalli and the Poor Knights Islands in case the missing boat had made down the coast.

That Thursday the raft wallowed lifelessly on the swells, its eight sea-beaten occupants at the end of their strength. Neil said later they had sucked each other's blood by mutual arrangement. Credibility is strained when he adds that someone had practised this on sleepers, evident from the incisions on their legs. He also claimed that Wetherilt had lost his mind that morning and had to be relieved of his command. In the Canadian press it was stated that the stewardess Mrs McGuirk, had had all the blood sucked from her breast until she died! These stories were violently denied by six of the others, but they serve to show the state that had been reached by some of the raft occupants.

A little after noon, the smoke of a steamer was sighted ten miles away: "As far as we could make out," said Neil, "she was heading in our direction. We were a crew of praying men, and we prayed with all fervency that we might be saved. At times the ship appeared to vanish. One man tied his white shirt to an oar and waved it. We shouted, too, with what little lung power we had left. Hearty cheers greeted our ears as the ship neared us and put out a longboat. Aided by its crew we boarded her and were at once supplied with food and drink as they rowed back to their ship, the H.M.S. *Penguin*, our empty raft in tow."

The Auckland public felt the disaster keenly. Out of a total of 189 passengers and crew forty-five were lost. When news arrived that the *Penguin* was returning with survivors of the raft the whole city responded with joy. A lieutenant on the *Penguin* told of locating the raft. On Thursday afternoon, when the ship was about sixty miles east-north-east of the Three Kings, and forty miles north-east of North Cape the bottom boards of a boat and other wreckage were seen in the water. Then the lookout man at the masthead sang out that a raft was in sight. At seven minutes past four the steamer was alongside the raft and it was seen that several on board were still alive. The sailors gave three cheers and the men on the raft responded feebly. Only one man was standing holding the signal flag. Three

131

were kneeling and the rest were in crouching positions. On board many were too dazed to give intelligible answers to questions about the missing lifeboat. Some stated that hours before a steamer had approached them, lowered a boat and then abandoned them. Others said a steamer had been sighted but did not mention the lowering of a boat.

The survivors were placed on pallets in the *Penguin's* chartroom. Steven Neil lay worn and scarred, in a deckchair by the bridge. Doctor McLean, the ship's doctor moved among them. Each man was lying in a different position to relieve the pain of cramped limbs. The skin of their faces was burnt and blistered, their eyes bloodshot and seared with brine. Sun and salt water had made their feet and legs too swollen and raw to bear the weight of blankets. Gaunt from starvation they had to be fed carefully as a sudden surfeit could be fatal.

As the *Penguin* steamed into the harbour, boats and launches put off in shoals and the Queen Street wharf was lined with thousands of people swarming over shed roofs, cranes, wagon tops and the rigging of ships. The man o' war lay out in the stream. The anxious friends and relatives of those still missing were kept in suspense. The Devonport ferry steamer *Eagle* was requisitioned to fetch the men from the *Penguin*. Jordan and the seaman Danielson had to be carried aboard on stretchers and the rest needed some assistance.

Wrapped in blankets in the *Eagle's* cabin, the raft survivors met the *Elingamite's* second officer, Renaut, and asked him eagerly for news of their shipmates and relatives. Neil learnt for the first time that his wife and son were saved and waiting for him on the wharf. Stooping over the emaciated fireman, Tom Mallins, Renaut held his wrist tenderly as he gave the names of survivors. After the horror of the raft, the joy of rescue and now these mixed tidings, the men were too weak to control their emotions. The return of the *Eagle* was greeted with loud cheering from the huge crowd, renewed each time a survivor walked down the gangway. There was a hush when the two stretchers appeared. Hansom cabs and an ambulance took six of the survivors to hospital, while Henry Wetherilt and Steven Neil, reunited with his wife and son, went off to a quiet Auckland suburb to recuperate in the fresh country air.

Chapter 12

FRED CHAMBERS, THE purser, was on deck at about half past ten on Sunday morning, 9 November. The *Elingamite* was going very slowly, her steam whistle blowing. He was standing on the port side aft when the ship struck. She appeared to strike forward. He heard the telegraph before she struck.

Mr Tole: "An appreciable time before?"

Fred: "Yes, I would say so."

Mr Hazelden, S.M.: "How long?"

Fred paused for quite a time before replying: "It would not be more than *four minutes*."

Tole: "You're not confusing minutes with seconds?"

Fred: "No, I don't think so."

Hazelden: "When did you see the rocks?"

Fred: "I heard the telegraph and then I looked around and saw the rocks. The ship was going forward all the time."

Tole: "How far would you say she went before she stopped?"

Fred: "About two lengths. There was a bump forward and she was brought up broadside on the rocks."

Tole: "Did you notice anything about the engines?"

Fred: "They had stopped before she struck at all."

Mr Hazelden was a stipendary magistrate, and Mr Tole represented the Customs Department. For the third time I was scanning the records of the inquiry into the *Elingamite* disaster. The discrepancies in times given by different witnesses began to weigh in my mind. There must be some reasons for such marked divergencies of opinion and I had a hunch that our diving knowledge might produce an answer to this puzzle.

Ted Allen, the donkeyman, was standing by the rails; the lookout man cried: "Breakers ahead". The captain said: "All right," and rang the telegraph. About *half a minute* later the ship went up on the land.

Tole: "What were you doing during this half minute?"

Ted: "I was looking over the side."

Tole: "What would be about the time from the ringing of the telegraph 'full astern' and the striking of the vessel?"

Captain Reid: "Two and a half minutes, as near as I could say. It would be about *four minutes* after she struck before she bumped seriously."

William Gunther: "I was walking up and down the deck when a passenger shouted: 'Look out.' Looking around I saw the rocks. The telegraph rang and about *half a minute* later I felt the vessel grazing on the rocks."

Henry Wetherilt: "From the time the telegraph rang to the time she struck would be about *two minutes*."

Ted Mulcahy (in the stokehold): "About *half a minute* after the telegraph rang I heard a grating under my feet."

Tom Tanner (at the wheel): "The captain ordered the helm hard-a-port and called for full speed astern. Telegraph rang at once, but continued to go ahead for *two or three minutes*, before she struck her port bow gently on the rocks."

Tom Mallins (stoker): "I heard the telegraph ring and *half a minute* later I heard a grating noise."

Harry Tallan (on deck): "The third mate worked the telegraph. The ship kept going for *two and a half to three minutes* before she struck."

Jim Morris (tram driver, on the well deck): "The time between the alarm and striking the rocks would be about *half a minute*."

The Nautical Court of Inquiry was held at Auckland from 28 November, nineteen days after the shipwreck, until 19 January 1903. During this lengthy period a large number of witnesses were called: three officers, three engineers, fourteen crewmen and thirteen passengers were closely examined, there being separate solicitors representing the captain (Mr Campbell), the officers (Mr Martin) and the engineers (Mr Cotter).

Captain Attwood told the Court: "I have been master of this steamer since July 1902. I was previously master of a sailing vessel for nineteen years and had been officer on various steamers. I have been trading for about two years on the New Zealand coast . . .

"I was called at 6 a.m. on Sunday, which was earlier than usual, because the vessel was nearing the land. The haze came down suddenly at 10 a.m. within a few minutes, but I knew where I was, having worked it out by dead reckoning. I ought to have been six or seven miles south of the South West King. When the fog came on

I sent for the chief engineer at three minutes to ten to tell him to slow the engines down. I could have telegraphed the message, but was afraid that if the engines suddenly slowed I would not be able, on account of the escaping steam, to hear the breakers, the fog signal, or anything else. I did not expect to hear anything, but one never knew what one might hear in a fog.

"At ten the engines slowed to four or four and a half knots; I then altered the course to east-north-east. By the compass the variation was 13°. I intended to begin to heave the lead at eleven o'clock and did not heave it before because I thought I was on the east side of the Kings. The lead would be no guide, as I supposed it was too deep. I was three-quarters of an hour on that course when the vessel struck. She was then going at four and a half knots and visibility was two ship-lengths. I saw the breakers on the port bow about that distance away, rushed to the telegraph and rang 'Full speed astern'. I ordered the helm hard-a-port, and rang three or four times. The telegraph responded from below to the first ring, but the engines did not seem to move. I went to the side of the ship. There did not seem to be any motion. I rang again, and Third Engineer Scott came on the bridge and reported that the engines would not move. I said, 'It's too late now, the ship is broadside on the rocks.' I told Scott to tell the chief engineer to bring up all his men to save themselves. I had not time to ask why the engines would not move. Had the engines been reversed when I first gave the order the ship would have escaped."

Evidence against Captain Attwood and the first officer, Mr Burkitt, was very heavy when it came to the details of navigation, lifeboat drill and the abandoning of the ship.

In presenting its decision, the Court stated: "When at 4 p.m. on Saturday the 8th it was discovered that the patent log had failed, no reliance could be placed on it to denote distance run. The set speed was therefore guessed at by the master and second officer and they estimated it at twelve knots, although during the previous day a speed of twelve and a half knots had been shown, and there were no conditions to indicate a lesser speed. On Saturday afternoon the weather became hazy and continued so throughout the night. At daylight on Sunday morning no more than two miles could be discerned. As the morning went on the weather became thick and foggy, and this fog so increased that at 10 a.m. not more than two ship-lengths ahead could be seen.

"It is necessary to here consider what was the position of the master at this particular point of time. His safety depended on his not having deviated from his course and not having overrun his distance. Since the wreck of the *Wairarapa* in 1894, no master should plead want of knowledge of the currents off the Three Kings; but knowledge of strong currents in the locality of the Three Kings, Cape Maria Van Diemen, and the North Cape, had been common to seamen in these waters for many years past. The *New Zealand Pilot* mentions that there is a current at the Kings of about three to five knots and the charts indicate it. The master could not rely on his log to indicate the distance run, and he could see no land, light, or mark by which to ascertain his position. One means he had of averting disaster was by sounding. If less than 100 fathoms was found he would know he was in danger. He could then feel his way, and his chart would enable him to estimate the degree of danger. He had on board Sir William Thompson's patent sounding apparatus, and he says he gave orders for it to be prepared, intending to use it at 11 a.m. He did not use it and the disaster to his ship was the result.

"A lookout man was stationed at the forecastle head, the fog whistle was sounded at intervals, and at 10 a.m. the engines were slowed down to 'slow ahead,' giving, it is said, a speed of four and a half knots. But the Court is of the opinion that, considering the number of revolutions (forty-four per minute), the pitch of the screw eighteen feet six inches, the fairness of the wind, and probable current, a considerably greater speed was attained. Although the master had found at noon on Saturday that he was two or three miles northward of his course, he appears to have allowed nothing for the set during this succeeding period of twenty-two hours; about 10 a.m. on Sunday he altered his course, which would put him still more to the northward and more up to the Kings. He offers no reason for this alteration except that he found a southerly set on a previous voyage and he judged it wise to make it. He had no reliable data on which to found a reason for so doing. He did not know the speed accurately; he had taken no special measures to ascertain it from the log after 4 p.m. on Saturday. He could see no safe distance, nor had he ascertained his speed when going 'slow ahead'. He was making for a passage between the Kings and the mainland, which is fifteen miles in width, if calculated on an area of safe water.

"After 10 a.m. the fog thickened until the master says he could not see more than two lengths ahead; and some of the seamen, and the lookout man in particular, gave a much less distance.

"At 10.45 the catastrophe happened. Some seconds before the lookout man saw the danger, the master, from his place on the bridge, saw breakers on the port bow, and at once rang the telegraph for 'Full speed astern' and then the lookout called: 'Breakers ahead,' and rang his bell. The wheel was put hard-a-port. The order to the engine room was repeated from below. The engines stopped, but

136

did not reverse. The master repeated the order more than once, but no movement came from the engines; and then the third engineer, who was sent for the purpose by the chief engineer, came on the bridge and informed the master, who then said with truth that it was too late. The vessel was then on the rocks ahead and also broadside on to rocks a-port. Not more than two minutes would elapse from the time danger was discovered until the vessel struck bow on."

The Court found Attwood had been guilty of grossly negligent navigation:

1. In driving full speed in fog until 10 a.m. on Sunday when he must have known he was near land.
2. In neglecting to take soundings before and after 10 a.m.
3. In altering his course without sufficient reason.
4. In proceeding at four and a half knots, possibly faster, without sounding, and
5. without carefully ascertaining the speed, yet relying on dead reckoning.
6. In guessing his speed since noon Saturday at twelve knots when everything pointed to a higher speed.

The Court held it a grave error of judgment on his part to allow No. 1 Boat to leave the ship half full. Both the master and the first officer were to blame in the failure to exercise the crew properly in boat drill, for the poor equipment of the boats and unsatisfactory state of tackle for lowering. Those in the boats should have stood by the rafts as long as possible and the master and officers should have kept the boats and rafts together at least until a concerted plan of action was arrived at. The Court ordered Attwood's certificate to be suspended for one year and made him pay £50 costs.

It was, more than anything else, the dispute over the failure to reverse the engines that caught my interest. During the Inquiry, I read, Captain Attwood had been vigorously defended by Mr Campbell, his counsel. Mr Campbell quoted the *Arizona* precedent, when it had been held that although there might be a series of blunders on the part of the master, if these defaults were not the cause of the disaster, his certificate could not be cancelled or suspended. He had submitted that in this case it was useless to consider many of Attwood's omissions unless they contributed in some way to the casualty. Obviously he was focusing everything on the failure of the engines to reverse.

If was also clear to me that this submission had a marked influence on the leniency of the Court towards Attwood, who might have been tried for manslaughter as was the captain of the *Kapanui* in an Auckland harbour collision in 1905.

The Court went on to sum up the engine-room controversy: "Not more than two minutes would have elapsed from the time the danger was discovered until the ship struck bow on. The master asserts that if the engines had gone astern when ordered, the ship would have been saved as she was two lengths (600 ft) from the rocks. The surviving engineers assert that when the order was given the ship was actually on the land and they suggest that the cause of the engines not working was either that the propeller was held externally or the bottom of the vessel was so injured by contact of the land that the tunnel shafting was thrown out of alignment and jammed."

The captain's defence, in building up the case against this unrefuted assertion of the engineers, brought the Court to some peculiar decisions which even the evidence presented belies: "No one on board outside the engineers perceived any touching or bumping as deposed by them." (What about the words of Morris, Gunther, Allen, etc?) The Court was of the opinion that "there was no grounding astern until after the vessel struck forward, as if the stern had been held it would not have gone on to the rocks." (I will shortly explain why I had good reason to feel this was a shortsighted view.) The Court held that the engineers showed reluctance to speak candidly about their engines and the failure to reverse.

For the engineers, Mr Cotter said: "Until an examination was made of the hull of the vessel, and the engines, no one could say that the engineers' opinion about the propeller being jammed was incorrect." He referred to reports by firemen, trimmers and the carpenter of a grazing action about half a minute after the telegraph rang; and to the influx of water in the after hold found by the carpenter.

Sixty-six years later we divers had the evidence Mr Cotter wanted. The next time I met Kelly I asked him about the propeller: "Kelly, do you remember the prop blades being bent?"

"Yes, each blade tip was buckled over. More than a foot from the edge. Those blades were bent and ragged. The prop was lying a foot off the slope that goes up to within about eighteen feet of the surface. I remember thinking what a queer shaped propeller."

"Well, it was high tide at 1.30 p.m. on the day of the wreck. I've also found out she was drawing 15 ft forward and 17 ft 10 in aft and was 310 ft long. So she hit at midwater. From where we saw the ship's engines and shaft, and the reports of the course before impact I reckon she would have skimmed right over that reef before hitting the rocks and swinging her stern in."

Kelly did some calculations: "At four and a half knots she would have covered two ship-lengths in seventy-two seconds, but she would

138

have been losing way with her engines dead, so that explains why it took two minutes until she hit the rocks, and why her stern was free to swing in. She would have covered three ship-lengths in that time at four and a half knots." Kelly concluded.

"Supposing they saw the island through the fog from two ship-lengths out as we are told, that is 600 feet. She would have clipped that reef with her stern within about half a minute, as it stands out from the cliff at right angles and she approached the island obliquely. I suppose we will never know the exact arithmetic of it all, but with our knowledge of that buckled prop at the foot of the roof, and the position of the engines, we could certainly have upset those Court findings."

"Yes," said Kelly, "those engineers really seemed to get mud flung at them for nothing. Fancy having a Court of Inquiry without a diving survey!"

Henry Wetherilt inferred that the engineers did not reverse because they had wedged their gears up to stop vibration on the way across. He based that claim on hearing some banging in the engine room during the brief minutes before the final impact. He knew a lot about engines as a marine surveyor. Captain Reid and he had jointly kept watch on the approaching rocks and down the skylight at the engineers.

Here is what Captain Reid told the Court:
"At the time I was directly beneath the bridge in the smoking-room with Dr Goldie and Henry Wetherilt. Dr Goldie had just been dressing my ankle, which I injured in Sydney. I was sitting near the steering gear. Suddenly I heard it move. Next I heard the telegraph ring. 'Hello', I said, 'we must be close up to something.' We all went out. When we got to the port rail the engines had stopped. Hanging over the rail I saw land through the fog. A good two ship-lengths ahead. I heard a hitting sound in the engine room. I said to Henry Wetherilt: 'It's all right, he'll back her off.' We waited some time and as the ship was not going astern, Henry went to look down the engine-room skylight. I again heard the telegraph ring. I said: 'Goodness gracious: are they not going to give the man his engines today?'

"Henry called out: 'How far are we off, Reid?'

" 'About twenty yards.'

" ' There's plenty of time if they give her the engines,' Henry said, still looking down into the engine room. 'Look over the side and see if you can see the discharge pipe.' I looked but could see no pipe. The vessel was still continuing slowly ahead, but easing as she went.

"Henry called out: 'How far are we off now?' So I replied again. Then I heard hammering of iron on iron. Once more Henry asked how far we had to go. I said; 'Ten yards, there's still plenty of time and there's deep water close up.' I called out to the passengers to hold on. The ship struck forward and rose about eighteen inches, skidding along a ledge of rocks and striking the cliff. I said to Henry: 'She's still all right—has not done herself any harm. It's not a hard bump and there's no sea on. She'll be all right yet, if they give her the engines.' Just then I heard a noise below as if a hammer being thrown on the plates. I said: 'She's all clear aft and she'll come off yet.' She was then still swinging round and her stern was still clear. 'Look out for the after derricks,' I called. 'If they go adrift they'll sweep some of the people overboard.' It was two, to two and a half minutes after the alarm that she struck. Within four minutes she was bumping seriously. By the time five minutes was up I was in number 1 boat.

To the Court, his friend Henry said: "I looked down and saw the engines were stopped. When they did not reverse I thought something might have been jammed. It was not unusual on long voyages to have the engines wedged up to take up the slack and prevent vibration. It flashed through my mind that a wedge had been inserted somewhere for this purpose.'

Kelly chuckled. "Funny to think that all the time those two were ducking to and fro the ship had already struck and was actually sinking."

"Yes," I said, "and Henry's deductions were proven quite groundless. Even Mr Tole stated that *no* wedges could have been used, as all evidence agreed that the engines were stopped within a few seconds of the order. Any wedges would have prevented this. He still got stuck into the engineers for not reversing, but this business about the wedges and hammering seems like a red herring, willingly taken up by all those looking for a scapegoat. Fraser, the chief engineer, was lost and the responsibility was his."

Kelly fished through some material he brought up from Dunedin: "I saw the effect of this propaganda in the *Otago Daily Times*. You sow a few seeds of rumour and that's enough. Look here at this."

The article read: "Jan. 21, 1903. It appears tolerably certain from evidence outside the engine room that the engines were not in good working order at the time. With regard to the suggestion that the reversing gear was wedged, we are not prepared to give an opinion but the alleged hammering heard in the engine room lends colour to the belief that all was not as it should have been. The extreme reticence of the engineers . . . strengthens the conclusion that there is something to hide. The only man who could have been held responsible paid for his error with his life . . ."

I was amazed at this editorial. "Talk about bias! And this in the face of Tole's rejection of the wedge business. Cotter, counsel for the engineers, also said that Joy's reversing gear could *not* be wedged anyway, and I can't understand why they accused the engineers of reticence. If they weren't responsible, why should they clam up anyway? Even Attwood admitted that he had never had any trouble with the engines or the staff."

"Well, what was the engineers' evidence like?"

"Read this one first. Jim Morrison was in charge of the engine room at the time of the wreck. As fourth engineer he had been on the *Elingamite* for thirteen months."

Jim Morrison's account is very full and straight forward:

"At a quarter to ten the chief engineer, Mr Fraser, came down and said Captain Attwood wanted him to slow the engines. At twelve minutes to ten, the chief rang the bridge to say the engines were being slowed. The vessel continued slow until ten-thirty when the chief engineer told me he would go up to the bridge and get the right time. Five minutes later he returned and said the time was twenty to eleven. So I put the engine-room clock on five minutes. Ted Allen, the donkeyman, then came down from greasing the bearings on the middle platform of the engines and as the water had not been siphoning properly to the forward sanitary tank, the chief sent him to see if the cocks were all right. The chief counted the engine revs; the number being forty-four. He had seldom done this before. After counting them he said: 'She's all right now; we must be past the Kings. I'll go up.' All orders to the engine room were recorded in our engine-room log-book, which the chief took with him when he left the ship.

"A minute after the chief had counted the revs, the order came: 'Full speed astern'. I answered it and reversed the engines. It took about a second to reverse. It would take seven seconds before she would begin to move astern. When the telegraph rang the chief had gone five steps up the ladder. He came back at once and opened the intermediate stop valve to give her full steam astern. He remained there until five minutes later when we were all ordered on deck. The chief worked on that valve *not* because the engines had stopped: it was a routine move to go full speed ahead. He saw she went half a turn and stopped."

Tole: "What part of the stern was scraping?"

141

Morrison: "The after part. You could feel it unmistakably. The telegraph rang several times at intervals of a few seconds. The chief answered the second ring and the third time he rang 'stop'. He then applied the auxiliaries to the dead engines—no effect. He told me to put the handle on the hydraulic pump. Just as I was doing this the second and third engineers came running down. After fitting the pump handle I entered 'Full speed astern' on the blackboard. The chief put her to full ahead again, but there was no movement. We put it down to something outside the ship holding the propeller just as we reversed. There was nothing loose in the engines. Not a spanner had touched them since we left Sydney. About forty-five seconds after the order 'Full astern' the chief engineer told me to plug up the air pipes from the after tank. It must have been holed as water was running into the engine room. I went to the nearby store to get a plug and there being none I went to the carpenter's shop next to it. This took one and a half minutes. That was the only hammering done, except to open the cocks on the pumps. When I returned the chief told me to go and tell the captain the engines wouldn't go. As I only had singlet and trousers on I asked the third engineer to do it. Returning below I met the chief and second engineer coming on deck. The chief told me to get a lifebelt on. The last I saw of the chief he was putting his log-book under his belt."

Then we have the words of the second and third engineers, Henry Arkins and Bill Scott.

Henry Arkins spoke first: "I was having breakfast when I heard the engines slow down. I went to the engine room. The chief and fourth engineers were there. The chief was by the levers. The fourth was putting a handle in the pumping gear. The third had arrived just before me. Just then the telegraph rang. The chief answered it and sent the third engineer to say the engines were jammed. This must have been caused by something outside the ship. I saw the chief go to the entrance to the prop shaft with a lantern. He tried everything possible to make those engines move. There was a slight bumping and grating from the after part of the ship and water was coming into the engine room pretty fast, so the ship must have been holed. I was not more than five minutes in the engine room. The hydraulic pump was started on the boilers to prevent them blowing up. Then we all came up from the engine room together."

Next the third engineer, Bill Scott: "The only trouble on the way across was Thursday afternoon, when the ram on the starboard bilge pump had broken off. That Sunday I was in my cabin when I heard the engines slow. Some time later the telegraph rang so I ran to the engine room. By then the telegraph had rung two or three times. The chief told me to tell the captain the engines would not move as the propeller was jammed. Before I left the engine room I felt bumps and heard the chief tell the second the engines had moved half a turn and then stopped dead. On the bridge the captain said, 'Very well, Scott.' I returned below at once. There was water coming out of the air pipe. The second told me to start the donkey and then to have a look at the bilges. I went to the stokehold and returned to tell the chief there was no water there. The second told me to open up the steam valve on deck. I did that and met Morrison, the fourth engineer, who asked me to take the chief's message to the captain as he wasn't properly dressed. I did so, one and a half minutes after having delivered the same message myself! The captain said this time: 'Too late—tell the chief and all hands to come up and get their lifebelts on.'

"From the time I left my cabin to go to the engines till I told the others to put on their belts not more than five minutes had passed. During that time the ship was bumping very heavily and at one time it seemed as if she would break in two. The only thing that would have been wrong inside the ship was the shaft being jolted out of line. There are seven bearings, a thrust block and stern tubes, all carrying the shaft, which revolves in these parts. The bumping could easily disturb them without there being much upset in the engine room. It would take a pretty severe jolt to do it, but the bumping was bad enough."

Then a fireman, Ted Mulcahy, said he was in the stokehold from eight to twelve on Sunday morning: "The ship had slowed down at about a quarter to ten and I was told to shut down the main damper and put the ash dampers in. At about 10.45 I heard the telegraph ring. The ship was going dead slow ahead."

Hazelden: "Before this ring did you hear or feel any sensation, bump, graze or anything of the kind?"

Mulcahy: "Not before the telegraph rang. While I was still in the stokehold the engines stopped, moved half a turn then stopped again."

Hazelden: "Could you tell from where you were that the ship held her way when the engines stopped?"

Mulcahy. "No, you couldn't tell from down there. When I heard the ring I went to the engine-room door about ten paces to see what the telegraph rang for. It stood at full speed astern. By the time I got there the engines were dead. The chief and fourth engineers were at the levers. I assumed it was the reversing gear levers, but they were all pretty close together and it was hard to tell from the door. They were not touching them. About half a minute after the ring

143

there was a grating noise and then a bump. The chief gave some order to the third engineer, who went on deck. The chief then picked up the log-book from the desk. I asked him if I should shut down the main damper. He said: 'Yes—and lock it, so the steam won't go off.' So I put the locking pin in the damper and went on deck leaving the engineers there. I heard no sounds of hammering."

Said Tom McColgan, the carpenter: "I felt no bump in my cabin. Hearing a commotion on deck I went up. Then I heard the telegraph. I saw the vessel brushing broadside on along the side of a high rock forty or fifty feet away on the port side. I went back to my cabin to put on my coat. Then I was sent to take soundings of the bilges so I went to my shop for the rod. The fourth engineer was there, trying to make a plug so I helped him. This took a minute. Then I took four sets of soundings on the port side. Forward it was dry but in No. 3 hold aft on the port side there was nine feet of water; it should have been three inches, so there must have been a hole somewhere. The water must have come in abaft of the engine room. Then I felt a lot of bumping. The stern had swung in towards the rocks. I reported the soundings to the captain who told me to help lower No. 1 boat."

Frank Peterson, the lookout man on the bow, offered a rather different viewpoint: "There were some twenty-five to thirty passengers on the forecastle but they showed no signs of anxiety. I was as far forward on the stem as possible. I first saw land on the port side—like a black cloud. I rang the bell, which was thirty feet away, and sang 'Breakers ahead'. The captain answered coolly, 'All right'. He may already have seen them. I then called through the ventilators: 'All hands on deck', to the crew. There was no impact until one or one and a half minutes after reporting."

If the engineers were reticent, then the first and second officers will seem almost mute. It must be remembered that neither was on duty at the time of impact. On the bridge were only Captain Attwood and Watson, the third officer, who was lost. Within five minutes Renaut and Burkitt were involved in getting the boats lowered and away. Most of their evidence was focused on these aspects where their responsibilities chiefly lay.

Frank Renaut the second officer, said: "I was on watch from midnight Saturday, during which time the weather thickened. I woke the captain and told him. He came to his cabin door and looked around. He said he didn't think it so bad as it appeared, but if it got worse, to call him at once. At 4 a.m. when the first officer relieved me it had cleared a little. I went on to the bridge just after 9 a.m. The captain asked me to work out our position by dead reckoning. Doing so I found our position eleven miles west and south-west of the Kings and our speed twelve knots. Visibility was two to two and a half miles. At 9.30 a.m. I went to my cabin and was writing up until the time of the wreck. When I heard the telegraph I went on deck. There were rocks right ahead and on the port bow two to three lengths off the ship. I went to the bridge. The captain and third officer were there. Before I got there the telegraph had rung several times. The captain ordered me to get the boats ready for lowering. I did not see the third engineer report *twice* on the bridge to the captain. I only saw him once and the ship had bumped by that time."

Len Burkitt, the first officer: "Having handed over my watch to the third officer, Watson, I had just got off to sleep when the casualty occurred. I awakened to the telegraph ringing repeatedly. Rushing on deck I saw the rocks on the port bow. Shortly after the ship grated on the port bilge. I went right forward to look for damage. There were rocks on the port bow but none actually ahead. The stern was not quite clear but not exactly on them. Not quite broadside on, but very nearly. Just as I got to the bridge the captain rang 'Full astern'. The engine room replied 'STOP'. I know the captain had already been ringing earlier. The third engineer came up to say the engines would not move. I then started directing the lowering of boats."

The trial had its lighter moments when the counsel for the engineers, Mr Cotter, drove poor Dr Goldie into a towering rage over a controversial piece of evidence which also shows how a well-meaning witness can be entirely wrong yet utterly sincere.

Dr Goldie: "I was in the smoking-room and about half an hour before we struck I had said: 'We're going straight for the Kings. We'll need our belts within half an hour.' This was half in joke and half in earnest.

"When I first heard the telegraph ring I went on deck. Vision was about three lengths and there were two lengths between the vessel and the rocks. I saw the chief engineer walking along the deck from the direction of the saloon towards the bridge. Seven to ten seconds after the signal to the engine room the lookout had cried: 'Breakers ahead'. The captain was on the lower bridge. (All evidence places him on the upper bridge.) I went along the foredeck and was the only person in that part of the ship when she struck. I heard no orders from the bridge until after she struck and there was no movement of the engines after the telegraph rang. At the time of impact the rocks were fifteen to twenty yards from the stern and it took a minute for the stern to swing around. I went to my berth to get my belt but the tapes were broken. I found another in an empty cabin."

Mr Cotter: "At the time you saw the chief on deck were you very excited ?"

Goldie: "No more than now."

Cotter: "Yet you told us you had said half an hour earlier you were going straight for the Kings."

Goldie: "Yes, but we were going so slowly I thought we would easily back out of it."

Cotter: "I warn you, you are taking away the reputation of an absent man." (The chief engineer).

Goldie: "I cannot help it."

Cotter: "Did you go below for a belt for a lady ?"

Goldie: "I may have done so but I don't recollect it. I remember going down for my own belt. I brought up two and gave one to somebody, but I don't remember if it was a lady or not."

Cotter: "As a matter of fact, doctor, were you not so excited at the time that you put the lifebelt on yourself instead of the lady ?"

Goldie: "Absolutely absurd: I did nothing of the kind."

Cotter: "Do you pledge your oath to that matter the same as your other statements ?"

After some legal quibbling, Goldie repeated his statement about the belts.

Mr Cotter: "He tells us he was no more excited than he is now."

Goldie: "No more I was!"

Cotter: "Supposing three other persons swore distinctly that at the time the telegraph rang the chief was in the engine room. Would you say that they were all mistaken ?"

Goldie: "I do not think I made any mistake. As soon as the bell rang I went to the door of the smoking-room and looking to the left the only person I saw on deck was the chief."

Cotter: "Did you know him ?"

Goldie: "Yes, he sang at the concert the night before and I gave him a bouquet of flowers."

Cotter: "And you say when the telegraph rang he absolutely walked away from the engine room ? You may have mistaken someone else for the chief."

Goldie: "Don't think so. I made the remark when on the raft that he was on deck when the telegraph rang. If I had had doubts, I wouldn't have mentioned that. It didn't strike me as anything unusual."

After this trial Captain Attwood was a broken man. Unable to resume command he obtained a job as tally clerk for a coal company. The pendulum of public sympathy, strongly condemnatory at the time of the disaster, swung heavily in his favour in later years.

In 1911, following the report from the H.M.S. *Cambrian* that the islands were wrongly charted, the Antarctic ship *Terra Nova* made a survey of the Three Kings area, placing the actual position of Great Island about one and a quarter miles further south, and a third of a mile eastward of the charted position. As a consequence the *Elingamite* Rehearing Act was passed in October 1911: "For a further enquiry as to the circumstances attending the wreck of the steamship *Elingamite*." The newspapers on 13 December carried the headline: "Nine Years Under a Cloud".

Before the Supreme Court in Wellington, Captain Watson gave evidence that "in connection with the finding that Captain Attwood's speed was twelve knots or more, I hold that it was about eleven and three-quarters. Had the West King been correctly charted Captain Attwood would have escaped altogether. The currents do not always tend in the direction of the charts and that used by Captain Attwood was more than useless, it was misleading."

Captain Attwood told the Court: "The *Elingamite*'s course was changed as I considered by dead reckoning that the vessel was abreast of the Kings about five to six miles southward. On the previous two trips there had been a strong southerly set but on this occasion it was northward. To have stopped the ship would have rendered her unmanageable and my calculations were made on the only charts available. I now know that they had carried me to a position of danger."

The Court, after referring to the mistakes in the chart, found that the case of negligence in navigation against Captain Attwood had not been proven; that the second charge, that he had allowed Reid's boat to leave without its full complement, was also not proven and there was no evidence of failure on the part of the captain for not standing by the rafts. He was acquitted on all charges.

His friends relate that Captain Attwood's relief was immense; "that next Sunday in church Ernest Attwood had his head held high." He established a business as a ship surveyor in Wellington and died in the 1930s.

Chapter 13

MY RESEARCH LED me from the history of the disaster to the early treasure salvage attempts. Something of value to our own quest might be learnt from their efforts. Although a great gulf of advanced technology separated us from the early divers, the inherent dangers of diving on the *Elingamite* were still the same. Our advantages were a better knowledge of what these perils were, and more flexible scuba diving equipment (scuba is "self-contained underwater breathing apparatus").

These early divers used "hard hat" equipment, which meant they had to descend a shot line, tugged down feet first by heavy lead-soled boots. The diver was clad in a cumbersome rubberized twill suit and his head was encased in a copper sphere into which compressed air wheezed, pumped fitfully through a vulnerable hose by a man-powered hand pump. At that time there was little scientific knowledge of diving technology and the serious effects of pressure on the human body. Divers approached their work in a hit or miss way, their guidelines being only what they had got away with before.

Man's early penetrations into the sea have always been painful and dangerous and progress has been amazingly slow. Until the nineteenth century the diving bell was the sole engine in use. In 1666, divers worked the Spanish Armada treasure ship *Florencia* in Tobermory Bay, in bells of air to a depth of ten fathoms. In 1715 an Englishman invented a leather diving suit, but it was not until 1828 that any major advance was made. Then John Deane invented the open diving helmet, in reality just a small diving bell which hung over a diver's shoulders. The wearer had to stay rigidly erect to keep the water level below his chin. Any inclination would be disastrous. Next Siebe attached to this "diving belt" a waterproof suit so that the diver could bend and stoop, and he developed an efficient surface supply pump. It was this same world-famed diving gear that the early *Elingamite* divers wore.

Just ten days after the *Elingamite* sank, the S.S. *Sterling* set out from Auckland with Captain Clayton, a marine surveyor for Lloyd's, Mr Burkitt, the *Elingamite*'s chief officer and Manuel Baker, a diver. They intended both to locate the wreckage for the purpose of the Nautical Inquiry and to search the coastline on their way north for the missing lifeboat: the east side of Great Barrier Island, round the

Little Barrier, taking in the Mokohinau and Fanal Islands, the Poor Knights and the Cavallis. This northern part of New Zealand is dotted with islands to which the southward current could have carried those thirty-five missing people, and the searchers were not abandoning the faintest hope.

The press reports stated:

"At 1 p.m. we were abreast of the Big King, but there was no sign of life. We then steered for the south side of the West King, and at 2 p.m. the same day we left the ship in the lifeboat with three hands, Manuel Baker, the diver, and Mr Burkitt, with Captain Clayton in charge. We pulled for the south side of the West King. The scene of the wreck of the ill-fated steamer was recognised by Mr Burkitt, who assisted Captain Clayton in sounding, grappling, and taking notes. A quantity of wreckage was soon discovered at 9 fathoms: broken tops of deckhouses, part of the port boat, and only 12 feet below the surface one of the derricks painted reddish buff, with goose-neck end up. We got a line round it, and dragged it up within 2 ft. of the surface, but it was too fast at the lower end to raise further. We supposed the gin and wire rope held it, but we could not see anything. Because of the current the diver, Manuel Baker, was unable to descend but he sounded all round the south side of the island, and we were all convinced that the ill-fated ship was under us. The scene was impressive, and we remarked that had the vessel struck some 40 ft. or 50 ft. more to the north she would have stove her bows and hit a perpendicular wall of rock with her stern, with 22 fathoms of water, say 12 ft. off, and if the collision bulkhead had collapsed she would have gone down in 22 fathoms at the bows and more at the stern in, say, less than a minute. Instead of that she missed the wall and went with a sliding glance along the ledge on the south side of the island with a wall of rock above them, the ledge nearest the wall taking the bilge and smashing it in as the vessel lifted and fell with the sea, and then sinking down on the next ledge, she filled and disappeared."

The search for the missing boat continued as far north as the Kermadec Islands and far out into the Pacific, but no sign of it was ever found. The Nautical Inquiry was still under way when the first treasure hunting expedition left early in January, 1903. The news of the lost bullion consignment had rapidly spread from Australia to the United States, but initially the recovery was in the hands of the underwriters who had paid out in full on the loss: Mutual Indemnity Marine whom Lloyd's of London represented through their local agents, Messrs. Campbell Ehrenfried and Co.

On 15 January the first expedition ship S.S. *Energy* returned with the glummest of reports. Helmet diver Warwick told the reporters that at the wreck site, despite the fine weather, there was a huge swell and an extremely strong current running. He had made several attempts to descend but found it impossible as he kept getting swept away. He was able to tell them that the *Elingamite* had slipped off the rock shelf on which she had first sunk and now lay in water thirty fathoms deep.

There followed a succession of five more futile expeditions. The second attempt was made aboard the S.S. *Young Bungaree*. Again unfavourable sea conditions and the wild wreck site made any diving impossible. When the *Young Bungaree* returned from a third failure the underwriters abandoned all chance of recovery. From then on it was open to the adventurers.

The first two such expeditions were organized by a Mr Gow of Wellington, who, with others, chartered and fitted out the auxiliary schooner *Emma Simms*. A news report read:

"September 7th, 1905. The *Emma Simms* has set sail to recover the bullion that went down in the *Elingamite*, off Three Kings, three years ago. A Wellington syndicate is exploiting this deep-sea treasure-trove. By arrangement with the underwriters the syndicate is to retain 75 per cent of any bullion recovered. The services of one Lee, an American diver of repute from Thursday Island, have been secured, and no grave difficulty is anticipated, as the steamer is lying in 14 fathoms. Aboard the schooner is a dynamo to power a 300 candlepower light which will guide the diver in the murky depths. The *Emma Simms* is in charge of Captain Tosswill and there is a crew of 8. The syndicate hopes to return with the gold within a month."

Five weeks later that expedition returned to Wellington, tail between legs. Mr Gow told the press: "Our attempt was euchred by bad weather from first to last and as the charter was for six weeks only, and the weather was as bad as ever, we tossed it in." At one stage their schooner was nearly driven on to the Great King while moored in the meagre shelter it affords. Using her engines and sails, she was able to slip her anchor and head out to sea. On another occasion they passed right over the body of the wreck. They were certain they could distinguish the form of the submerged vessel beneath them. When about to prepare for diving operations the swell came up again and the schooner had to put to sea.

"There had been no further chance to do anything practical," said Mr Gow. "Treasure seeking at the Three Kings is a gamble on the weather. Given good weather an expedition still has to face the currents, the usual perils of deep diving and the risks and chances of submarine gold fossicking amongst crumbling wreckage." Mr Gow was convinced that the treasure could be got at in fair weather and organized another expedition, chartering the tug *Pelican* from the Devonport Ferry Company.

After another lengthy search I unearthed the following newspaper report:

"The party left Auckland on February 8th, 1906, and spent a week under the shadow of the West King. The wreck site was located without difficulty, but it was impossible to operate on the first day after arrival, owing to the heavy sea. On the next day the sea moderated, and Percy Leigh, the diver, descended to the wreck, the first of five descents in all. He reported that there was very little left of the steamer beyond the fragments of the hull. When asked if he found any trace of the treasure, Percy Leigh replied: 'Absolutely none: all trace of it had disappeared. The gold was in wooden boxes, enclosed in an iron tank or strong-room. I located the spot where the tank had been, but the tank, as well as the gold, had entirely disappeared. I made a careful search among the wreckage, but I was unable to discover even a coin to hang on to my watch chain. The treasure, more than £17,000 worth, had evidently been swept down the shelving rock into deep water, where it will remain scattered for all time!"

Despite this pessimism Mr Gow was unconvinced that it was impossible to recover the treasure, and though he made no subsequent effort, having lost a considerable amount on those two trips, he always stoutly maintained that the gold was there, and could be got at. A later report said:

"As the result of a skit written about the wreck, a rumour went around the colony some time ago that a party of smart Americans had secured the treasure, and, without reporting their find, had returned to America. The story was apparently as reliable as many others connected with the land of the Stars and Stripes."

Less than a month later, a Queensland syndicate chartered the same ship, the *Pelican*, and set out "to rescue the bullion".

Herald, 14 March: "This latest attempt has been organised by Mr J. N. Parkes, his son, and Dr MacDonald, who have had considerable diving experience on the Queensland coast. The party left Auckland on March 6th and anchored at Tom Bowling Bay at

7 p.m. on the 7th to avoid reaching the Three Kings in the dark. They crossed over in the morning, arriving at the wreck site at 1 p.m. The sea was too heavy with a fresh southerly so they anchored back at North West Bay. On the morning of the 9th they sailed across to the West King, but there was too much sea. On the 10th it moderated, being fine and clear with a light southerly, but at the wreck site there was too much swell, and all they could do was take soundings. The 11th was a perfect day. By 6 a.m. the steamer was moored head and stern, but shortly after running the kedges out the ebb tide set in very strongly and it was found that the moorings would not hold and the steamer was dragging. Captain Gardiner considered it would be imprudent for the diver to descend, especially as a kedge had been lost and lines carried away. A further attempt was made that afternoon to moor, but lines and kedges would not hold, although the diver was ready.

"On the 12th—after a lot of risky boatwork, the ship was moored in position. The cage in which the diver was to descend, protecting him from the current and from sharks, was slung to a davit on the port side, a wire rope being taken to the winch, owing to the lack of a derrick aft. The cage was slung over the side, but it was difficult for the diver to enter and use it conveniently. Eventually a descent was made. At 11 fathoms a signal was made by the diver to heave up. On reaching the surface he was seen to be in trouble. Quickly he was taken on board and undressed. Part of his woollen cap had got into the exhaust vent of the helmet, thus preventing a free escape of air. The diver was in danger of suffocation." (This would cause his suit to balloon and shoot him rapidly to the surface. Compressed air expanding in his lungs and suit could well have killed him instantly with an air embolism.) "The expedition decided to give up and return at once, requiring more gear."

When I read this report I recalled that old son of a diver, Mr Harper, at Leigh, who had told Kelly and me with a snort of indignation about that "ex man o' war man—a shallow water man. When it got too deep for him he had shut the exhaust valve on his helmet."

This might be all right in shallow depths for a quick ascent, but the pressure difference at the *Elingamite* site was too great. Scornfully old Mr Harper said: "He never got to the bottom. Just roared to the surface with bleeding eyes and coughing blood. They had to steam flat out at sixteen knots down to Helensville for the nearest doctor, with a north-wester behind them and black squalls chasing them." Miraculously the diver recovered from the air embolism.

The Three Kings' loneliness was not disturbed over the rest of

1906. Prospective treasure hunters were learning that the best time of the year was in January, and it was in early 1907 that the seventh expedition set out. Captain George McKenzie, of Auckland, owner of the auxiliary schooner *Huia*, fitted her out at the Kaipara for a three-month expedition, put his cousin, Captain Dan McKenzie, in command and engaged as diver, Mr E. Harper who had accompanied two of the previous *Elingamite* expeditions and was a hotel keeper at Little Omaha. A Lloyd's representative, Captain Willis, accompanied the expedition to protect the underwriters' claim. The terms under which the previous expeditions undertook the search was the right to seventy-five per cent of the recovered specie. In the case of the *Huia* expedition, because of the known hazards, the underwriters agreed to give eighty per cent to the organizer of the expedition, of which diver Harper would get fifteen per cent. Then came the newspaper report with Captain McKenzie's message:

"Good luck; have recovered £1,500. Hoped to recover lot. Heavy swell at present prevailing making it impossible for diver to work."

As soon as possible the press sent a man up to Mangonui to interview diver Harper on his initial success:

"It is evident that the *Elingamite* when wrecked, sunk on a rocky pinnacle and smashed to atoms. Every porthole was broken out and the strongroom and treasure boxes smashed. Mr Harper is sure that the treasure was never previously located. The wreck now lies in 22 fathoms of water. Standing on her bow great submarine gullies are visible below. The work of securing the treasure is very strenuous, as the coins have corroded and are sticking together in mounds. A number of silver spoons and forks bearing the Huddart-Parker brand were also brought up, one fork with gold coins lodged between the prongs. When Mr Harper returns he plans to take down a heavy hammer to break up the heaps of coins.

"Mr Harper has a splendid record as a diver, and is looked upon as one of the best men in his profession. Reared on the Thames River, London, he soon came into prominence wherever diving operations were to be carried out, and was, when quite a young man, engaged in the East in salvaging work. One of his first serious tasks was in going down off Colombo to a sunken steamer, which he succeeded in raising and taking to Bombay. Afterwards he was engaged in various diving operations in the East, including the laying of great 25-ton stone blocks for a breakwater in Colombo Harbour. He then came to New Zealand. Before the wreck of the *Elingamite*, Mr Harper was engaged in harbour works at Wellington. He was a man very keenly interested in his work, and from the moment the

Elingamite sank he made up his mind to secure the treasure which went down in the steamer."

Captain Willis said: "On the 14th January after touching bottom at fifteen fathoms and walking down what had the appearance of a grassy slope, Mr Harper had located a portion of the wreck in seventeen fathoms of water. As far as he could see the remainder of the wreck lay on an angle sloping down into deep water. On the following day five descents were made and Mr Harper then reported that the gear of the vessel was in a general state of 'smash' and she was completely flattened out. At half past ten next morning (January 6) the diver brought up a number of coins and reported that he could see no signs of the bullion boxes and the coins were lying loose over the surface of the iron plating, in about twenty fathoms of water. At 11 o'clock Mr Harper again descended and remained below till noon, during which period he sent up some additional gold and silver coins. Shortly after coming to the surface Mr Harper complained of deep water pains, and being taken on board the *Huia* he fainted. Restoratives were applied and every possible attention was shown to Mr Harper. He was much better that evening, though he was still evidently suffering considerably from the effect of being in such a depth of water for a long period. By the 8th Mr Harper had completely recovered and he resumed diving operations."

"It had been arranged," said Captain Willis, "that on no account was Mr Harper to stay below more than fifteen minutes at a time. The necessity of observing this precaution was impressed upon him by both Captain McKenzie and myself. On that and the following two days further sums of money were recovered. Then, owing to a strong swell and the shortage of water, our party returned to Mangonui to refit. As soon as the weather is suitable we shall return to the scene of operations."

When Kelly and I had interviewed Mr Harper's son at Leigh he had given us many of the details recorded here, including a humorous sidelight.

Just before they arrived at the Kings the barquentine *Elverland* had foundered. Becalmed and drifting past the islands in a thick December fog she had struck the Farmers Rocks and sunk. The crew had landed safely on the Great King, while the captain had rowed, with others, down to Houhora for help. When the *Huia* appeared the castaways had thought it was a rescue ship. Tough old salts, they had deliberately set out to extract the utmost in sympathy from their deliverers, tearing their clothes, and bedaubing themselves with grime. Touched by their pathetic condition Captain Willis, the Lloyd's agent, had given the first mate his second-best suit, to Mr Harper's delight. After some delay from bad weather, the *Huia* set out on what was confidently believed would be a total recovery of the treasure. Where six divers had failed to find a single coin this sixty-year-old veteran diver Harper had located the money pile.

The next newspaper report told of his last dive:

"The treasure boat *Huia* arrived at Mangonui on January 23, bringing the body of the diver, Mr E. J. Harper, who died from heart failure. On January 22 he made his first descent since the *Huia*'s return to the Three Kings in quest of the *Elingamite* gold. He went down three times, and each time sent up some of the treasure. Harper was in great spirits and very sanguine, and on the occasion of the third descent he stayed down about 30 minutes. When brought to the surface he complained of his heart, and asked to be taken on the *Huia*. On reaching the vessel he collapsed and though every effort was made to save his life, he died shortly after two o'clock. The treasure sent up for the morning's work was valued at about £800, half of it being silver and the balance gold. This additional £800 secured brings the total amount recovered up to £2,500, and of this the diver's relations will receive 15 per cent, according to the contract."

· " 'Diving operations,' related Captain Willis, 'were resumed on January 22, when the launch with the diver and party on board left the *Huia* and proceeded to the scene of the wreck about half-past eight in the morning. Mr Harper went down twice and on each occasion was signalled at the expiration of 15 minutes. But he remained below, 23 minutes on each descent. When he descended for the third time he was very cheerful, being in excellent spirits and apparently in the best of health. He was signalled as usual at the end of 15 minutes, and he replied "all right". Although he had been strongly warned against remaining below for a long period he persisted in doing so, and on this occasion he had been down 33 minutes before he came up. I was on board the *Huia* at the time. Mr Harper complained of being ill when he came to the surface and was at once conveyed by the launch to the *Huia* where every endeavour was made to bring him round. After a time he commenced to show signs of recovery. The efforts at restoration were continued and he still showed some signs of rallying. A consultation was held, with the result that Captain McKenzie left the ship to pick up the big lifeboat. I continued the use of restoratives in the meantime with satisfactory results. Captain McKenzie returned to the ship in less than half an hour. Shortly afterwards, despite our continued exertions, Mr Harper showed signs of collapse.'

"Speaking of the disregard paid to the strong advice not to remain below more than 15 minutes, Captain Willis said that one of Mr Harper's sons gave him the signal to come up, but as he did not respond, said that nothing could be done. 'My father will always have his own way and he's on to the treasure now.'

" 'It should also be stated,' said Mr Willis, 'that Mr Harper, when he came up, ascended in the usual way, and it was not until he stepped into the launch that it was known that anything was the matter. He then complained of being ill and made a remark to the effect that it was foolish to remain so long under water.'

"An inquest was held on the body at Mangonui. The evidence disclosed the fact that deceased had over-exerted himself on the third occasion of going down, and that accidental death, no blame being attachable to anyone, was returned.

" 'I should like to express my deep regret, which was shared by all on board,' said Captain Willis, 'at this sad termination of Mr Harper's career. Personally, I had the greatest respect for him. I consider him to have been one of the best and bravest divers that I have ever had anything to do with. I never met a braver man, and it was just through his persistence and his extreme desire to make a success of the expedition that he met his death. All possible precautions and care were taken, and if all the doctors in Auckland had been there they could not have saved his life. The deceased's sons have expressed their thanks for the kindness shown by Captain McKenzie and the crew of the *Huia* and for the sympathy extended to them.' "

I obtained much more accurate information on the diver's death from *The Log of the Huia*, by Cliff Hawkins. This showed that he had spent forty minutes below on his last dive and not thirty-three as Captain Willis had stated.

The very year that Harper died of the "bends", physicist John Haldane published his diving tables in England, which showed unmistakably what men could and could not do underwater.

I gave the figures from the *Huia* log-book to Kelly. Horrified at the extremely dangerous pattern Harper had followed, Kelly showed me what Harper should have done. According to the lastest diving tables his first descent required a six-minute halt at ten feet before surfacing to let his nitrogen-saturated system approach normal without the fatal formation of bubbles in the tissues and along the spinal cord. His second descent was much worse: had he allowed an interval of three hours or more he would have been safer. As it stands a second descent to that depth after only twenty-two minutes on the surface, would require a halt at twenty feet of fifteen minutes and another at ten feet of twenty-one minutes. After the third dive Harper should have stopped at thirty feet for nineteen minutes, at twenty feet for thirty-seven minutes and at ten feet for seventy-one minutes, a total decompression time of 127 minutes! From this it will be clearer why, in our own diving work, we had to space our dives from the first light to dusk and observe the most stringent decompression procedures.

After Harper's death the *Huia* returned twice more, raising a further £300 in coin before giving up for the winter. The *Claymore* sailed from Auckland on 14 December 1907, having on board Captain Dan McKenzie, and two divers, Clarke and Leigh. (They had made earlier trips.) On their first day's diving they raised some £700 of specie before deteriorating weather forced them to put back to Tom Bowling Bay for shelter. After repeated efforts to get back to the Kings, the *Claymore* was eventually forced to shelter in Mangonui.

In the first days of 1908 she returned to the wreck site, but the divers were able to work only for a day and a half, obtaining about £200 more of the specie. On the last day diver Clarke went down three times, in a desperate bid to raise more coin before the weather drove them away. From his last descent he surfaced fit and well but shortly before boarding the *Claymore* he complained of a cramp in the arm and pains in his feet. Diver Leigh made another descent and then the diving launch returned to the ship.

The wording of the newspaper report shows the ignorance of "bends" current at that time:

"Mr Clarke was then found to be feeling the effects of compressed air on the lungs, but this was relieved by means of a hot bag, and he seemed to be merely suffering from the usual inconveniences which are common to the diver's calling. The weather becoming dangerous, it was decided to return to Mangonui. On the way across in the night, with no indications whatsoever of collapse, diver Clarke expired."

The *Elingamite* had claimed her second diver. For some reason this fatality was lost to all the popular historical records and it was only by the slenderest chain of coincidence that I managed to track it down. At the time of writing I have another rumour to verify, that Percy Leigh returned on a later trip, and he too died of the "bends".

So it was little wonder that the *Elingamite* was abandoned for over fifty years, her location forgotten, her treasure supposedly beyond human reach. Then in March, 1957, a modern scuba diver took up the search: a professional Auckland skindiver, Les Subritzky, grandson of the skipper who had sailed his schooner *Greyhound* to the rescue in 1902. Les dropped down to 200 feet and spent some twenty minutes exploring the scattered wreckage. He had not the least idea as to where the bullion lay and all he could find that was recognizable were some parts of her cylinders. The remainder of the vessel had been swept away by the sea's action and huge boulders, which had tumbled down the sloping seabed, made it impossible for him to carry out a thorough search for the treasure. He was amazed to find a solid steel shaft, nine inches thick, that had been broken and twisted like a mere strand of wire. All he recovered was part of one of the *Elingamite*'s brass ventilator shafts.

On resurfacing he found that the current had swept him 200 yards down from the dinghy in which his friend, Harry Pope, awaited him. The weather, in true Three Kings fashion, had worsened considerably and the fierce tidal rip had him in its power. Rapidly he was being carried towards some jagged, wave-lashed rocks. Luckily Pope spotted him from some seabirds wheeling round his head. Just in time to stop him from being hurled on to the rocks, he pulled Subritzky into the dinghy. Despite his narrow escape he said he had no regrets. A dive on this famous old wreck had been one of his main ambitions. But he had no wish to return.

Book 3

Chapter 14

ONE HUNDRED AND twenty feet below our flippers fourteen plugs of gelignite, linked by cordtex and electric detonators, erupted in the money pile. Kelly's knuckles were still white on the handle of the plunger as our aluminium boat tossed on the huge swells and bounced with the backlash from the cliffs. "We're still floating," I broke in. Lolly pink mao mao kept bobbing to the surface all around us, spinning in the seething eddies and whirlpools of the tide-race. The blast had upset their air sacs bringing them helpless to the top.

"Wonder if we got the big groper," said John Gallagher, as we sat there in the dense mist blanketing the West King and wiping out our ship *Lady Gwen* cruising at a safe distance. We felt sorry for the fish, but Peter Clements and I were burning to dive down to see the effect of the explosion on the *Elingamite* skeleton. There would be no vision down there until the current had swept clear the great mushroom of suspended particles and black corrosion hanging over the wreck. So we pitched and bucketed and waited in our dinghy moored by a shot line and buoy to the *Elingamite*'s propeller shaft.

The day had finally arrived when Kelly, movie camera, explosives and beard, drove into Auckland. On his way through Wellington he had inveigled the loan of a sturdy aluminium boat for our expedition's use and now all that remained was to sail away over the summer sea to the Three Kings. We had a whole fortnight to prepare, from scratch, our carefully planned full-scale assault on the bullion. Getting away from New Zealand turned out to be the most gruelling, nerve-wracking battle that any of us had waged in our lives. Right slap-bang before Christmas it started. In theory we had a fortnight until our departure on 31 December, but we were to find that this allowed us in reality only five business days.

It all began the Friday night of Kelvin's arrival when our syndicate met at John Pettit's home to set things in motion. John, Jag, Kelly and I all signed an impressive legal document John had had prepared by a solicitor. This duly apportioned the treasure amongst us; it established our *Elingamite* syndicate as a legal entity and appointed Kelly and me as managers, able to negotiate with the underwriters. The cold, legal document dispatched, we warmed heartily to this reunion of treasure addicts after a year's humdrum existence and it was with difficulty that we forced ourselves to keep conviviality to a minimum and get on with the planning.

We were in for a shock. There was a nagging doubt, John said, whether Larry Walker would have his scow the *Lady Gwen* ready in time. Just in case of a let-down he was trying to obtain a trawler, but Marine Department regulations were an obstacle: "No diving gear on licensed fishing craft". What a tragedy for us if we could not get to sea because of red tape!

At the meeting we dished out jobs. Jeff, a supermarket manager and our cook, was the ideal man to handle food supplies, and he was now thoroughly experienced at catering for expeditions. His only mistake was to be the two huge bags of onions. Jag, the engineer, would arrange for our supply of fifty scuba tanks, seven air storage cylinders, a second 16 mm movie camera for topside sequences, a diving ladder, an extra case of explosives, detonators and electric cable. With his nursery business at full pre-Christmas throttle, all John Pettit could do was arrange our wine supply, obtain some steel ammunition boxes to hold the bullion, and undertake to get all the equipment and supplies to Awanui, 300 miles away, in one of his delivery trucks. The rest was over to Kelly and me.

We desperately wanted an air compressor to refill our scuba tanks. Already in the last month we had scoured New Zealand from Invercargill to Kaitaia for such a machine, but there was no hope. We now resolved to offer up to N.Z. $600 for one, or N.Z. $200 for a fortnight's hire, but we *had* to get one if we were to be prepared for a major bullion strike. Each of us had ideas and leads we would follow. We were embroiled in the compressor problem when our two new expedition members bounced in: Peter Clements and Jaan Voot. We were lucky to have these two divers along, both on a no-share, voluntary, just-for-the-adventure basis. Both were as experienced as any diver we knew, having begun, like Kelly and me, some fifteen years before in Canterbury. The four of us had often dived together off Stewart Island, Kaikoura and in the Marlborough Sounds, and we knew one another's capabilities well. Both these men had an excellent grasp of technical matters; Jaan being an engineering graduate and Peter an expert on heavy machinery. Peter has the most irrepressible, buoyant good humour you could possibly maintain on a tough diving trip, and Jaan an intensity and eagerness which had won him those two eighty-pound plus kingies on our early spearfishing jaunt to the Kings when we first discovered the wreck.

With all this engineering aptitude around I took a plunge into the

162

airlift problem: "Come on Kelly, tell us what you've decided on."

In short, and everyone accepted his experimental evidence, we wanted desperately a powerful water pump to power a gold dredge/ water jet combination. "I've got one in the glass house," said John. We dashed out in the dark to examine our lucky break, but John's water pump wasn't there. "Some bastard's pinched it," swore John with a lovely cadence, and we all went back inside. Kelly and I would have to hire or buy a pump but the type we needed might be a little hard to locate.

Next we discussed the range of lifting gear, ropes, marker buoys and other paraphernalia on our lists, which Kelly and I were to track down. Jag had constructed a special buoy system for mooring over the wreck site. Four yards of heavy chain would fasten it securely to the propeller shaft so that no tide-race could shift it. Jaan undertook to pick up a pneumatic boat for emergency use and a specially prepared diver's medical kit, including morphine and syringes to kill pain in case one of us was stricken with "bends" or mauled by a shark. Pete would bring a tape recorder. We later wished he hadn't! Finally discussion turned to our colour movie plans and TV releases, also part of the syndicate venture. "We must have a lighting system to restore the colour down there," I said. John reckoned he could borrow a lovely little Honda generator, and Kelly told us he would jack up a set of floodlights using sealed beam headlights. When this meeting closed in the early hours of the morning, we had an anti-climax: a weekend in front of us; there was little we could do in Auckland. Kelly and I were very worried about the untested movie camera housing. Would it focus truly? Would all our framing be wrong? There could be a dozen bugs to jeopardize our film and turn us into raving lunatics thereafter for not having bothered to test it. So, although time was pitifully short, we grabbed our diving gear and tore up to Cape Rodney where a sonar buoy was being moored by a marine research group which I belong to. I had heard it was breaking loose. We would do a thorough practical test, with Kelly filming me placing extra concrete slabs on the two moorings. Holding the one hundredweight blocks I made some very rapid descents to eighty feet, and the movie camera whirred beautifully as I wrestled them across the sandy floor and into position.

Next evening we sat in front of a TV set in Auckland. On the news came our underwater sequence. Conditions had been terrible, as it was a heavy storm that had disturbed the buoy, and we had dived in the aftermath, a heavy jostling swell and turbid yellow water. Kelly beamed when the screen showed the whole procedure spot on. At first attempt we had successfully put some film through the TV pipeline. The following day we purchased N.Z. $320's worth of colour film and spent the evening discussing filming techniques with Lynton Diggle, a National Film Unit cameraman. That was all the movie preparation we could spare time for.

The remainder of that week, Kelly and I worked like tornadoes trying to obtain gear. We hunted desperately for the type of water pump we needed but no such pump could be obtained. "A 4,000 gallons an hour machine?" As he scratched his head, the hire pool man pondered: "Well, there's one." He pointed to a huge Goliath on four wheels employed in road building, but seldom mounted in a dinghy for use in heavy seas! It was a very lucky break when we located components of a high-power, low-weight model at MacEwans Pumps, which they kindly undertook to assemble in three days, ready on Christmas Eve. When Kelly collected our water pump, a 300-pound monstrosity, the Christmas spirit was well under way in every Auckland business house. This was to make our quest progressively harder as what had seemed to us business hours became increasingly a matter of smirking office girls, smiling char-ladies and clinking bottles from behind oak-panelled doors. But we did manage to get the sealed beam lights, special strong ones to resist pressure. We had a last session with Muir Douglas, the embattled Auckland manager of the insurance company now under-writers of the bullion, after which we emerged duly appointed salvage agents.

Nowhere could we obtain the 200 feet of one and a half inch hose we needed to jet water into the wreck. Then I remembered the fire brigade. A friendly chat there and we emerged with exactly the right stuff—condemned fire hose in three lengths. The brigade had a kindly regard for treasure hunters as this hose is not released to any of the industrial concerns who clamour after it. At the same time as we chased pumps, hose and lights, we were fighting a running battle to obtain a compressor, on six fronts. After endless phone calls, visits, engaged calls, locked doors, "I'm sorry buts" and exorbitant prices, we found the trails had gone cold. At the last minute we found one in pieces—a demonstration model which we sent off to Jag's Hamilton engineering works in the hope that he would be able to fix it in time.

Forewarned by the oversights of earlier expeditions, we made proper arrangements for TV releases, newspaper and periodical rights to the story. We bought strong duffle bags to hoist coin in and we took out equipment insurance. We chased for hundreds of miles around a city which was rapidly slowing down for Christmas and the New Year. For us those days were a nightmare of pavements, parking meters, staircases and phone calls, in the midst of Christmas shoppers and the traffic mêlée. Our feet ached, we starved ourselves to save time and our minds whirled to keep track of all the minutiae and to make snap decisions. We longed for the silence and peace of the undersea and that thought drove us to extreme efforts.

As the clinking glasses and raucous laughter level grew, our hopes faded. We needed an outboard. We still didn't have a compressor. A surface supply hookah might do the job. The two business firms concerned in these quests were both on third floors, a block apart, and in both cases the boss "was out—back any minute". As the day ticked by we took turns to maintain an ambush in the office of each boss. We waited interminably: we *must* get a hookah pump; we *must* have an outboard. Desperate, Kelly and I would plunge downstairs to race up to the next building to try to catch the other absent "back-soon" boss. After another half-hour, we decided to split forces and wait on each man alone. Off we galloped again. The conviction that our treasure hunt must have the right gear drove us to frantic levels of determination. Perhaps not having eaten all day maddened us even more, but things had approached a vaudevillean farce when I passed Kelly dashing up some stairs as I plummeted past him in a lift.

We roared with laughter at this stage. All Auckland seemed to be bent on inebriation. Sorely tempted to join in the swill, we stuck to our guns and decided to withdraw. There were still vital requisites, but the city was a maddening jungle and we were glad to escape and head north, laden with gear: boat, water pump, fire hose, two movie cameras, film, pneumatic boat, explosives, morphine and high hopes. Over the festive period all we could do was relax and collect our sanity. Kelly worked at assembling the water pump outfit and building the floodlights, while down in Hamilton Jag was hopelessly engaged in repairing our compressor, chasing others, borrowing storage tanks and talking customers out of hiring his firm's rental scuba tanks. "No good diving at Christmas: water's always murky and you won't feel fit enough anyway."

At long last we all arrived at Awanui on the last day of 1967, both Jeff and John having collected traffic tickets for overloading on the way. Our first sight of the *Lady Gwen* was the funniest moment in years. Our ship sat flat on her lady-like bum in a mangrove swamp by a grassy bank: ming-blue and buff, an ungainly, squarish wooden lump, with some sort of telephone booth or outhouse perched on top of the cabin-engine room shed. This we gathered, served as the wheel-house. To our discomfort we were to learn the *Lady Gwen* didn't have an outhouse.

"Are we going to the bludy Kings in that?" Jeff queried in his broad Lancashire-lad accent. As things turned out, we very nearly didn't! In searing heat and humidity we sweated and heaved. Our chain of five divers (six until Kelly found the excuse of filming us!) stowed fifty scuba tanks into the bilges; we lashed our logpile of storage cylinders to the deck, we fought over the four bunks, stacked supplies in every corner, put the explosives right up on the bow, grunted the water pump aboard, and shoved the aluminium dinghy on top of the cabin. A tarpaulin was rigged over the foredeck to provide extra sleeping room. This was shared by a vast room-sized ice box filled with all our steaks, white wine, butter, champagne, beer and other perishables.

At last we were ready for sea. All we needed was the ice. Huge chunks were awaiting us in a nearby fishing co-operative depot's freezer. Off Jeff and Jag went in the stationwagon to fetch them. Shortly they returned grim-faced. "No ice?" "Someone's pinched it."

Larry, the skipper, got on the phone. It turned out some fisherman had opened the freezer, seen this fine heap of ice and decided he might just need it on his Christmas holiday jaunt.

"Could ice stop us after all this?" To freeze another batch would take a day and if we didn't leave soon the tide would again sit the *Lady* back on her chuff. We were dogtired now and aching from slinging air tanks around. Nothing is worse to handle than these unwieldy cylinders. Holding a pressure of one ton per square inch each is a potential bomb if not treated carefully. With weariness and defeat we felt like broaching the white wine in our sorrow. But Larry was still trying. With commendable guts he aroused from bed the boss of the rival fishing firm and extracted from him the whereabouts of the key to the freezer. In a flash three divers had a mountain of ice at the foot of the now sinking gangplank, just in time to catch the night tide.

Our excitement was electric as the *Lady Gwen* rumbled and bullied her way down the creek through the mangrove swamp. I marvelled at Larry's skill at navigating in the dark such a serpentine maze. But it was not long before I realized his technique was simply barge and bluster. The staccato roar of the twin diesels shattered the stillness of the inky night, ducks flapped and fled as the *Lady* with her dish-shaped rump bumped and sloshed from bank to bank, backed off, accelerated and charged again. Nothing could stop the old girl now and those new engines throbbing mightily under her deck engendered our first respect for her. We were grateful to be heading seaward when the tide was already ebbing.

"She's got a ton of guts," Jag observed as we stood on the bows, dodging overhanging mangrove branches and marvelling at her progress. Another glimpse of our new skipper's whimsical sense of humour appeared when he leaned from his "outhouse" and flicking

166

wheel spokes to yell: "Who wants to drive?" Strangely appropriate as going downstream in the *Lady* was like a trip in a colossal bulldozer. "But what will she be like at sea," I wondered. To avoid the answer I decided to copy Jag's habit and sleep all the way there. Nipping below I grabbed a spare corner of the cabin floor, unrolled my sleeping gear and swallowed a seasick pill. But the accumulated excitement of a big trip was too much for my brain and I soon awoke and took a stroll on deck. The New Year was creeping in as the *Lady Gwen* wallowed northward on a calm, moonless sea. Beneath the awning two divers slept on deck. Peter on a camp stretcher, Jaan, pessimistically, on the upturned pneumatic boat. Wisely too, as the low freeboard decks rolled awash and the cold seas swirled around them. I decided it was too hot below in the cabin and lugged my sleeping gear up on top of the ice box far above the waves, a fortnight's tucker under me if the *Lady* subsided while I was asleep.

Mornings start very early at sea at the beginning of the year and this one was no exception. I awoke to our skipper Larry saying: "The old spud barber is doing a helluva moan down there among his pots and pans." True, our cook, Jeff, didn't warm too kindly to his galley. A real chef, he is a stickler for having things set up properly from the start, and he'd had better facilities in our tent perched on a cliff edge than on this expedition in the *Lady Gwen*'s poky galley. With his usual good nature, John Pettit got to work with hammer and saw, and while Jeff chuckled at Larry's new term for a cook, a set of kitchen shelves, a table and plate rack materialized. We'd drawn up a duty roster and it was Pete and John's turn for fatigues. But most of the cabin floor and every bunk was still huddled with sleepers—not an inch to move in preparing breakfast.

"Your first duty," said John to Pete, "is chucking these bums out of here." By eight in the morning we had all crammed back into the cabin for our first meal of peaches and cornies, garlic steak and tomatoes, eggs, bacon and black coffee. With Jeff on board we would eat like kings even though the accommodation was sub flop-house standard. And the fatigues men made an alarming discovery: when Jeff first stepped on board he had cleaned up the cabin, sending ashore all spare gear lying around. With the skipper's dirty plates he had sent ashore most of ours. We meekly ate our peaches and steak off all manner of vessels, but no one muttered any hate towards our cook.

We didn't see the Kings appear. We strained ahead for hours during the crossing, as the time of arrival is never sure with the powerful currents that sweep unpredictably across the course. Gradually the brilliant sunny day dimmed as a northerly sea mist came up ahead of us reducing vision to five miles. The closer we drew to the islands the denser it grew, until we were peering into a white-out. We were there—off the Three Kings. We groped in to anchorage beneath the huge cliffs of the Great King, under a gloomy sky, skeins of mist hanging down through the pohutukawas and trickling down to the shoreline. The sea was calm enough, we agreed as we lunched, but conditions would be worse at the wreck site. After discussion and sounding out Larry's feelings about poking around the Kings in a fog, we decided to give it a try. The fog was lifting in patches and any day at the Kings when the sea is calm is precious. We might only get halfway down to West Island, nine miles off, but it was better than sitting at anchor and venturing nothing. On the way down, comfortably fed, I climbed into a cosy bunk, having had so little sleep on the ice box. Just as I was dropping off in the early hours, the cook had woken me to get his morning food supplies. So now, in a vacated bunk, I dozed off again.

After twelve months dreaming about it West Island seemed even more unreal when I awoke to see it, tilting and glinting through a thick mist. *Lady Gwen* heaved, lurched and spun a half mile off the wild tide-race as we stood off to size up the situation. The light south-west wind was causing the swells to crest and break over the wreck site, but after watching the danger area for a while, we noticed that there was about a twenty-foot gap between the diving area and where they broke out of control and smashed in a seething mass of white up on to the rocks. There was a chance that two divers could swim in and make a plunge upcurrent of the wreck and reach the bottom before the current caught them. Fortunately it was running northward, otherwise any error would sweep them on to the jagged reef protruding at right angles to the island, just south of the wreck site. As it was they would be carried clear of the island towards New Caledonia.

If we ventured nothing we would have wasted a valuable day. If only a small buoy and light line could be moored to the wreck today we would be able to dive at any stage of the tide, whether tending north or south, as we could haul ourselves down the line. This would enable our permanent buoy and heavy shotline to be rigged later. It certainly seemed worth a try and we were so eager to see the wreck again that there was no lack of volunteers to take on what was a pretty hair-raising dive. In fact Kelly told me afterwards that when the *Lady Gwen* rounded the corner of West Island and nosed in towards the wreck site, Pete, the only newcomer to the scene burst out: "Christ! Is that where we're going to dive!"

John Pettit and Jag togged up and the *Lady* steamed in. Abreast of the wreck site we pushed the aluminium boat off the cabin top and it smacked down into the sea twelve feet below. "Great, these tin boats!" said Larry. Rowed by his son Tom, who willingly accepted the job of boatman, the little boat soared and sagged towards the wreck site on that foggy white day. From the ship it looked no bigger than the seagulls screeching above us as the divers prepared to descend into that confused zone of white froth and translucent blue water above the wreck. Backwards they somersaulted and disappeared trailing a nylon line. To us now it seemed hopeless to dive. The surges had increased in force and the dinghy kept dropping from view. On several attempts they were swept away, like Les Subritzky, but they wore yellow life vests and the dinghy soon plucked them out of the current. *Lady Gwen* took them in tow and released them upstream of the wreck. They had to flipper madly to reach the bottom before being swept out to sea again.

Through the fog we watched, amazed that our dinghy could live in such a welter of confused water. Larry told us that line fishermen up here had often found it impossible to get a line to the bottom, using heavy window-sash weights for sinkers. The movie camera was whirring in our ears, when a cry went up: "They've done it!" There was an orange speck streaming out from the wreck site, then two small figures wriggling into the boat.

As John came on board he reached into his hood and spilled out a handful of black coins. Down in that maelstrom he had managed to relocate last year's coin reef. The line was now lashed to the prop shaft beside it. Jag, who was itching to get at the propeller, had a big surprise for us. It was not as big as we had estimated. Each blade would weigh between one and two tons. Nor, luckily, was it cast in one piece. Each was bolted on by sixteen nuts. The blade edges were so rough and jagged from impact that it must have been stopped while rotating.

As we sailed back to the anchorage at Great King we discussed plans for the next day, while Jeff cooked our New Year's dinner: a great mass of Chinese food in our genuine Chinese *wok*, to be washed down with cold champagne. We'd made it back to the *Elingamite* and already some more coin was aboard. "If the weather holds we go right to work in the morning, blast hell at the coin reef and get some good film," Kelly said.

And Jag added: "A good charge in the prop-boss, and maybe we can unscrew the nuts and raise each blade separately!"

"No use making films and getting props if we don't get the loot," I insisted, and everyone agreed.

Tuesday was the weirdest day of my life. Strangely calm at first, the wind came up as we sailed down to West Island. An eerie sea mist fumed around each island and with some uncanny power of its own crept out over the sea, despite the moderate breeze. As the island loomed up my mind flashed back to the parallel conditions as the *Elingamite* had crept at four and a half knots through the whiteness that Sunday morning sixty-six years before: "It was like a transformation scene in the theatre: a rift in the fog, a precipitous cliff like a snowclad mountain charmed us to look at it for a few seconds. Then it struck me we were making straight for it. White breakers were foaming and heaping not two hundred yards ahead. A shining blue light puzzled us momentarily, this being a phosphorus shine in the breakers," said survivor Steven Neil.

Suddenly out of the mist a black shape loomed straight towards us. A naval fisheries patrol launch was on to us. "God! What have we done?" "Some regulation broken?" The boys looked flabbergasted, so I told them not to worry. I guessed it would be Sir Douglas Robb. With his family link with the *Elingamite* he had told me he would try his darndest to get up there somehow to watch us at work and now, by good luck, he had intercepted us just as we arrived for our first big day. Running side by side our piratical craft and this spick and span naval ship made an unlikely pair. Sir Douglas waved from the flying bridge and seamen whirled a throwing line in the air. Curving out across our decks the sisal line was grabbed by the divers and hauled in. Up came a sodden sack: two dozen cans of lager. "Best wishes from Sir Douglas," the navy skipper loud-hailed us. Enthusiastically we waved our thanks. It was comforting to have another ship in the area.

None of us will ever forget that morning. To make matters worse at the wreck site a furious eleven-foot spring tide was careering past in rips, whirls and eddies. Out in the mist Pete and I bounced around in the dinghy while in the boiling sea beneath us Kelly and Jag toiled. First they had to moor the permanent buoy system to the propeller shaft: two forty-four-gallon drums, properly clamped and ring-bolted, one hauled ten feet below the surface, the other bobbing loosely. The first would keep the shot line near vertical in the current, while the free one would mark its position. This system overcame the problem we had had the previous year, when the current had pulled our light buoy right under and strung it out at a useless angle for ascents. They were also to lay the first gelignite charges in the coin seam and around the prop blade and Kelly was to try and snatch some movie sequences of the action. As we waited under the towering cliffs it was frightening to look out towards the open sea into a blank curtain of mist. Somewhere out there the *Lady Gwen* and the navy ship were cruising. "What if they lost contact with the island?" I thought, mindful of the plight of the raft survivors in this very region. Pete voiced my fears:

"Hope they can find their way back to us; we didn't bring any tucker."

As we waited, Kelly and Jag were having a tremendous struggle below: "Each time a wave swept past 120 feet above, the chain we were trying to shackle to the prop shaft would snap tight with a crack, threatening to slice off any unwary fingers. Struggling to keep tension on the rope and do up the shackles at the same moment, Jag and I had little time to worry about the treasure, but we did glimpse rows of milled edges of half-crowns poking from the solid coin seam we had been forced to abandon last year.

"In the boat overhead we had a double set of charges all prepared for laying once the buoy was secure. When the shackles were tight and the rope securely fastened to the chain we glided up our new roadway to the surface and grabbed the charges and movie camera. I filmed Jag as he came down festooned with plugs of jelly and cordtex. Quickly we dug holes under the coin seam and pushed in the plugs. The violent wave motion was already breaking some of the plugs and see-sawing the thin plastic coating on the cordtex across the sharp edges of steel and rock. Without wasting a second we swam up the slope to the propeller, trailing the electric detonator wires which by now were hopelessly tangled and bunched. Up there we each shoved a heap of plugs under the propeller boss. While I connected the detonator leads, Jag scouted around finding rocks to pile against the charges to confine the force of the explosion to the propeller. Out of air, but the job completed, we dashed back up our rope trailing the main firing cable to the surface."

At last the job was done. The two divers piled back into the boat. Kelly tossed his big movie camera into the bow. "Pretty dark with no sun."

"Big groper down there," spluttered Jag.

We had to clear the water now as anyone in the blast area would be killed by the shock wave. Master-blaster Kelly assured Pete and me we would be quite safe in our aluminium refuge, but the *Lady Gwen* had to cruise well out of range as the blast might damage her broad expanse of bottom. Our skipper's parting comment had been: "Be careful you don't blow the bloody wheels off us."

The plunger in Kelly's hands rammed home. The boat leapt bodily as a sledge-hammer blow thudded into us. The fourteen plugs of gelignite and cordtex had detonated in the money pile and around the prop. As we waited for the avalanche of current to clear the murk, brown scum and gas bubbled to the surface amidst the widening red carpet of dead fish. Kelly describes this moment of excitement:

"With cold, salty fingers I connected the leads to the firing mechanism. Doubts ran through my mind. Would the charges go off or would the motion down there already have broken the wires, pulled out detonators or chafed through the skin on the cordtex? I pushed home the plunger. A reflex kick slammed back up my arms as the shock wave from the explosion below hit the boat. A fraction of a second later a thunderous rumbling roar echoed from the towering cliffs. My instant reaction was that we had started a landslide but I soon realized that the shape of the cliffs focused the noise back at us as we sat astride the explosion. It was now Wade's and Peter's turn to descend as soon as the water cleared. We wondered what sort of transformation the charges had made in the coin reef."

"Watch out for sharks," Kelly said comfortingly as Pete and I tumbled backward from the upcurrent side of the boat, gripping masks and coin bags. We snatched the buoy line as we were whisked past, and flapping in the current like washing on a clothes line we hauled ourselves down through the sliding avalanche of water. Sharks often react hungrily to underwater blasts we knew, as we finned downwards. All these injured fish would make a marvellous banquet. As soon as my eyes hit the wreck I forgot all thoughts other than sinking down into that reef of intractable bullion we had to leave a year ago.

Pete saw a grey nurse shark glide in towards my unsuspecting fins. When it veered his way his grip tightened on his diving knife. Poor Pete! His first dive on the famous wreck and no time for sightseeing. I led him straight into the bullion crater and to work. As seconds are valuable at depth we both set to, raking, plucking and scraping coins into our canvas shoulder bags. A chink, chink behind me told me Pete must be in luck, too. Beneath my mask great black lumps of coin were scattered everywhere among jagged steel plate which threatened to skewer me. Even at this depth the powerful swell jostled us to and fro among the rocks and debris. The blast had done a magnificent job. A car-sized rock had shifted a foot sideways. Huge boulders were split and shattered. The ship's skeleton had been flung at grotesque angles all around the fringe of our coin seam.

My sack was half full when my diving knife prised loose a huge chunk of black coin. Plumes of bubbles billowed from my regulator exhaust ports as I heaved it into the sack. This was fantastic! A glance at my instruments: air gauge and decompression meter both told me I should soon be on my way up. Actually it was better below than in that foggy, wild place sagging and bulging away up above our heads. Despite frantic efforts I could not move the bullion bag. Close by a huge 300 pound stingray kept flapping over Pete's head. He grabbed it by the nose and swung it neatly away. Like a runaway Persian carpet it flapped into the buoyline, and kept fluttering around it confused and useless. I signalled to Pete that my air was getting low and our decompression meters were nearing the danger zone. Behind him our usual seventy-pound groper was gulping down wounded fish and two sharks circled. Visibility had improved to 150 feet now and our twin plumes of bubbles curved far above us in the tide-race. It hurt, but there was no alternative. I fixed a marker buoy on my bulging coin bag and took off up the shot line. Planing upward on the current I met Pete at ten feet for our routine five-minute stop. Pete's bag looked very heavy. His eyes spoke amazement at my empty hands. Jubilant I signalled that I had too much to raise but it was a nagging pain to have to leave so much silver below.

Together on the shot line we plunged and crashed in the surges, spinning and buffetting into each other as we waited for the DCP needles to wind back. The changing water pressure as the big swells passed over us caused us a lot of pain; our ears kept popping and masks flattening as we see-sawed from five to twenty-five feet. At last the red needle signalled our deliverance and we bobbed to the surface. My yell of excitement scared hell out of Tom the boatman, who thought I had been injured.

"It's as big as a leg of mutton," I gabbled as waiting arms yanked me aboard the *Lady Gwen*. Everyone was agog for news of the effect of the explosion. "Fantastic bloody sight," I exulted drunkenly. "Pull up the bag—bring up that bag," I yelled, to no one in particular. Out in the dinghy two men heaved and swore as a great weight slowly inched up from twenty-two fathoms. Our movie cameras whirred and tape reels spun as on the heaving deck of the *Lady Gwen* the coin sacks were emptied. A cascade of silver poured out. We danced around for joy picking up stray beauties and raving. These coins were in first rate condition; coming from the big mass there was no corrosion. In this one descent we had raised over 130 pounds weight of pure silver. Nearly twice as much as on the whole of the last expedition. One lump weighed nearly 100 pounds. No wonder I couldn't get off the bottom. Where the rope was attached the bag was badly ripped. We had almost lost it.

The navy boat *Maroro* was moving in close by. The mist, lifting higher, bathed everything in a blinding white light. Grabbing a coin, I piled into the sea and swam across to meet Sir Douglas, handing him a fresh souvenir in return for the beer. I pointed out to him how the ship bearing his mother and brother had rammed obliquely into the island; how the boats were launched and their probable course over to the Middle King. Sir Douglas sketched for me where he thought the landing place was for the seventy-three survivors and I resolved to make a trip down there later between dives to examine the spot. From where we were, half-a-mile off the wreck site, it looked even worse than close-up. The old lumbering *Lady* fussing around her tin chicken kept vanishing behind the swells that flexed over the sea to thunder into the West King. The air was white with spray and streamers of mist trickled down the cliff face and smoked around the corners of the island.

From their comments I knew the navy crew were flabbergasted at our diving in such conditions. When the time came for me to return to our ship, the mist had shut in again, blotting out the island. The *Maroro* felt her way in. When the island burst into view the *Lady* had gone! Anxiously I searched for signs of wreckage, but we met her around the other side, where years ago Captain Reid had rowed Boat 1, expecting to find a landing.

Everyone had now made their morning dive and we were all decompressing. Over lunch they told me that the next three divers, John, Jaan and Jeff had not done so well, getting only an eighth of a bag each. There was more coin there, but it was tightly compressed and needed loosening. Master-blaster Kelly had then ducked down on a bounce dive, the first of many. (Provided he only spent a couple of minutes on the bottom laying charges, he would avoid decompression troubles.) He had put a really heavy charge into the seam. For good measure he had poked in all the old broken plugs that had failed to detonate earlier. There had been a huge "WHAM"—the biggest yet.

When the next three divers had gone down late that afternoon they found the explosions had cleared, revealing utter chaos: too much "omph". The conglomerate coins were all loose now but widely scattered. We could see that if our blasting continued to open up such masses of silver, progress would be painfully slow gathering them up. One thought obsessed us: somewhere down there beneath that rubble was a ton and a half of bullion. At this stage our gold dredge contraption would come into its own.

Talking it over, back we sailed to the anchorage. After another memorable meal and plenty of good wine to fête our big haul, we were invited over to the *Maroro* moored alongside. Into her tiny wardroom the nine *Lady Gwen* men filed, guests of the captain and Sir Douglas. Such hospitality and sociability is most unexpected at the Kings, but this Tuesday had been a day packed with surprises. We were very happy, equally tired and glad just to relax away from our coin-blackened, wet-suit-flapping workhorse. When we admired their trim little vessel the skipper modestly explained that she had been refitted so often she was like the axe he had from the Battle of Hastings: three new heads and two new handles.

That night the *Maroro* sailed down to New Zealand leaving us to the customary Three Kings isolation and taking with them our first TV film. This really set things going at home. When we returned many a questioner wondered how we'd managed to get the film back while we were still up there. After this unforgettable Tuesday ordinary narrative would fail to convey the activity of the ensuing days. The repetitiveness of our efforts, our high moments and our setbacks, our frustrations and fading hopes, are best expressed through the immediacy of my diary pages, begrimed with coin corrosion and salt spotted as they are. The following are diary excerpts linked by straight narration.

Wednesday 3 January: Fine, a light westerly, seas calm. An early start. Jag and I, finding ourselves on fatigues slyly suggest: 'Let's skip a cooked breakfast and make an early start today with the gold-dredge. Looks like the wind might strengthen.' There were some strong protests from John Pettit at missing on a cooked meal. I hope he can dive as well on peaches and cream.

As I write we're headed down to the West King. Everyone is scribbling in diaries or leafing through girlie magazines. Jaan is still asleep on deck, missing out on a fine breakfast.

Dive One. Jag and Kelly have descended to lay a string of charges in the wreckage. Pickings are lean in the coin seam. They are hoping to open up new deposits where the other bullion boxes have spilled. We are excited because today we shall set to work our powerful water jet and gold-dredge combination. We are wise to have skipped breakfast; should get a lot of dives in today, and we may strike the mother lode.

On the next two dives my optimism was dented; that string of blasts revealed no new coin masses and thick rubble now covered our original deposit:

Dive Four. Kelly and Jag are rigging the water jet and hoses in the dinghy as we lie off the Princess Rocks for lunch. Jeff has just plunged in for a nude swim. What a brave, clean cook we have!

5.00 p.m. Kelly has been down and tried clearing the coin seam with the water-jet. Catastrophe! The whole system is a complete flop. The less we think about it now the better for morale . . . Jag has just bobbed up with one gold coin—found in a niche twenty feet away from the silver seam.

5.45 p.m. Sad Dive. Pete and I moved a lot of loose rubble in the coin seam with limited success. It was cold down there—very: 14·4° C. First we fossicked widely without result. Pete then worked at one hole, delving blindly down between two plates and scooping

175

coins into his bag. This is the hole John said had suddenly appeared beneath his hand. There must be a hollow space beneath the wreckage. Have to blast it. While working down in a hole, Jag says a ray came right at him. Later, when a rock slipped down on him, he thought it was a ray and reacted vigorously. These two rays are always prowling the site. Five feet across they would weigh over 200 pounds and are quite dopey with over-eating blasted fish. Jaan pushed one off by its nose and as it flapped off he noticed it had two barbs on it, which is unusual. After each dive Jaan is building up a big drawing of the wreck site using an underwater pad and compass to take notes. Today has been a big blow to our hopes: no mother lode, only twenty pounds of bullion raised and the failure of our water-jet system.

That night in the cabin I asked Kelly to set down his thoughts on this failure: "Designated 'master blaster', up till this point my diving time had consisted mainly of digging holes and cramming in charges which grow progressively bigger as we try desperately to uncover the mother lode. The site now looks like a battlefield with bomb craters gaping at regular intervals amongst the wreckage. Occasionally new lumps of coin have appeared but not the vast quantities we're longing for, and we have loosened a very large area of bottom.

"Today the time came to try the dredge. I descended through the tide-race as Tom cranked the pump into life in the boat overhead. On the bottom I watched the canvas hose as it filled and stiffened. Damn! Halfway down there was a twist in it and the water was not getting past. The increasing tidal pull was bowing it out in a gigantic horseshoe. Ascending to midwater I struggled with the hose trying to untwist it. Finally with a rush the water surged through.

"Back at the bottom I opened the tap and started sluicing. It was working well and I soon had a yawning hole lined with scattered coins. I switched the water off and as I gathered them into my bag I noticed that my action had stirred up a great cloud of corrosion. Undeterred by the growing obscurity I started again and had soon increased the size of the hole considerably. Visibility was now reducing to zero. A great mushroom of Indian ink was rising. I moved further down the slope and resumed jetting but was again enveloped in clouds of blackness. I realized that it was not only the dredge that was stirring up the muck. Despite the depth the switchback wave motion, aided by the current, was eroding the edges of my excavations and generating the murk. Atomized by the explosives the degenerate iron corrosion was dyeing the water like soot. I shut off the dredge and swam up. Thirty feet from the bottom

The tally of gold and silver after a successful morning

An inquisitive
mao mao approaches
a diver excavating
coins from the seam

Wade Doak with
two half-sovereigns
in his mask, for safe
keeping, and hands
full of silver

Sometimes the coins were welded by corrosion into a hard mass which broken open, showed many of them in excellent condition after sixty-six years

Wade Doak stands on one of the bronze propeller blades salvaged from the *Elingamite* in January, 1969. The jagged edge of the blade in the foreground gives a clue to the mystery of the wreck which was overlooked at the Court of Inquiry

my mask burst through into clear blue water. Below me boiled a great sepia cloud that writhed and billowed with the motion of the water. I realized with dismay that it would be at least half an hour before there was any visibility down there, for as fast as the current carried it away more was generated. Our dredge is a wash out: $300 down the drain!"

My diary continues on Thursday:

Fine, hazy, streaks of cloud. This could mean a wind is coming up so an early start. Not much time for sleeping on this ship. Programme today includes lots more blasting after that mother lode and a major assault on the prop. Later we must rendezvous with the *Roa* for a fuel transfer.
Over the Wreck site: Conditions are shocking here today. A huge swell is surging in with tremendous backlash and white water right out to the buoy and around it. We are on the verge of tossing it in for the day but the weather is still fine and sunny. Days like this are all too rare up here. Kelly and Jag have decided to make an attempt to descend. They want to blast the prop and open out the coin seam.

Out at sea where the swell was gentler they got into the boat with all their gear on and were towed in towards the wild West King. A hair-raising trip as the dinghy kept surfing down on top of the *Lady Gwen* and then slewing around violently. Once cast off, Jaan rowed the two divers over to the spinning buoy. Without the twin buoy system it would have been impossible to operate under such conditions as it was the only means of holding the boat back from the surf. As we stood off and watched we feared some swells might break a few yards earlier, right over the boat. Kelly went down, set one lot of charges, climbed aboard and fired it. Then both he and Jag descended to set more charges. From this point, standing off on *Lady Gwen* I made on-the-spot notes:

10.00 a.m. A terrific *wham*. The mightiest yet. I glance up at the island summit. A huge slab of granite is poised to fall on the wreck site. So loose only the wind seems to hold it there. They're kicking the giant in the shins. Will he retaliate? Three tiny, audacious figures out in a cockleshell belting hell out of the sea-floor to filch the precious metals from beneath his fist. Now the boys are waiting for the water to clear. In their minds dreams of coins, sharks, severed prop blades . . . Each big swell coming over them threatens to swamp their boat. What a helluva place this is: the remotest island in the whole lonely chain, way out in the Pacific. There's a big blowhole keeps puffing and bellowing spume back over them, and acres of white water on all sides. Of course the spring tides are contributing a fair bit to the confusion. No one would dive here just for money!

10.10 a.m. They've gone down again. Just Jaan tossing there above in the boat. Beside me in the warm sun Pete says: 'How steady the old *Lady* rides the swells out here.'

Then Larry leans from the wheelhouse: 'Hey Jeff. Come and drive for a while and I'll make a cup of tea.'

'If that's a bludy hint I'll brew a pot.' Jeff looked quite flummoxed. Must have taken Larry seriously for a minute.

10.30 a.m. Jag's up. We're moving in to pick them up. Smiles: Jag has some coin. We empty them on deck. It is rare to see sixpences, and threepences among the coin—and three shiny gold half-sovereigns.

'Why do we always find them along with the small change?'

'They're from the gold hole.'

'What about the prop?'

'Well,' Kelly tells us, 'we swam up there but couldn't find it for the murk. We'll have to leave it to John and Pete.'

When those two came up John flashed a gold coin but they had no news of the prop. They had left it too late in their dive and could not go up there. So it was over to Jaan and me to check it. *Our Dive*: Jaan inspected the prop then worked at Pete's coin seam, while I dug in Jag's gold hole. I gleaned a few dozen coins, poked in all the holes and prospected up and down the coin seam: now quite a deep trench with stray coin scattered everywhere. Jaan brought up a large brass bolt from the prop. He reported that one blade was virtually ripped off, retained by only two bolts and they were loose. Great news!

As prospects of our finding the mother lode dimmed this brass prop grew in importance. It would be worth up to N.Z. $2,000 in spot cash. On one blade the incredible power of our explosives had sheered off sixteen bolts, each two inches in diameter and weighing ten pounds.

At the anchorage we rendezvoused with Ray Jose of the *Roa* to transfer drums of diesel. After tea the friendly *Roa* skipper shared our wine and a yarn with us. Five months back Ray and his son had been rescued from their sinking trawler just near here, during a big blow. His story showed us just how tough it could get around these islands.

Just off the Great King the *Dolphin*'s engine had broken down

178

and they were adrift in fifty-foot seas. The steep waves were breaking along the crests. With the mounting force of the gale whole tops would drop off and it was impossible to go over the mountains of ocean. To act as sea anchors kapok mattresses, a fishing net and cray buoys were strung out on the anchor warp as the boat reeled and pitched. Ray explained that in this weird region the seas are often worse in the lee of the islands than to windward. The 40-foot *Dolphin* was swept thirty miles in twenty-four hours, and yet for roughly half that time they had stayed within sight of the Great King.

Luckily an air force Orion had located them and directed the liner *Kuala Lumpur* to their rescue. Only once a year does a ship go along this path. The final touch was amazing: Five weeks later the derelict *Dolphin* had drifted toward the coast and anchored herself just beyond the surf by her trailing warp. The salvors found her a reeking mess of rotten crayfish and fuel oil. As he leapt on to the ladder of the liner Ray told us he had thought: "Better a live coward than a dead hero." But we had no doubts about this blue water sailor who does all his cray fishing fifty miles from land.

That Friday my diary reads:

The day of the propeller. Today we must determine whether Captain Attwood was right, or his engineers. Did the *Elingamite*'s engines fail to reverse through a mechanical fault or was the captain's command too late, the prop having struck a rock while still turning? It is fine, sunny and clear. What tremendous good luck we're having with the weather! This morning all seven divers have made descents but our haul is pitiful. More blasting is the only answer. The bulk of the bullion *must* be nearby beneath the mounds of corroded plate. Jag comes up with another piece of gold: 'There's a whole colony of crays moving in to eat the dead fish. Must tell Ray Jose to put his cray pots down.' Kelly and Jeff surfaced really glum about their results, so John has tallied their booty: 75 uncorroded half-crowns! This is a useful morale booster and from now on after each dive the boys are counting their hauls to cheer themselves up. A far cry from last Tuesday! Jaan is really trying too hard. On his second dive, after finding a gold coin, he stayed below too long. Pete, who had dived with him, surfaced first, grabbed the emergency scuba set always at hand and carried it down. Jaan was hanging on the shot line to decompress and his own tank was empty. Waiting for his decompression meter to tick back he had to stay at 10 feet for 20 minutes. We certainly don't want any 'bends' up here. With the nearest decompression chamber for treatment two days away, it would be fatal. Jag has just surfaced again with next to nothing. He's angry and wants to blast something.

Friday afternoon: It's sweltering hot. While we're toasting our chilled bodies in the sun the *Roa* has come alongside. Ray Jose is offering to haul up a prop blade for us. Larry isn't keen to do this with the *Lady Gwen* as it is too risky without the right gear. Ray says the *Roa* has a winch and boom that can lift a ton at least. This jolts us out of our sun-baked lethargy. Poor Kelly, for the fourth time today, hops below to shackle a rope from the *Roa* to a bolt hole at the base of one blade. Everyone is at fever pitch. Why? Only a blasted old prop but this is a tangible piece of the *Elingamite* and she's in such a mess it is often hard to believe we do have a ship down there. Our own property too! The *Roa* has the line around her winch drum. She's heeling over and tugging like hell. The boys on the *Lady G*, cameras poised, hold their breath. The winch has stalled. Again they heave. There is a danger that even a moderate swell could suddenly put a huge strain on the *Roa*: the blade, having lifted, might begin to fall just as the ship rises. A third attempt seems to have jigged the blade up and down, but clearly the *Roa* can't do the job. An anticlimax, but we've learnt two things: we'll need a hefty boat and lifting gear before those blades ever gleam in the sunlight; and our prop is very valuable.

6.30 p.m. Sufficient time having elapsed we've made our last series of dives for the day. A meagre yield of coin has come up. Before leaving another set of charges has been placed around the last two remaining blades and along the coin seam, so that it will have all cleared by tomorrow morning. Who knows, when next we dive a shining carpet of coin may be laid bare. Still we dream about that mother lode. From close examination the boys are sure that the prop was turning when it hit. So much for those engineers' integrity at the Court trial. At the anchorage the sea is a burnished mirror of calm. As Jeff readies our meal, steak and pineapple sizzle in the *wok*. The sun glares in the cabin door on warm faces; the aroma of wine and garlic attracts the gulls that hover around the stern while the massive wooden rudder jiggles and thumps lazily in its pintles. No one dares set foot on the cabin floor while Jeff is cooking. His huge razor-edged cooking knives flash menacingly on the chopping board. Those precious knives that no slushy on fatigues dare wash in hot water or else . . . Even the skipper keeps clear of our cook. Two to a bunk our crew huddles, sips cold beer and waits. A mark of our deep appreciation of Jeff's cuisine is our utter respect for his rule: 'Keep out of me bludy way, mate!' And as his fingers fly among the food I muse:

What sea cook washes himself from head to foot twice a day and scuba dives between times? On a diving expedition there is only time for one real meal a day and a good cook is as essential as a good ship. As we turn in I notice a misty halo around the moon and long wisps in the sky: a sea change in the offing. 'We must make a really early start,' says Jeff. 'Quick breakfast and off down to the wreck.' I agree as I'm on fatigues again.

Chapter 15

I AROSE AT 5 a.m. on that grey Saturday morning to a chorus of abuse from the crew. The instigator of the early start, Jeff, swore the loudest. He had rigged his bed on the ice box lid, which had to be removed so I could get at our breakfast supplies. By 6.15 we were steaming flat out for the wreck site and munching breakfast. Kelly commented that one blast yesterday had shifted a twenty-ton boulder about nine inches, laying bare some davits.

"Yeah," I growled, "and I didn't have time to draw my legs into the boat before they fired the shot!"

True to character, Jaan Voot never once arose in time for breakfast. Notoriously a late-to-bed and later-to-rise man, it was amazing the way he could adapt shipboard life to his normal living pattern. On our first series of dives the silver was still coming up. Goldfinger Pettit scratched up two gold coins. I got forty half-crowns. "Where is that mother lode: the one and a half tons of silver?" we asked. Talk in the cabin at lunchtime was to place really big charges all over the place, as the weather might break soon. Our big storage tanks still held enough compressed air for thirty-six more descents, so our air supply would out-distance the weather.

Pete told us: "Kelly launched the boat this morning without screwing the bung in. For half an hour he sat over the wreck site like this, perched up in the bow to pay out the detonator lead. When I climbed over the stern things started to happen!" Jag was satisfied. On his first dive of the morning he had found every blade of the propeller lying separate: three quite close together, the fourth twenty feet away. The boss was splayed out and beneath was a deep crater. All the metal was gleaming bright.

Soft-hearted Kelly told us that as he sat in the dinghy "this poor little crab was groping over the floorboards. Must have come off some wreckage we'd hauled up. I felt sorry for him and flung him back into the sea. Then I realized he was drifting down to where the charges would soon erupt."

Not a cap full of wind. As the morning went by we realized this was the calmest day we had ever known at the Kings. We were able to dive straight down from the *Lady Gwen* actually moored to our buoy during the slack water. None of the usual strenuous dinghy trips to and from the wreck site. Ascending I was able to swim straight up to the diving ladder. Even Larry was infected with our eagerness to have a good look around now that the conditions were kind. He paddled around in the dinghy examining those awful cliff faces and reefs at close range: Meek and harmless the sleeping giant that for three hundred and sixty-four days of the year was a skipper's nightmare.

Between descents Kelly took Tom in for his first skindive. Fancy starting your diving career at the *Elingamite* site! Snorkeling inshore in waters that we had never before seen calm, they spotted the boilers and engines, heaps of twisted wreckage and two more prop blades! Kelly quickly returned for his scuba gear but he found the blades were only cast iron, probably carried up for'ard as spares.

Awaiting the passage of time for our next descent I decided to swim ashore. I wanted to land on the West King to get a new angle on the shipwreck. Jaan Voot and I slipped overboard and as we swam over the dark, jumbled wreckage under the shadow of the island, I recalled phrases from the day of the disaster.

10.40 a.m., Sunday, November 10, 1902:
"Ahead I saw a great green mass with white in the foreground. Another moment we saw breakers and realized we were running into a huge cliff." . . . "The fog drifted apart. A great cliff towered high above the masts." . . . "The rock sprang suddenly out of the dense cloud." . . . "An onrushing rock wall." . . . "A great ringing of the captain's bell, a grating on the rocks, then a crash as if the bottom of the ship had been knocked in, followed by a scraping and grinding as of the keel on the rocks."

At the cliff foot the sea surged up over the matted kelp. We rode it in and snatched a hold as it sucked back. Before the next one hit we had clambered clear of the sea, the first men to land on this ledge since Passy the Portuguese cook, who had tried to swim in from the wreck with a line in his teeth. Around my neck was an amphibious camera and light meter. As we explored the shelf we were amazed to find so much wreckage: iron, brass and bronze, flung up to forty feet above sea level and firmly embedded in every chink and cranny by the sea's action. All we could prise loose was the case of a brass padlock.

Our next series of dives produced one gold coin, a little more silver, many more blasts and a feed of crays for lunch. We noted that crays thrive on explosions. On this calm sea Larry just let the ship drift off the island. Even in such placid conditions the ocean weather is peculiar: as we relaxed in the sun it began to look bad. A fog bank moved in, the horizon and island whited out and then, one hour later, it was glittering and fine again and hotter than ever. Lying off the island we noticed the ship was spinning end for end in a giant whirlpool and this right out on the open sea!

To fill in time before our next descents we moved down to the Middle King where we hoped to find the landing site Sir Douglas had described and get some movie footage of the spot. Sir Douglas Robb's mother had written: "Imagine a narrow inlet, the sea having broken through the cliffs on one side, a ledge as hard and sharp as rocks are made some twenty feet above sea level, the sea roaring on three sides, the spray dashing up on to the ledge and seabirds screaming and screeching all night long in the fog and rain."

As the stern of our aluminium boat rode up the rock face on the swell we leapt ashore, the boat nipping quickly out on the backwash. How could they have managed to land the three boatloads of survivors on those jagged, weed-slippery ledges? We found the hollow in the rocks where Mrs Robb had huddled with her little son, Connal. We saw the water trickling from a crab-crammed fissure in which the survivors had found moisture and a little sustenance. Our ears were pierced by the screams of seabirds protesting at our intrusion. From pools mosquitoes swarmed for their first drop of human blood in sixty years, and the huge, bold crabs came scuttling forwards waving outsized pincers.

Two miles to the east lay the well-wooded Great King Island to which one raft carrying eleven men had drifted. Beyond it to the north the blinding blue sea and sky merged in the heat. We shuddered as we remembered the accounts of the eight survivors on the other raft which had drifted helplessly for four days sixty miles to the north in this same heat. Somewhere out there eight others, including the stewardess, had died of thirst or flung themselves overboard, maddened from drinking seawater.

When we climbed on board the *Lady Gwen* to return for our next series of dives we were grateful for the safety of our ship and the cold cans of beer in her ice box, after one hour on the Middle King. At 6.00 p.m. Kelly, Jaan and I went down for our third dives of the day. I got about a dozen coins. Jaan did quite well just scooping up everything from one hole—stones and all. We came up to ten feet and spun on the buoy rope in the rip. Kelly was first to disappear, legs last, into the dancing dinghy. Jaan followed. As I had been working deeper I had to stay another chill five minutes, ten in all. My diary records: "What a hell it is to get changed in the evening when the boat is under way, all the bunks are taken, and you're on fatigues!"

I wrote that evening: "This may have been our last day. We seem to have come to the tail end of the fine spell and it looks as if a south-east change is coming. Where, oh where is that mountain of silver? And one more day would make such a difference to our film. It is a week today since I left my home, but it seems like months. The cook is giving us a double ration of steak tonight. And don't we need it! A most strenuous day: Landings on two islands and three dives."

We were all yarning in the cabin as I scrawled my notes. Suddenly a weather bulletin came over the radio: A series of lows and easterly winds. This was the worst wind for the Three Kings.

"All hands on deck," had a new meaning to us semi-sailors as we stowed all our diving gear down the for'ard hatch, unrigged the deck canopy, and lashed the boat securely on top of the cabin.

"What's the old scow like in head seas, Larry?"

"It's exactly like water skiing: slam, slam all the way."

Even Larry looked grim. The sense of remoteness produced an unusual tension and thoroughness in our crew as we readied the *Lady* for sea. Divers are notoriously casual when it comes to seaman-ship. Familiarity breeds contempt for the usual terrors of drowning. But storms: that was different.

As Larry drove her bows into the teeth of the gale we all snuggled down in the cabin to get some sleep in before things got any worse.

Sunday morning we awoke to a jobbling, easy sea. We had sailed right out of the storm. Back at the Kings the *Roa* radioed to say she was still in the thick of it. Ray would ride out any storm rather than come home fishless. Months later he was to ride out up there the hurricane that sank the *Wahine* in Wellington Harbour!

As we cruised down the Northland coast in the warm sun we set to work tallying our haul. The steel ammunition boxes were emptied on deck. While Kelly filmed, we slaved. I entered totals of each denomination as the boys sorted and counted. A gruelling hot occu-pation it was. The decks were too hot to stand on so Jeff kept sluicing them down with a bucket, spattering us in the process with black filth off the coins. As he stood with a poised pail John Pettit looked up lovingly: "Can I help you fix some lunch, Jeff?" Jeff enjoyed the hint.

Back to the entrance of Walkers Creek and we slithered and ground upstream slightly ahead of the tide—"We took it up with us," Jag reckoned—and nudged into the landing and its hurdygurdy junk pile and old boats, long, green grass and mangroves, lots of bare kids and a few excited welcomers. We were too tired to unload, but a swim and a fresh shower soon got us going. By evening every-thing was packed. We swigged our last cans of beer around the ice box with Larry and Tom and then headed south with 10,000 *Elingamite* coins. The rest is still up there—somewhere.

185

Just the other day I read a verdict on the gold ingots left in the famous *Lutine* wreck: "In our humble opinion this affair is one in which the sea is very likely to let men succeed if they agree to pay the price. To recover the treasure great capital is needed . . ." That fits the *Elingamite* bullion very nicely. Our *Elingamite* syndicate can find many feasible schemes for blasting all that wreckage, sucking all the debris up and passing it through screens. There certainly is a fortune down there, but at the West King, raising it would cost too much: a high risk investment.

Even so we shall return from time to time to collect our propeller blades and scratch around for the odd coin or two.

Appendix 1: The Whaleboat Chase

As ARTHUR THOMAS of Houhora tells it: "We received first news of the wreck when Mr Burkitt, the first mate landed No. 2 lifeboat upon a small sandy beach near Farmer's Point on the eastern side of the lowlands leading to Mt Camel.

"There was a Maori settlement over the hills upon the eastern shore of Houhora Harbour and it was here that the party rested while Mr Burkitt crossed with the aid of a Maori and dinghy to our side. My father, agent for the Northern Steamship Company, was thought to be the best one to see and it was here that the story was told: The *Elingamite* had been wrecked the previous day; No. 1 and No. 2 lifeboats had picked up their full quota and decided to head for the mainland with a view to getting help; other boats launched and fully laden had headed for the Big King; a raft with sixteen aboard was adrift.

"It was known that a sister ship, the *Zealandia* had left Auckland for Sydney and would be passing the North Cape at 7 a.m. the next morning; could she be intercepted and diverted to the Kings? Thoughts naturally turned to Peter McIntosh, a big, powerful man who had previously had a whaling station on the island off Cape Karikari and still owned his favourite boat, the *Tainui* (now in Auckland Museum). Upon being approached he was quite willing to give it a go and got to work on the crew right away. We had to get the boat out of the creek where it was moored and by the time this was done and the odds and ends checked up it would be about midnight. We still had to get out of the harbour and through the heads before getting a clear run to the cape so I would say it would be about 1.30 or 2 a.m. before we were able to turn north.

"We were most fortunate in having a really good breeze, about south-south-west and by keeping well off shore were able to romp along under mainsail only. When about five miles due east of the North Cape we sighted a column of smoke over the horizon, slightly astern, and it was not long before the masts and funnel showed up.

"Realizing that we could not possibly intercept her Peter altered course to north-west with the hope that we could get close enough to be seen when the *Zealandia* altered her course direct for Sydney. The hull became visible and got larger as we closed the gap.

187

Eventually, we hoped, passengers or someone would be likely to get their binoculars to have a last look at New Zealand. Our sail was lowered and a signal—a red camera cloth supplied by Chick Northwood—was fastened to a halyard and pulled up and down the mast. After a while the ship turned and came straight toward us; after she slowed down we tried to get alongside but were whisked away like a feather by her reversing propellers. Finally they threw us a line and we were able to pull alongside near the bow.

"It was quite impossible to be heard from the boat owing to the hissing of escaping steam so a rope was lowered and Peter was hauled aboard to deliver his message. Upon his return he was accompanied by a very large tin of biscuits, half a cheese and a bottle of whisky. The *Zealandia* then went on her way to the Kings and we headed for the North Cape.

"As the wind had dropped to practically nil and what there was came offshore we rowed and arrived off the cape in the late afternoon; there is a reef which pokes out easterly from the tip of the cape and to save time and effort Peter took us through a narrow passage. He was quite familiar with this short cut to a nice, calm little bay but his crew were not and certainly had the wind up. After landing in the bay it was decided to stay the night so the boat was hauled above high water mark, turned upside down and with the help of the sails provided a good shelter. We did not get much rest however, as during the night one of the party awakened to say that a big ship was signalling not a great distance off shore. She was brightly lighted and stationary. Peter said he had never seen a ship of that size so close in and so, being a bit wreck minded (or 'wreck happy' to use a soldier's phrase) it was decided to investigate. The boat was dragged into the water and away we went.

"After rowing some distance we saw the masthead lights of another ship coming up the coast toward us; this proved to be the *Clansman* on her way to search for the raft. The big ship, of course, was *Zealandia* returning to Auckland with survivors from the Kings. Her signals were for the *Clansman*. After they heard our story we were hoisted aboard, boat and all, and headed for the Kings; during the trip a man named Abraham was stationed up the mast to keep a lookout for the raft. I do not know his nationality but he was a coloured man and reputed to have wonderful sight at night but nothing was found.

"It was daylight when we arrived at the Kings and went slowly along the inside but saw nothing until we reached the point where the wreck occurred; very little there too, just odd things close in to the sinister black rock, sliding up and down on the surge. What a dirty dismal hole for a ship to be wrecked. A boat was launched to investigate but could not get in close enough on account of the surge.

"The *Clansman* continued around the island and proceeded fairly close in on the outside toward the Big King and it was after we had gone quite a distance that lots of wreckage appeared and continued in volume. After we had passed the Big King, it appeared to have a definite north-easterly set and the *Clansman* followed this for some distance before heading for Houhora."

Appendix 2: The Austrians

IN THE AFTERMATH of the shipwreck the charges against the misconduct of the Austrians did not go unchallenged.

In Auckland through an interpreter, Austrian Yovic Pribicevich spoke for his ten countrymen:

"We were all on deck at 8 a.m., up forward keeping a lookout with the sailors. After the ship struck we assisted in getting the women and children into boats. At this point Captain Attwood ordered the men to man the boats. We tried to get into Boat 1 which was not full, containing ladies, but some of the sailors and firemen pushed us back. Captain Attwood then interfered, saying that the lives of the Austrians should be saved just as much as their own. He gave orders to allow us aboard. Seven of us got into Boat 3, with Captain Attwood, one in Boat 1, and three in Boat 6. Despite reports all eleven of us survived. Had Captain Attwood not intervened we would all have had to remain and drown. Some of us jumped into boats already pulling off, others leapt into the water and climbed aboard.

"We all come from coastal districts, know how to handle boats and were pleased to handle an oar. There were six oars to a boat, four being used at a time. One of our men, injured in getting aboard, lay under the seats unable to help. We took off our coats to row and bail. We were glad to let the thinly clad English sailors borrow these for a few hours but they refused to return them until the *Zealandia* rescued us from the Middle King.

"On the rocks there was a keg of whisky and some plugs of tobacco but none was allowed for us. The sailors even took our tobacco from us. One Austrian, Mijo Bovich, in Boat 1 with the women and children, rowed for six hours. A lady (compare Miss Maybee's story) gave him a spell occasionally, while the other five men took turns on the remaining oars."

At his embassy, Mr Langguth, Austro-Hungarian Ambassador, conducted an inquiry into the charges against his countrymen. Not a single one could be substantiated and all were withdrawn. Captain Attwood forwarded a statement that they had worked well and willingly, and he was not aware of anything on their part to call for blame.

With the order for passengers to take to the boats two foreigners, not necessarily Austrians, were hurrying forward amongst a number of other passengers. "I simply asked them to stand aside and not to come so fast. They obeyed immediately."

Captain Reid added that he would not specifically accuse the Austrians. There were other foreigners aboard.

Mr McGeorge, a passenger, pointed out two Austrians he had seen assist in lowering the boats.

The ambassador stated: "A certain section of the people in this country take every opportunity of attacking Austrians because they are foreigners. They are seafaring people. Would English passengers on an Austrian shipwreck, ignorant of the language, unable to understand orders given, stand aside while others saved themselves? Some Englishmen think no one else but themselves possessed of manly qualities."

Yet, at the time of the disaster, statements such as these were made:

Reid: "Two Austrians tried to rush the boat and we kept them back." Donaldson: "An Austrian, who appropriated two lifejackets, was jammed between one of the lifeboats and the ship and sank" (all eleven survived!). Neil: "I hit the Austrian mighty hard on the point of the chin." F. Banks: "There were some Austrians in Boat 3 who proved a bit troublesome. They would not bail or help with the oars until forced to. They seemed too terror-stricken to do anything." Tallan, A.B.: "I saw an Austrian leap overboard and believe he drowned." Henry Wetherilt: "There were two Asiatics there and fortunately my small knowledge of Arabic enabled me to address them pretty roughly and restrain them from rushing the boat. As soon, however, as it touched the water they dived off and got in."

Appendix 3: Case of the Twisted Blades

January 1969:

It is a dim vaporous day off the West King Island. Midsummer, yet we can see our breath. A long, greasy swell skeined with mist rolls in from the south-west. We are all shivering in our wet suits: Kelly Tarlton, myself and the three Johns—John Gallagher, John Young and John Pettit.

Everyone is impatient. We have dived down to the *Elingamite* again and found the propeller blades still lying on the rock slope, tossed at odd angles by our explosive charges a year ago. Larry Walker has nearly completed the rigging of the derrick.

Kelly is ready to go down to shackle the wire cable through one of the nine boltholes on the palm of each blade. Oh to get this $3,000 prize aboard while the unearthly calm lasts! Such perfect conditions are essential. Peter Sheehan, at the wheel, must position *Lady Gwen* directly over the wreck where white water and breakers usually rage. Kelly plans to free-fall in a gliding arc, landing fair on top of the blades. For five minutes we watch his bubbles streaming to the surface. Then his head breaks through and "OK" he yells. The winch chatters and the cable "brrrs" through the pulley. Through the surface we can see a dark shape looming up. The *Lady Gwen* lists over and bobs on the surges confidently. In a blaze of multi-hued marine growths, the palm of the blade emerges.

By midday four propeller blades are sparkling in the sun. Bent like bananas, huge chunks have been smashed from the leading edges: They were certainly turning when the *Elingamite* hit!

On our last dive Kelly secured a maker's nameplate from the ship's engines and John Pettit found the *Elingamite* bell. These and other relics have been deposited in the New Zealand Maritime Museum which we have established at Whangaroa on the Northland coast.

At the present time souvenir sets of our coins are selling briskly and a display of the *Elingamite* treasure is touring Australian cities. For Kelly and myself the treasure has changed our lives: We are now able to devote all our time to diving, photographing the undersea world and writing about it.

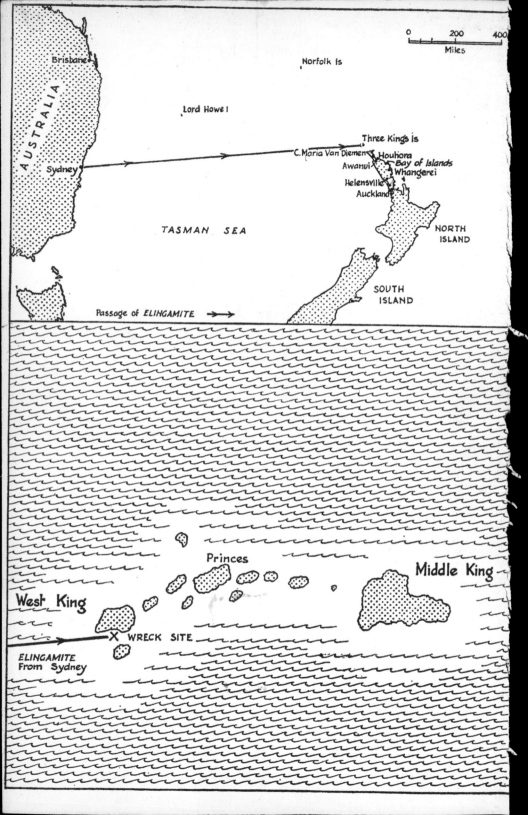

Brisbane

AUSTRALIA

Norfolk Is

Lord Howe I

0   200   400
Miles

Three Kings Is

C. Maria Van Diemen
Houhora
Awanui
Bay of Islands
Whangarei
Helensville
Auckland

Sydney

TASMAN SEA

NORTH
ISLAND

SOUTH
ISLAND

Passage of ELINGAMITE ➤➤

Princes

Middle King

West King

X WRECK SITE

ELINGAMITE
From Sydney